Slavery, Memory, and Religion in Ghana, *c.* 1850–Present

Based on a decade of fieldwork in southeastern Ghana and analysis of secondary sources, this book aims to reconstruct the religious history of the Anlo-Ewe peoples from the 1850s. In particular, it focuses on a corpus of rituals collectively known as 'Fofie', which derived their legitimacy from engaging with the memory of the slave-holding past. The Anlo developed a sense of discomfort about their agency in slavery in the early twentieth century, which they articulated through practices such as ancestor veneration and spirit possession, and by forging links with descendants of peoples they formerly enslaved. Conversion to Christianity, engagement with 'modernity', trans-Atlantic conversations with diasporan Africans, and citizenship of the post-colonial state coupled with structural changes within the religious system – which resulted in the decline in Fofie's popularity – gradually altered the moral emphases on legacies of slavery in the Anlo historical imagination as the twentieth century progressed.

Meera Venkatachalam holds a PhD in Social Anthropology from the School of Oriental and African Studies, University of London (2007). She has conducted post-doctoral work at the Centre of African Studies, University of Edinburgh. Her writing has appeared in *Africa* (journal of the International African Institute) and *Journal of African History*.

THE INTERNATIONAL AFRICAN LIBRARY

The International African Library is a major monograph series from the International African Institute. Theoretically informed ethnographies, and studies of social relations 'on the ground' which are sensitive to local cultural forms, have long been central to the Institute's publications programme. The IAL maintains this strength and extends it into new areas of contemporary concern, both practical and intellectual. It includes works focused on the linkages between local, national, and global levels of society; writings on political economy and power; studies at the interface of the socio-cultural and the environmental; analyses of the roles of religion, cosmology, and ritual in social organisation; and historical studies, especially those of a social, cultural, or interdisciplinary character.

Slavery, Memory, and Religion in Southeastern Ghana, *c.* 1850–Present

Meera Venkatachalam

International African Institute, London

and

CAMBRIDGE
UNIVERSITY PRESS

University Printing House, Cambridge CB2 8BS, United Kingdom

One Liberty Plaza, 20th Floor, New York, NY 10006, USA

477 Williamstown Road, Port Melbourne, VIC 3207, Australia

4843/24, 2nd Floor, Ansari Road, Daryaganj, Delhi - 110002, India

79 Anson Road, #06-04/06, Singapore 079906

Cambridge University Press is part of the University of Cambridge.

It furthers the University's mission by disseminating knowledge in the pursuit of education, learning and research at the highest international levels of excellence.

www.cambridge.org
Information on this title: www.cambridge.org/9781107519169

© Meera Venkatachalam 2015

First published 2015
First paperback edition 2017

A catalogue record for this publication is available from the British Library

ISBN 978-1-107-10827-1 Hardback
ISBN 978-1-107-51916-9 Paperback

Contents

List of Figures

Acknowledgements

This book has its origins in a PhD thesis submitted to the Department of Anthropology and Sociology of the School of Oriental and African Studies (SOAS), University of London, in 2007. As with any long-lasting academic undertaking, my debts are numerous. Financial support came from a research studentship offered by SOAS and several fieldwork awards administered by SOAS and the University of London between 2002 and 2007. I was extremely fortunate to have J. D. Y. Peel as my doctoral supervisor. This project took shape under his guidance, and the intellectual insights that he brought to my research have been significant. Over the years at SOAS and the University of London, I have also benefited greatly from attending the lectures and seminars of Louis Brenner, Richard Fardon, Paul Gifford, Richard Jeffries, Murray Last, John Parker, John Picton, and Johan Pottier, which added great value to this project. Upon completion of my thesis, Murray Last and Birgit Meyer suggested some very useful rewrites, which in due course, improved the structure and readability of this book.

In 2009 I was awarded an Economic and Social Research Council (ESRC) postdoctoral fellowship at the Centre of African Studies (CAS) at the University of Edinburgh. At CAS I was able to draw upon Paul Nugent's expertise in Ghanaian and African history as draft chapters of my doctoral thesis metamorphosed into this book. At CAS and the wider School of Social and Political and Science at Edinburgh, I am grateful for the contributions and support offered by several members of staff, especially Barbara Bompani, Jennifer Curtis, Joost Fontein, Tony Good, Charlie Jeffery, Tom Molony, James Smith, Isabella Soi, and Wolfgang Zeller.

In Ghana, my field research would not have been as successful without Barbara and David Tettey, to whom I am indebted for providing me with a home base in Accra over the last decade. I have been overwhelmed by all the help offered to me by the Tettey family and their friends, particularly Emelia Agyeman and Jennifer Amevedzi. In Anlo, my numerous informants who so generously gave me information over the years always made me feel welcome. I am very grateful to the Agboado, Amegbor, and Nyamesi families of Anlo-Afiadenyigba for their hospitality, and for the many enjoyable spells of fieldwork they facilitated in Ghana's Volta Region and Togo throughout the years. The final leg of research was made easier on account of the encouragement and goodwill of Irene Odotei and Kojo Amanor of the Institute of African Studies at the University of Ghana; I also picked up useful advice and information from Kojo Opoku Aidoo, Edward Nanbigne, Moses Nii-Dortey, and Samuel Ntewusu.

Numerous other friends, researchers, and well-wishers propelled this project through its various stages in several different ways. I thank: Mawuli Adjei and Sela Kodjo Adjei for helping with Ewe translations in the final moments; (the late) John Compton of Forfar for taking such an interest in my research and travels; Girish Daswani for sharing his astute scholarly insights on Ghanaian religion; Rita Duah-Sakyi for introducing me to Ghana over a decade ago; Tim Gros in Accra for his steadfast friendship; Jeanette Rehnström for her company during my first visit to Ghana; Martin Tsang for the most inspiring discussions on African and Afro-Atlantic religion; Abraham Vanderpuye for assisting with my last chaotic spell of archival research in Accra; Mawuena Abrotta, George Adadevoh, Victoria Agboado, Julius Akoto, Leila Chakravarti, Sharik Choudhury, Iván Cuesta-Fernández, Setri Dzivenu, Ingie Hovland, Malika Kraamer, George Kyeyune, Angela McFarlane, Louise Müller, Amy Niang, Eugene O'Doherty, Sang Park, Mette Steen Petersen, Jenny Roger, Elisabetta Romani, Eleni Sideri, Paul Swanepoel, and Marianna Volpi for their inputs at one stage or another; and finally, once more, a very special thanks to Louise Müller, without whose timely interventions and late-night Skype calls, this book would not have been *this* book. I am indebted to my family: my aunt, Stella, and my late uncle, Shankar, and my parents, for more than they can imagine.

I was delighted to discover that the reviewers for this book were Sandra Greene and John Parker; the insights they brought fine-tuned the discussions presented in the following pages. I also extend my thanks to the production team at Cambridge University Press. It has been a great pleasure to work with Stephanie Kitchen of the International African Institute (IAI), whose patience and professionalism at managing academic authors are truly remarkable. Miles Irving very kindly produced the maps. James Brisson designed the cover. Mike Kirkwood's masterful copyedits enhanced the quality of the text. Ken Karpinski oversaw the production process with great efficiency. Once again, I thank J. D. Y. Peel – this time in his capacity as an editor of the IAI's monograph series – for his enthusiasm for this project, and for his unflinching support over the last eight years.

Glossary

Most non-English words used in this work are Ewe, though a number of terms in other West African languages have also been used. All words below are Ewe, unless indicated otherwise. This glossary is intended for English speakers, and alphabetical ordering follows the English language. This list is not an exhaustive list of all foreign language words used in the following pages, but a Glossary of the most frequently occurring non-English words in the book.

Ewe uses the Roman alphabet supplemented by the following international phonetic alphabets: Đd, Ɛɛ, Ƒƒ, Ɣɣ, Ŋŋ, Ɔɔ, Ʊʊ. (I have not used these in my text). The presence of certain sound clusters (Dz, Gb, Kp, Ny, and Ts) make Ewe a rather difficult language to learn. The tilde (~) mark nasalises vowels.

I stick to the Anlo dialect of Ewe as far as possible.

I use Anglicised spellings throughout the book. Instead of Aŋlɔ, I write Anlo; instead of trɔ̃ I use tro, and adaɖaɖa is adadada.

The final 'e' at the end of many Ewe proper nouns should be pronounced 'é'. French spellings include this marking, while English spellings do not. In this text, Lomé is Lome, Sacrebodé is Sacrebode, and Kpalimé is Kpalime.

The plural of most Ewe words are attained by adding – *wo*, usually at the end. I follow this convention.

Ab(e)rewa	Anti-witchcraft movement; deity in the Anlo-Ewe Gorovodu pantheon; wife of Kunde
abusua (Twi; pl. *mmusua*)	matrilineage
Ada	One of the deities of the Yewe cluster
adadada	'cooking for Ada' (deity); part of the funeral rites for a dead Yewe initiate
adeha	'hunting group', casual supplicants of Gorovodu shrines, who organise ritual events, and are closely associated with the cult, but are not initiated into it

aduru (Twi; pl. *nnuru*)	drinking medicine
adze	witchcraft
adzeto	owner of witchcraft, witch/wizard
Afa	Divinatory system of the Anlo-Ewe; a knowledge system; also revered as a deity
afedo	local patrilineage
afedo-me	ancestral house
afeme	house, home
Agbodedefu	a ritual associated with a Yewe cult, where a ram is sacrificed to the sea;
agbota	a ceremonial role within some Anlo cults, in particular Fofie
agumaga	divinatory apparatus used by an Afa diviner
ahe	uninitiated members of any cult associated with shrines in an informal capacity
aklama	unique personality traits and distinguishing features of an individual
akonkofo (Twi)	a social group in Asante of the early colonial period, consisting of wealthy businessmen, who often rebelled against the fiscal policies of the *Asantehene*
akple	cornmeal porridge staple of the Anlo
alaga	The state of going wild within the context of the Yewe cult, in reaction to insults
Alegba	protective deity, the guardian of ritual knowledge, the gatekeeper of the Anlo-Ewe pantheon
alomevi	person acquired through working with one's hands; one of the many terms used to refer to a slave in the late nineteenth century in Anlo
Amaka	one of the deities of the Yewe cluster
amatsi	a combination of ceremonial herbs and water
amedzodzo	process of sponsoring a descendant
amedzoto	*Ame* = person, *dzoto* = ancestral part which makes up an individual, or ancestral sponsor
amefefle	bought person, someone acquired through the slave trade
amegasi	soothsayer
ametsiava	war captive, prisoner-of-war, enslaved person; also an ancestor who has died a premature death, usually attributed to human agency

asafohenega	war chiefs of the left and right wing of the Anlo army; borrowed term from Twi
Asantehene (Twi)	the Asante king
asekyere (Twi)	'pedigreeing', the offence of exposing or referring to an individual's non-Asante ancestry
atike	medicine
avadzi	war stool, symbolising one's slave-owning status in society
Avleketi	One of the chief deities of the Yewe cluster, the Goddess of the Sea and wife of Hevieso
avlesi	a sub-category of Yewe *vodusi*, pledged primarily to Avleketi
awadada	*awa* = war; *dada* = mother, war-chief of the Anlo, in charge of the central wing of the army
awoamefia	title of the paramount chief of the Anlo, which translates into 'he who lives in seclusion'
awoba (or *awowa*, a loan word from Twi, pl. *nnwowa*)	pawn or indentured labourer
batakari	tunic worn by northern peoples
bayi (Twi)	witchcraft
Blekete/Brekete	Drumming rhythm; a Gorovodu deity; an anti-witchcraft cult; a type of ritual knowledge
boko	Afa practitioner
bome	the abode of unborn souls
dasi	a sub-category of Yewe *vodusi*, pledged primarily to the serpent Voduda
dufia	chief of a *duto*
duko	city-state, chiefdom
duto	town or village, generally not as big as a *duko*
dzidzidome (Mina dialect)	born-betweens, category of people with male slave antecedents and free mothers in Mina society.
dzingbe/dzingoli	the sky
dzo	magic, medicine, protective measures used to combat witchcraft
dzogbe	destiny, the mechanism which charts out the specific path the individual has to follow during his or her lifetime; *dzogbe* may also refer to those ancestors who have not

	followed the path of destiny and linger on as unhappy presences
dzoto	mother and father parts, and ancestor souls, which go into the making of the *luvo*
Eda	one of the deities of the Yewe cluster
Evegbe	sense of 'Eweness', Ewe identity, oneness of Ewe people, the Ewe language, Ewe nationalism
Eweme	'Ewe inside', the central Ewe belt
fetatrotro	cow sacrifice, associated with Gorovodu cult
fiamanya	uninitiated members of the Fofie cult (translation, 'unknown queens')
fiasidi	initiate of a *troxovi* shrine, akin to *trokosi* (translation 'woman fit to marry a chief')
foasi	ceremony associated with the Nyigbla cult in the 1800s, by which two or more initiates from each Anlo clan could be recruited into that cult
Fofie	cult associated with slave ancestry, organised around a deity from Kete Krachi
fofiesi	pledged to Fofie, term used to describe a full-fledged initiate of the Fofie cult
fome	lineage, family
gbogbe	breath, or the force which kept the body alive
goro	kola nut
Gorovodu	cult associated with slave spirits from outside Anlo, and forms of medicinal knowledge derived from outside Anlo
Hevieso	thunder god; head of the Yewe pantheon; husband of Avleketi
hlo	clan, organised patrilineally in Anlo
hlofia	leader of a *hlo*, or clan
hlokponu	clan house
Hogbetsotso	festival held annually during the first weekend of November in most large Ewe towns to mark the peopling of Eweland after the mythical exodus from Notsie.
home	a pawned individual, though the word is also used for a bought person
hozi	stool of wealth
hubono	Yewe shrine owner
hunku	sacred palm nuts, part of an Afa diviner's apparatus
husunu	a male Yewe initiate, a *vodusi's* counterpart.

juju	(Colloquial) magic, witchcraft, medicine
klu	generic term for slave (word used in context of religious servitude, and also for a prisoner-of-war)
Kodzogbe	the world of the living
Koku	protective deity found in Anlo
kope	settlement comprising several patrilineages
kpele	divining beads
kpokpo	novice Yewe initiate, usually living in the shrine for a period of confinement. On completion of the period, they are known as *vodusiwo*
kpoli	signs of non-kin determinations/life signs, made by Afa divination
Kunde	an anti-witchcraft cult; head of the Gorovodu pantheon; husband of Ab(e)rewa; a slave-spirit
luvo	the physical elements of a person, believed to have powers special to an individual; *luvokuto* refers to the soul of death, while *luvoagbeto* refers to the soul of life
Mami Wata	a mermaid; a water spirit revered all over West Africa, whose worship is believed to generate success and mishaps in equal measure
Mamma	protective deity which was brought into Anlo in the 1980s from Nigeria
Mawu	the supreme God in Christian Ewe culture; one of the many Ewe *trowo* in some Ewe sub-cultures; along with Lisa the original cosmic couple in Ewe-Adja-Fon myth
Mawufe	the abode of Mawu; heaven
Mawusubosubo	Sunday service; Worship of Mawu (the Supreme Being)
medzi	one of the sixteen signs made by Afa beads as they are cast during divining sessions
midao	a Yewe priest, usually one step above *vodusiwo* and *husunuwo* in the Yewe cultic hierarchy.
minao	a Yewe priestess, usually one step above *vodusiwo* and *husunuwo,* in the Yewe hierarchy
nkwankwaa (Twi)	youngmen; a social class in Asante which arose in the nineteenth century, largely as a

	result of the cocoa boom and colonial economy
nukpekpe	Yewe initiation ceremony
nuvo	evil
nuvuvu	mouth opening, after which spirits speak freely through a person, generally used within the contexts of cultic initiation, especially Gorovodu and Fofie
Nyigbla	patron deity of Anlo and war god
obosom (Twi; pl. *abosom*)	natural forces transformed into deities
odonko (Twi; pl. *nnonkonfoo*)	generic term for slaves in Asante from the northern grasslands
ohoho (Twi; pl. *ahoho*)	free stranger resident in Asante from a neighbouring Akan kingdom
otani (Twi, pl. *ntafo*)	term used to refer to Muslim traders in Asante
senterwa	from the English sentry; minders of the possessed Gorovodu spirit mediums
sofo	from the Twi *osofo*; priest, especially in the context of Gorovodu cult; owner of Gorovodu god-objects
sosi	a sub-category of Yewe *vodusi*, pledged to the thunder god, Hevieso
sro	spouse; also means pledged in ritual contexts
suman (Twi, pl. *asuman*)	word used to refer to man-made deities, like protective charms and amulets
togbi	elder, grandfather
togbui	ancestor
togbuiwofenoli	ancestor who has led a dissatisfied life
tokomefia	ward chief, subordinate to the *dufia* or town chief
tro	deity, used mainly to denote ancestral deities in Anlo
troklu	initiate of a *troxovi* shrine, generally male
trokosi	initiate of a *troxovi* shrine, generally female
trosi	pledged to the *trowo*, term often used to describe Gorovodu spirit mediums in Anlo
troxovi	*tro* = deity; *kono* = unfruitful, lost (i.e. lost to parents and dedicated to deity); *vi* = child; literally, deities that took children.
Tsiefe	the world of the ancestors
vide	a little bit
vodu	deity, usually referring to nature spirits

Voduda	serpent deity in the Yewe cluster; companion of Avleketi
vodusi	pledged to the *voduwo*, used for a female initiate of Yewe shrines
Yewe	cult associated primarily with nature spirits, organized around Hevieso (Thunder), Avleketi (Sea), and Voduda (Serpent)
Yewegbe	ritual language spoken by members of the Yewe cult
yewesi	'pledged to Yewe', generic term for all Yewe initiates
zikpi	stool
zikpifeme	stool house
zizidzela	Nyigbla shrine initiates

1   Ghosts of Slavery?

While travelling through Anlo-Ewe villages in southeastern Ghana more than a decade ago, I came across several shrines dedicated to various local deities, known generically in the Anlo-Ewe dialect as either *voduwo* or *trowo* (sing. *vodu* and *tro* respectively). The outer walls of these shrines were adorned with colourful representations of mermaids, serpents, priestesses and priests, and visual depictions of the many spiritual entities in the Anlo-Ewe religious imagination. The images on the walls of one shrine complex near the northern Anlo town of Agbozume caught my particular attention. This shrine complex was located a good distance away from the centre of town. It was one of many rooms around a rectangular courtyard occupied by members of a single extended family. A pictorial story unfolded on two adjacent walls within the shrine. In the first picture, several slaves – chained together in single file – were being led away by men armed with guns, swords, and machetes. This procession of slaves and their captors was headed by the leader of the armed men, who carried an elaborately decorated stool on his shoulders. The image seemed to invoke a victory parade. The confidence and sense of jubilation present in the first image was conspicuously absent in the second one, which appeared to depict a more solemn, contemplative theme. The same warriors were now gathered around this stool and their slaves, bent on their knees with their arms outstretched, in a gesture implying subordination, anxiety, and worship. Not only were the slaves and the stool the focal points of the second visual composition, but they were also much larger than the warriors who had enslaved them. The slaves looked upon their former captors menacingly, while the faces of the warriors wore worried, distressed expressions. These two images made very little sense to me at that moment.

Later that day, I made my way to the local market. I became acquainted with an initiate of this shrine complex, who introduced herself as Adokomesi. She was in her late sixties, and maintained a small stall in the market, selling boiled rice and vegetable stew during the day. She explained to me that the cluster of deities to which that shrine complex was dedicated – known collectively as Fofie or Krachi Dente – were extremely influential spiritual entities all over Anlo.[1] Fofie referred not only to a collection of divinities, but also to a specific type of worship organised into a well-defined religious network across several towns and villages in Anlo, with a number of similar, if not completely uniform, beliefs, rituals, and practices. In the town of Agbozume alone, a large number of casual supplicants and committed initiates identified with the Fofie religious network. Adokomesi proceeded to tell me how she had come to be associated with Fofie.

Centuries ago, my ancestors were rich and prosperous. Some of them were merchants, while others were warriors. They frequently travelled out of Anlo to the slave markets in the north, to either capture or buy slaves. They kept some slaves for themselves, and sold the others at coastal markets. During one such expedition, they captured an Akan woman, and brought her here. She served her masters faithfully for several years. Her masters (my family) kept her very well. But she became just like a child of her master: she started worshipping her master's *voduwo* and *trowo*, and forgot her own people, her original home, her culture, and most importantly, the gods of her homeland. She married her master, bore him several children, and eventually died here in Anlo.

The slave master's family made a big mistake. They did not know how to perform her funeral when she died, as they were unfamiliar with her Akan funeral customs and the laws of her homeland. So they were not able to please her in death, and she remains an unhappy presence. All *voduwo* and *trowo*, including hers, are jealous beings. They need constant attention, sacrifices, and devotion. The slave master's family had encouraged this slave woman to forget her own gods. Those gods are angry with us, her descendants, and are demanding our attention now. I now represent her and devote my time to worshipping these Akan gods. I was renamed after her gods during an initiation ceremony. In fact, the name I bear is unheard of in Anlo and Eweland. It is associated with Akan gods, suggesting that my forefathers kept Akan slaves. As well as praying to our slave-owning ancestors, we must honour the slaves that our family owned in the past, because they worked hard for us. Master and slave have now become one through this worship, and we, their descendants, can be happy.[2]

As Adokomesi's account immediately suggests, the Anlo-Ewe have a special fascination with slavery as a collective experience in their past. The Fofie shrine with which Adokomesi was associated had about seventy other members in the town of Agbozume, known as *fofiesiwo* (sing.

---

[1] Fofie is a Twi word, which appears to translate as *fo* = people, *fie* = household. In the Akan calendar, Fofie is also the term for the fourth ceremonial Friday of the month, dedicated to the worship of Akan *abosom* (sing. *obosom*; Twi: deities or spiritual beings). (In the Akan calendar, a month has 42 days.) Fofie may also be used as a proper name in Twi-speaking regions, to refer to persons born on that particular Friday. The term in Anlo refers to a number of deities that are believed to originate from the Twi-speaking Akan areas of Ghana and the northern savanna. It is used also to denote a form of worship associated with these non-Anlo deities.

[2] Interview with Adokomesi, Agbozume, 12 August 2000.

fofiesi).[3] These women had pledged their lives, as Adokomesi had, to worshipping the various spiritual entities associated with their slave ancestors. Other *fofiesiwo* I became acquainted with also emphasised similar concerns with respect to the slave-holding past. Through their descriptions of Fofie worship, they articulated a curious mixture of emotions with respect to the Anlo agency in the practice, which included fear and apprehension in relation to the slave ancestors, combined with a sense of nostalgia for the prosperity the slave trade had brought their society in the past. *Fofiesiwo* claim that they are descended from once-prosperous slave-owning families. Most of the peoples that the Anlo enslaved hailed originally from the inland Ewe-speaking areas, referred to locally as 'Ewedome' lands, and areas that are currently the northern and Ashanti regions of modern Ghana, and parts of central and northern Togo.[4] These slaves would have been acquired between the late seventeenth and nineteenth centuries: primarily by Anlo merchants who traded salt and textiles in exchange for slaves from the slave markets that lay between the West African forest belt and the savanna; and secondarily as a result of the many military skirmishes between the Anlo and their various neighbours. Female slaves, in particular, were retained and incorporated into Anlo society. The Anlo preference for enslaving women was one they shared with other African societies of that era: apart from control over labour provided by a slave, the institution of slavery was also a legitimate and convenient method of enlarging a lineage or entourage (Akyeampong 2001b: 67). Land was scarce in Anlo: prestige and status were therefore realised through the control of people. Female slaves usually 'married' their masters, and were valued immensely by the latter for their reproductive capabilities. Anlo men, as a result, fathered children with slave women, which worked to the advantage of the former in establishing their credentials as individuals with large numbers of descendants.

Fofiesiwo also claim that enslaving peoples in the past had caused practical and spiritual problems, which they are trying to rectify through a series of ritual and religious performances and practices. They point to the fact that their ancestors – the Anlo slave masters – pursued a strategy of integrating their slaves into patrilineages and other local institutions

---

[3] *Si* (Ewe = wife/spouse of, implying a 'spiritual' marriage between supplicant and deity in this context). *Fofiesi* loosely translates into 'pledged to Fofie', or spiritual wife of the Fofie deities.

[4] 'Ewedome' or 'Awudome' (trans. 'Ewe in the middle') strictly refers to the Ewe chiefdoms of the central Ewe belt, sandwiched between the coastal Ewe zone and the northern Ewe zone. The Anlo, a coastal people located in the southernmost belt of Eweland, use the term rather loosely to describe any non-Anlo Ewe-speaking area located north of their chiefdom.

through marriage.[5] For the non-Anlo slave women, membership in Anlo society was contracted through their social roles as slave wives. Marriage to an Anlo man, however, imposed a number of other regulations upon the newly integrated member: in addition to observing rules and taboos of the patrilineage, these assimilated slave wives would also have had to worship deities and gods associated with the patrilineages of their masters. Ancestral deities and localised spirits occupy an important position in Anlo religious thought, as the Anlo believe that, just like themselves, their slaves would have had strong links with the ancestors and divinities of their distant northern homelands. By forcing their slaves to worship Anlo gods – in order to identify with and integrate into their masters' patrilineages – the Anlo had led their slaves to displease their ancestors and gods. They believe they have created a condition whereby their slaves were not only geographically displaced from their homes, but were also subjected to a programme of forced acculturation and assimilation. By 'Anloising' their slaves and their immediate descendants, the Anlo had deprived them of their identities and their uniqueness, which was tantamount to denying their very existence. They had condemned their slaves – to whom they owed much – into oblivion, turning them into invisible elements of Anlo social history. Generations later, therefore, the Anlo believe they are incurring the wrath of their former slaves and their long-forgotten gods for precisely these historical misdemeanours. Fofie worshippers, who are typically the descendants of slaves and their Anlo masters, believe they must now appease the long-forgotten gods of their slave ancestors, through the medium of prayer, to make up for generations of neglect.

In addition to the sense of fear that the Anlo feel in relation to their slave-holding past, narratives of *fofiesiwo* demonstrate the development of a particular moral logic with respect to the 'lessons of history' as they are locally construed (Boddy 1989: 417). Slave holding was formerly equated with wealth: slaves were money in the past. Owning slaves was a measure of the social standing and financial worth of an individual or a lineage. Claiming descent from a slave owner is a matter of great prestige in society, and the Fofie cult, while acknowledging the harm done to slaves in the past, also simultaneously celebrates this other aspect of slavery. The Anlo retrospectively believe that the period of slave holding and slave trading in their history – from the 1720s to the 1880s – coincided with an economic golden age, during which their chiefdom prospered from the revenues obtained through the trade. The demise of the slaving era was brought on in Anlo gradually after 1807, when the

---

[5] Anlo women belonged to their natal patrilineages throughout their lives, and did not assume membership of their husbands' patrilineages upon marriage. Slave wives could be integrated into their husbands' patrilineages, as they had no kin in Anlo.

British abolished the trans-Atlantic trade. Anlo came under expanding British influence during the late nineteenth century, and in the 1870s it was integrated into the Gold Coast colony. Steadily worsening financial conditions became a feature of post-1870s Anlo, and continued into the colonial era. The inability to generate money and wealth within the deteriorating post-slavery economic climate led the Anlo to draw their own conclusions based on the events of their recent history. They developed the belief that their slave ancestors, in collaboration with their Ewedome and northern gods, were angry with them, and had begun preventing them from accumulating wealth. The Anlo came to believe they have fallen from a more prosperous period in their past; Fofie worship provides a platform for pacifying the slave ancestors and their angry gods, who are held directly responsible for this fall. Aspects of Fofie worship, and the emphasis on the well-being of slave ancestors, appears to be an Anlo attempt at making amends for the past through a series of ritual, sacrificial, and practical measures.

Are the residual effects of slavery to be found only in Anlo-Ewe country? Virtually all West African societies, from the chiefdoms of Anlo to the kingdoms of Asante and Dahomey, owed their prosperity largely to participation in the slave trade. The acquisition of people through raiding, warfare, and from internal West African markets, may have accelerated in the region as a result of the demand for slaves created by the trans-Atlantic trade. As the domestic economies of these societies also relied heavily on slave labour, the large-scale incorporation of bought people, slaves, and ethnic outsiders into local kin and social structures was widely practised in African societies, as people were valued particularly for labour and their reproductive abilities in these people-poor societies. Scholars of West Africa broadly concede that discussing any aspect of the slave-holding and slave-trading past is a stringent cultural taboo. This is not to suggest that West African societies have forgotten or are psychologically unscathed by the legacy of slavery. A growing corpus of academic literature agrees that West African societies appear to have developed a range of different emotions in relation to their agency, role, and participation in the slave-trading and slave-holding past, emotions which find demonstration through diverse cultural mechanisms such as ritual and religious practices, aesthetic expressions, and social norms.

A comparative analysis of this literature suggests that the nature of the concerns developed by West African societies fall into three broad descriptive categories. In the first case, certain societies appear to be troubled by the social expulsion and exclusion of people through the slave trade. In such societies, a number of ritual mechanisms and oral traditions record extreme remorse at selling one's own people, especially kin and children, into slavery. Shaw (2002) argues that the slave-trading era was characterised by the breakdown of social cohesion and trust due to the rampant raiding and kidnappings in Temne society. These unsavoury memories are encoded in divination techniques and ritual knowledge, reproduced through asymmetrical gender relationships and kinship structures, and played out in the political sphere in post-colonial Sierra Leone where witchcraft and stories of cannibalism serve as metaphors for the same kind of exploitation that slaves would have endured as victims of predatory slave dealers. Similarly, Argenti (2006) argues that the masking performances of the *fulengan* society in the Oku chiefdom of the Cameroon Grasslands display an etymological link between masking and slavery: choreographic and dramatic features of these masquerades recreate the violence and deception involved in the act of selling kin into slavery. In the Dahomean heartland, the Fon appear to be concerned with the well-being of the souls of the people that they had sold into the trans-Atlantic slave trade: Herskovits tells us that during ceremonies associated with the cult of the royal ancestors in Abomey, there were always libations poured for those members lost to the community through slavery (Herskovits 1938).[6]

Secondly, smaller, non-centralised groups of people, placed typically between or at the boundaries of aggressive states, lived in perpetual fear of enslavement. Located at the fringes of the Dahomean kingdom, the Gen, AJA, and Hueda peoples of the Middle Slave Coast lived in constant fear of capture, which found articulation in the creation of ritual objects, anthropomorphic statues known as *bocio* (Blier 1995). The *bocio* are figures tightly bound with cords, gags, and strings of cowries, objects that were visual signifiers of the slave trade. Rather than providing aesthetic enjoyment, these statues were meant to awaken a negative disquiet in their audiences. Called *kannumon* or 'the things belonging in cords' (ibid.: 26), they reflected individual disempowerment and social breakdown to which the peoples of the Middle Slave Coast had become accustomed during the height of Dahomean slave raiding.

In the third instance, some societies have developed fears about the effects of the incorporation of large numbers of foreign slaves into society. Measures have been put in place to uphold the achieved status of assimilated slave descendants. Those concerned with the plight of incorporated

---

[6] A notable exception to this scenario is described by Charles Piot (1996). The Kabye of northern Togo were notorious for selling their kin into slavery. In 1909, German ethnologist Leo Frobenius noted that children from that society were usually traded in exchange for cowries. These transactions were usually undertaken by mothers' brothers of those sold into slavery. Maternal uncles were the family members who were regarded as the most affectionate and trustworthy, and who exercised ritual, social, and moral control over the pre-pubescent children of their sisters. Piot noted that members of the Kabye community within which he conducted his fieldwork continued to discuss this aspect of their past quite openly, and joked about it casually (Piot 1996: 31).

peoples were usually slave descendants themselves: their attitude towards their slave origins is generally one of shame; they seldom acknowledge this aspect of their past openly, usually resorting to elaborate measures to conceal it.[7] The Fulbe, an agro-pastoralist people in northern Benin, had a discrete category of person in their society, known as *maccube*, which loosely translated into slave. The descendants of the *maccube* are known as the *Gannunkeebe*, indicating that slave ancestry is ascribed in Fulbe society. The *Gannunkeebe* seldom respond directly to historical questions which relate to their slave origins, and their elders do not consciously pass down verbal narratives of slavery to the youth, favouring a complete rejection of this aspect of the community's past (Hardung 2002). Elsewhere in West Africa (from Niger to the Republic of Benin and the Gambia), slave descendants negotiate a number of strategies to cope with the stigma that host societies attached to their slave antecedents, from migration to concealment (see Bellagamba 2009; Hahanou 2009; Rossi 2009).

Closer to Anlo, the Asante and the Akan in general also appear to be concerned with the absorption of slaves into institutions and society. Many able office bearers were products of unions between slaves and free people, which resulted in the Asante state setting itself up as the guarantor for the achieved assimilated status of such people. The Asante rule *Obi nkyere obi ase* (Twi: one does not disclose the origins of another), maintained – and still does in Asante customary law – tremendous importance (Wilks 1975: 86). This rigid stance on not exposing one's slave origins is the norm not just in Asante, but also in the broader Akan belt: what we find in this cultural zone in general, is an artificial state of amnesia, induced either by the state machinery or societal laws (Poku 1969; Wilks 1975; Klein 1981, 1994; McCaskie 1995).

Ethnographers of the Anlo and southern Ewe have noticed that these closely related peoples seem to be deeply distressed over the manner in which they forcibly assimilated peoples into lineages through slavery in the past (Rosenthal 1998, Wendl 1999, Venkatachalam 2012, Rush 2013). Rosenthal's study of the Ewe of southern Togo suggests that these societies commemorate their slaves through their engagement with

---

[7] Some recent work has begun to suggest that slave descendants in some parts of West Africa spoke quite unabashedly about their pasts, as in the southern Ewe case. In an article written in 1999, Susan Rasmussen argues that the 'slave narrative' genre in Africanist scholarship needs to be re-evaluated. Through her analysis of two narrative accounts – one a former Tuareg slave and the other a former slave owner – she is able to illustrate that the slave voice is unashamed of the servile past, while the aristocratic voice expresses a sense of remorse at her agency in enslavement, her privileged position along with her subjectivity in history, as well as her class positioning in relation to slave descendants (Rasmussen 1999).

two religious orders, the Gorovodu[8] and Mama Tchamba. Rosenthal interprets the southern Ewe engagement with these orders as an elaborate culture of guilt that has developed in accordance with the dynamics of local history: the spirits of northern slaves have become the gods of the descendants of their southern masters, and the master–slave equation is inverted through the act of possession, generations after the demise of slavery. Through the practices of the Tchamba cult, the neighbouring Mina of Togo (immediately east of the Ewe), also revere slave ancestors in a similar manner, through spirit possession and a corpus of ritual measures aimed at the appeasement of their foreign-born slave ancestors (Wendl 1999). In southern Eweland, initiates of these analogous orders are neither reluctant to acknowledge the debt their communities owe to slavery, nor unwilling to admit their own slave antecedents. Thus, the ability to engage with the legacy of slave origins openly – albeit within the context of religious networks – appears to be a distinctive southern Ewe cultural trait, somewhat extraordinary when viewed through the comparative lens of West African ethnography.

Religious Change and Slavery in the Historical Imagination

This book revolves around two interrelated themes, which are dealt with in tandem with each other: (1) the relationship between memories of the slave-holding past in the historical imagination and an evolving Anlo identity over the twentieth century; and (2) religious change through Anlo social history.

My first thematic focus is the working of memory in the Anlo historical imagination. Anthropologists and historians have formerly treated history and memory as antithetical, diametrically opposed means of accessing the past (Lambek 2002: 54). History was meant to signify a record of events, written by a historian, and generally treated as a well-preserved discourse, immune to distortions. Memory, on the contrary, was believed to be its disorderly counterpart that manifested itself through folklore, myth, and even ritual, and was prone to constant distortion. In tracing the recent development of the Fofie cult in Anlo through available sources, this study is also addressing the complementary relationship – and tension – between memory and history, between the methods associated with the study of orality and historiography. It thus also interrogates the convergent and divergent spaces inhabited by Africanist anthropologists and historians.

---

[8] Gorovodu deities continued to be revered in contemporary Anlo, though their worship is configured in a manner that is very different from the practice in southern Togo, where Rosenthal conducted her research.

How have memories of slavery been constructed, and then reproduced by successive generations in Anlo social, cultural, and religious
landscapes? Firstly, I am interested in the mechanisms and the cultural
apparatus through which information about slavery is passed on and preserved – in other words, in the 'particular modalities' through which the
Anlo construct their relationship to their past (Cole 2001: 104). In Anlo,
the past is remembered through a variety of means: in discursive and
non-discursive ways; it is explicitly verbalised in accounts and codified
in non-verbal gestures; it is embedded in the landscape and embodied
in ritual. Secondly, I wish to explore the relationship between the functioning of social memory and identity. I am not concerned solely with
contemporary identity as a static phenomenon in the present; rather, I
am interested in the evolution of an Anlo identity as a continuous process
over the twentieth century and how it developed in definitional terms in
relation to peoples of slave origin in the chiefdom, a process which was
undoubtedly influenced by the space occupied by memories of slavery in
the Anlo psyche.

What exactly constitutes the subject matter of memory, and how can
we determine that a people are indeed remembering the past? Anthropologists agree that remembering in the strictest sense is an individual
activity, as memories can only be possessed by the individual in his or
her mind. Ethnographic knowledge is traditionally generated by informants in the form of answers to questions posed by the anthropologist.
Informants' replies take the form of discursive verbal narratives, where
they are usually explicitly aware of what they are saying, in response to
questions of the anthropologist. Individual narratives of the slave-holding
past have informed much of my research on the Fofie cult, and such narratives of *fofiesiwo* and their families have occupied centre-stage in this
ethnography. Scholars have often made a crucial distinction between the
memories individuals possess, dividing them into autobiographical and
semantic memory (Bloch 1998: 117). Autobiographical memory consists
of episodic memory, typically experienced by an individual during his or
her lifetime. Semantic memory constitutes generalised knowledge about
the past, taught to members of the community; these memories can be
either practical or theoretical, part of a larger corpus of the tradition
learnt from just being in society. Historical memory, the events of a more
distant past, is considered a subset of semantic memory. Autobiographical and historical memory, of course, cannot be studied, or retrieved, in
isolation from these other memories (ibid.: 121–4). Over the course of
a period of time, autobiographical memories usually become assimilated
into semantic – and historical – memory (Laidlaw 2004: 4), and they
are difficult to disentangle from one another. The distinction between
autobiographical, semantic, and historical memory is negligible within
the context of the Fofie cult: metanarratives and micronarratives merge

in the most unlikely ways, while contemporary family histories are juxtaposed to regional events in chronologically incompatible sequences.
Anlo 'memories' of the slave-holding past varied, depending on who was
entrusted with their narration. Memories of the slave-holding era focused
on the nature, personalities, and homelands of the women the Anlo once
enslaved, not dissimilar to Adokomesi's account furnished above. While
the basic gist of the stories about slavery remained roughly constant,
the details shifted depending on who voiced them. For instance, *fofiesiwo*
in the act of trance, when possessed by the slave spirits, lamented the
ill-treatment of slaves in Anlo; Fofie shrine-owners boasted the number
of slaves their ancestors owned or captured in war, a reflection on how
wealthy their families were in the past; accounts of Ewedome women
living in Anlo were concerned with Anlo 'savagery' in the past. Individuals from the same lineage will often narrate factually different accounts
about the same shrines, idols, ancestors, and slave spirits. These accounts
are chronologically and temporally distorted, as demostrated in Karin
Barber's (1991) study of *oriki*, or Yoruba praise poetry. As in the case
of *oriki*, their historical variegation is ignored, and although they contain
references to historical moments, they are not arranged in chronological
order, and older units are not separated from newer ones. While there
may be elements of truth in these narratives, the truth value in itself is
not important; what is important is that they are being kept alive by the
community in some recognisable form. For many *fofiesiwo* (and indeed
initiates of other cults), 'discovering' their connections with the slave
spirits (or other *trowo* or *voduwo*) was preceded by recurring periods of
sickness, which was alleviated upon joining the cult(s) in question; in
such cases, memories of these illnesses fused with their experiences of
being possessed by slave spirits, their own life histories, and fragments of
memories of historical slavery in Anlo. Bodily memories of illness were
such overwhelmingly traumatic experiences that they came to influence
how biography and social history were remembered; all these three categories merged in the narratives of initiates until they were completely
indistinguishable from each other.[9]

The erratic nature of individual memories therefore makes their truth
and analytic value about a past suspect. In *On Collective Memory* ([1950]
1992) Maurice Halbwachs argued that memories could be produced collectively by societies, in dialogue with the social frameworks within which
they are generated. According to him, collective memories are also essentially unstable: they are constantly reworked in keeping with 'the politics
of the present'. Therefore, given their shifting nature, memories need to

---

[9] This is not dissimilar to what Kleinman and Kleinman (1994: 714) observe in their
study of victims of trauma and political violence in Chinese society during the Cultural
Revolution.

be anchored through acts of social commemoration in order to be made truly memorable. Paul Connerton (1989) extended Halbwachs's thesis further, suggesting that assumptions and experiences about the past are conveyed not only through what have come to be regarded as 'conventional' historical methods such as oral transmissions and written sources, but are also replicated through habit memory, or 'the capacity to reproduce a certain performance' (Connerton: 1989: 22) through mnemonic activities. While Connerton agreed with Halbwachs that the distinction between individual and collective memories was insignificant on account of the fact that they were being constantly modified in dialogue with each other, Connerton went on to suggest that when the past was not remembered cognitively through such rituals and commemorative acts, it was being actively embodied in them (ibid.: 41–71). Included in these embodied habit memories were a broad range of (predominantly non-discursive) phenomena such as bodily gestures, socialisation, and other commemorative rituals that 'explicitly refer[red] to mnemonic persons and events, whether these are understood to have a historical or a mythological existence' (ibid.: 61).

Inspired by Connerton, a number of anthropologists have set out to show how the past has been encoded and embedded in non-discursive forms. Comaroff and Comaroff (1992: 38) argued that habits, mannerisms, and fashions, 'the bodily microprocesses', evolved in tandem with the larger social and political trends, 'the broad historical macroprocesses' associated with every historical epoch; characteristics of the latter, therefore, are imprinted upon the former. We have several ethnographic examples where slave descendants have internalised their servile statuses in their bodily gestures, mannerisms, accents, and expressions (Hardung 2002 on the *maccube* in Fulbe society; Rossi 2009 on the Tuareg). Bodies in themselves serve as mnemonic devices for key historical events in a number of societies. In northern Madagascar, the Antankarana royal descent group drowned to their deaths while in battle with the Merina; they now return as *trumba* spirits during a bathing ritual, enacting the instant they lost their lives, as they enter Antankarana bodies (Lambek 1996: 245–6). The Sadah, the rulers of Yemen, who claimed descent from the Prophet Mohamed, sought to replicate a particular type of personality, who was to have all the attributes of what they considered a worthy monarch (vom Bruck 2005). Essentially, the history of the Sadah was preserved through personal memory, and aspects of this history – such as relations with other interest groups and members of society – were constantly reproduced and replicated by successive generations. Sadah personhood – which was essentially the product of imitation – was defined through personal memory, with monarchs aspiring to replicate one another. *Fofiesiwo* reproduce history in a similar fashion, as they re-enact the lives of the slave ancestors and their relationships with their

Anlo masters. The bodies of the *fofiesiwo* serve as sites of memory in themselves, where experiences of slavery are actively embedded, selectively resurrected, improvised, and transformed, especially through the act of possession. Upon death, a *fofiesi* will be replaced by another family member from the same lineages. They, therefore, take on the attributes of one or many slaves kept by their lineages in the past, and hence inherit the personal relationship(s) the slave(s) had with her/their *trowo* from non-Anlo regions. After the initiation ceremony, the *fofiesi* is no longer her old self, but is meant to represent the slaves her family owned in the past. *Fofiesiwo* therefore actually re-enact history on some level, by bringing back individuals from a bygone age into the present.

Anthropologists have argued that in certain societies, instances of remembering are not expressions of individuality or recollections of an individual's thoughts, but rather ritual affirmations of relationships between either disparate groups of people, or, between the living and the dead (Lambek 1996; Cole 1998b, 2001), an idea that holds currency in the case of the Fofie cult. Cole observes that for the Betsimisaraka of eastern Madagascar, communication with the ancestors is a fundamental part of daily life, and seemingly mundane tasks – from farming to travelling – are incomplete without involving the ancestors in some capacity. Ancestral memory is not a heroic history of events (Cole: 1998b: 614), but rather a process which strengthens relations between the ancestors and descendants to mutual benefit. Cattle sacrifice, the cornerstone of Betsimisaraka life, is termed remembrance in local parlance, through which people renegotiate their links with the dead, as well as strengthen social order. To remember is more than to recollect a simple fact: it is to define the place of those who remember in the world, in relation to other cosmic agents (ibid.: 616). Following Bartlett (1995), Cole argues that by negotiating and fortifying one set of relationships, the Betsimisaraka forget other historical events: this explains their silence on topics such as the violence associated with French colonialism (which, in their conceptualisation of local history, threatened social order), a subject which Cole set out to study at the beginning of her sojourn in Madagascar. Cole contends that in their efforts to ensure the continuity of their own ancestral histories, the Betsimisaraka had incidentally incorporated and subordinated the French colonial period into their own historical narratives. Dual processes of 'deliberate forgetting' (Cole 1998b: 621–3) and 'incidental remembering' (ibid.: 624–6) had gone on to make this possible. However, French colonialism was not entirely erased from the Betsimisaraka historical psyche, and certain events could – and did – trigger a revival of memories of the episode. In Anlo, Fofie worshippers' memories of the slaving past are largely based upon genealogical accounts of their lineages (explored further in Chapter 4). For Fofie practitioners, the act of remembering is also tied with the ritual acts of revering the slave ancestors and their gods on a daily basis, through prayer, libation, possession, and sacrifice, in personal, lineage, and communal shrines: these acts create ancestral energy in themselves, which certain Anlo lineages deem necessary for their well-being. In a sense, the memory of slave holding is intimately linked with the memory of these slave ancestors, real or imagined, and generating knowledge and memories about slavery is indistinguishable from performing these ritual acts themselves. Ceasing to perform these ritual acts within the framework of the Fofie cult would eventually result in extinguishing the memory of local slave holding, and the slave ancestors, in Anlo.

In 2002, Rosalind Shaw argued that certain non-discursive forms in the Temne cultural landscape were in fact memories of the slave trade (Shaw 2002). She extended the distinction that Anthony Giddens made between discursive and practical consciousness to memory: according to Giddens, discursive consciousness referred to what an actor can express verbally; practical consciousness referred to the ability of the actor to access the *durée* of the action, without being able to express what s/he knows about it (Giddens 1984: 41–9). Practical memories, according to Shaw, refer to knowledge about the past embedded in the cultural landscape, of which people are aware, but to which they are unable to give expression. Such practical memories about slavery and the slave trade, according to her, can be, and have been encoded in key institutions, and have affected things as diverse as divination techniques, gender relationships, kinship patterns, and relationships between politicians and diviners in post-colonial Temne society. This approach suggests that ritual constitutes as well as preserves a culture's long-term memory; encoded within ritual, therefore, are cues that reference historical incidents.

There is little doubt that the ritual environment can be a repository of knowledge about the past, created and shaped by events of the past, and influenced by processes and practices of the past. Both ritual and habit memories (and there is an obvious relationship between them) are shared cultural knowledge, transmitted over time, through learned social practice. The content of both these memories – such as knowledge about the past, experiences, and activities that commemorate it – are, as far as this study is concerned, best conceptualised as something passed down from generation to generation in the form of 'tradition'. Often 'invented' to suit the ideological needs of the present (Hobsbawm and Ranger 1992), tradition contains factual distortions; it is warped as it undergoes a process of sedimentation and layering over time, as memories and lingering collective experiences come to be superimposed upon each other (as seen in the works of anthropologists who studied habit and ritual memories – see Lambek 1996; Cole 1998a, 1998b, 2001; Shaw 2002). Spirit possession, acts of divination, and the tending of ritual objects in Fofie shrines are all part of either ritual or habit memories; they are historically created processes, and members of a society may access the historical knowledge encoded in them or implied by them at differential rates, depending on a range of factors such as their positions, statuses, and socialisation.

Slave Coast religion has been described as a 'vortex' by Dana Rush (2008), on account of its ability to incorporate and thoroughly amalgamate influences, ritual techniques, and deities from the forest and savanna belts and trans-oceanic routes. It is helpful to think of Anlo historical memories of slavery in the past as 'vortextual' phenomena – aspects of discursive and non-discursive memory merge; in the production of ethnographic knowledge, historical narrative and ritual action often complement each other in complex ways in informants' accounts of the past; there is no one way of accessing the past that takes supremacy over the other. Combinations of autobiographical, historical, and semantic memories interplay with ritual and habit memories in interconnected yet multifaceted ways. It is the nature of these interconnections that this study attempts to explore and deconstruct.

Anthropologists such as Blier (1995), Shaw (2002), and Argenti and Röschenthaler (2006) argue that slavery and the slave trade were tremendously disturbing episodes in West African history, which have left behind extremely unsettling legacies that pervade the ritual consciousness through a series of fragmented, disconnected, artistic or ritual expressions. Argenti and Röschenthaler (2006: 35), using psychoanalytic models, argue that memories of slavery, like other memories of extreme violence, were experienced in the social psyche belatedly. Societies failed to deal with the consequences of the event normally – that is, in the immediately aftermath of the event: instead, they 'dissociated' from the pain caused by it at that point in time. Argenti and Röschenthaler go on to suggest that the slave trade will infringe upon a society's psyche as 'repetitive, intrusive experiences' (2006: 35), at various points in the future and in unrecognisable forms. These legacies of slavery, which manifest themselves in different ways, through discursive and non-discursive forms, are neither strictly memory nor history, and are best referred to ambiguously, as a 'body of experience' (ibid.) which implicitly refers to the past. That there is a robust corpus of information, 'a body of experience', about the slave-holding past stored in what Tobais Wendl terms the 'ritual consciousness' (1999: 122) in Anlo is undeniable. 'Ritual consciousness', according to Wendl, runs parallel to mainstream historical consciousness, and generally seeks to engage with problematic and sensitive issues, which societies find difficult to address openly. So where there is a general silence about the slave-holding or trading pasts, as in the case of the Mina, studied by Wendl, elaborate ritual performances enact and encode aspects of the morally problematic nature of the practice as envisioned by the society in question. In Anlo, however, there is considerable overlap between the ritual and historical consciousness, and there is considerable movement of information about slavery between the two spheres. We are, nevertheless, confronted with a chronological 'memory' puzzle in the case of the Anlo. 'Memories' of slavery would leave the Anlo ritual consciousness and enter mainstream historical consciousness somewhere during the early twentieth century. We know that a slave-related religious order (also called Fofie) existed in Anlo as early as the nineteenth century (Greene 1996a: 67; Akyeampong 2001b: 69). A combination of factors allowed for the reconfiguration of an already existing religious order into a cultic network which permitted the elaborate discussion of local slavery in the 1930s, decades after the abolition of domestic slave holding. It would appear that something noteworthy happened in 1920s Anlo: the very mechanisms for reproducing *habitus*[10] vis-à-vis the memory of slavery, became defunct (De Boeck 1998: 31), resembling what Richard Werbner (1998: 1) described as a 'memory crisis'; instead, the ghosts of slavery which were dormant in Anlo society were stirred up, and they were destined to intrude into the Anlo consciousness as a set of disconnected, disturbing experiences as outlined by Argenti and Röschenthaler (2006), until they were reconfigured into some meaningful schematic forms of expression that could be reproduced to serve as reminders of slavery as the Anlo would deem appropriate to their existential needs at some moment in the future.

Exactly when and why did the Anlo-Ewe develop strong moral sentiments against slave holding? As the early twentieth century progressed, they came to be deeply troubled by the part they had played in enslaving people in the past. The evolution of the Fofie cult, from the 1930s to the present, serves as a window on the shifting discourses on slavery in the Anlo consciousness: it also tells us about changing relationships between the coastal Anlo and their northern slaves, from the era of pre-colonial slave raiding to post-colonial Ghana; it documents the transition of various northern and Ewedome peoples in the Anlo imagination from slaves to citizens of the same nation state. Fofie also serves as a framework through which the Anlo access and engage with conversations about slavery with descendants of slaves from across the Atlantic: ideas of inequality, poverty, and human dignity are central to this exchange of ideas on slavery, forced mobility, and destiny. During the 1930s, Anlo memories of slavery came to focus on the contributions of slaves to their lineages and society; they also sought to emphasise the suffering they (as slave masters) had inflicted upon their slaves. Further, they came

---

[10] *Habitus* in Bourdieu's terms is the ability to reproduce the past. It is embodied history, which is 'internalized as a second nature and so forgotten as history, and is the active presence of the whole past of which it is the product' (Bourdieu 1990: 56).

to think of enslavement as a practice that was morally problematic, as it had robbed slaves of their connections to their own homes, families, and ancestors, all the things that completed and humanised people in Anlo religious thought. Interestingly, these ideas about the ethically problematic nature of slavery were constructed not in the language of European abolitionism, but through local religious institutions and Anlo perceptions of their own versions of history and their ideas of moral progress. Sedimented upon this local discourse on Anlo slavery would be other narratives, generated against the backdrop of conversions to Christianity; conversations with diasporan Africans (initially freed slaves who returned to Anlo, and later tourists in the African diaspora who arrived in search of their roots), and discourses on abolition that were promoted by the colonial and post-colonial state, adding to the layered, multi-faceted nature of memories of slavery and the slave trade in contemporary Anlo. Eventually, aspects of the slaving past that have made the Anlo uncomfortable would be 'sequestered' – to borrow a term from Bayo Holsey (2008) – or omitted from the public sphere. Discussions of slavery and the slave trade in the public sphere and in the post-colonial educational curriculum contribute significantly to this process, leading to the formation of new sets of memories through entirely new media.

The second thematic focus of this book is religious change. Religious activity is the medium through which the Anlo remember slavery in their past, and participation in the Fofie cult is one of the main ways through which concerns about slave holding in the past are articulated. The Fofie cult, with its corpus of practices dedicated to the well-being of the peoples the Anlo once enslaved, is one of the many religious cults in Anlo, and functions in accordance with the dynamics of the religious system. Situating the Fofie cult within the contemporary Anlo religion system is one aspect of this study. One of the most significant contributors to the study of Ewe religion is Albert de Surgy (1981; 1988), and his work provides a valuable catalogue of deities, cults, and human players in the Ewe religious landscape. Michel Verdon (1983) focuses on the Abutia Ewe, located north of Anlo. Though Verdon's study is focused on the political and social structure of the Abutia Ewe, it makes a significant contribution to an understanding of the differences between the religious practices of various Ewe sub-groups. Nadia Lovell (1993; 2002), who studied the Ouatchi (Watchi) Ewe of Togo, assesses the importance of kinship for religious participation, a study which has helped place Anlo attitudes towards kinship and inheritance within the broader regional context.

These studies of Ewe religion and religious history have tended to analyse the development of 'indigenous' religious practices in isolation from their engagement with the world religions, enforcing a rather unhelpful emphasis in the academic literature. Christianity has become an integral part of the West African religious landscape and worldview, and any study of the evolution of indigenous religious practices has to take this factor into account. Most recently, studies by Rosenthal (1998), Baum (1999), and Allman and Parker (2005) have continued this trend, documenting the evolution of 'indigenous' religious practices in various West African societies, while not adequately accounting for the multiplicity of conversations between indigenous African traditions and the world religions. This situation has arisen, in part, because sources for the construction of the African religious past are so different, giving rise to separate research trajectories. Most studies concerned with indigenous religion are put together through meticulous fieldwork, resulting in the analysis of locally construed histories (see Lorand Matory 1994 on the Yoruba; Rosenthal 1998 on the southern Ewe; Baum 1999 on the Diola). Equally, significant studies of West African Christianity have tended to concentrate on how Christianity was indigenised, while ignoring parallel developments within local religious traditions (see Peel 1968b; Adogame 1999; Soothill 2007). There have been very few attempts to construct West African religious history as a dialogue between the world religions and African 'traditional' religion (Meyer 1999; Peel 2000). These histories of religion in West Africa, continue to focus on mission history, inevitably using missionary accounts as their initial baseline – and these histories contained an inherent bias: they carried very little information or analysis on actual indigenous religious experience, and exhibited a tendency to marginalise developments within the sphere of African traditional religion. The story of the evolution and development of indigenous religion is therefore abruptly cut short upon mass conversion, and the history of indigenous religious practices has become a footnote in the development of African Christianity or Islam, leaving us with an inadequate picture. I attempt to trace the evolution of practices related to the Fofie cult in their most recent form, from their institutionalisation in Anlo during the 1930s to the present. I treat Anlo Christianity and 'traditional' practices as part of the same structure, preferring not to distinguish between the two traditions. This history of Anlo religion attempts to reconstruct why Fofie and the themes articulated through engagement with the cult became moral and existential concerns in Anlo religious history when they did. I also attempt to provide an explanation for religious change in Anlo in the *longue durée*, to try and account for: (1) how indigenous religious practices and Christianity developed in tandem over time; and (2) why certain cults and strands of Christianity gained popularity at some points in the chiefdom's history, while others fell from favour with their devotees during other times. This explanation of religious change seeks to critially engage with theories and arguments that present conversion in terms of cultural rupture, power relations, and modernity (Horton 1971; Fisher 1973; Ifeka-Moller 1974; Mudimbe 1983); instead, drawing upon recent ethnographies by Baum (1999), Meyer (1999), and Allman and Parker (2005), I argue that local perceptions of history, changing notions of identity, morality, and destiny within the colonial geo-political context, along with formations of pre-colonial, colonial, and post-colonial sub-jectivities informed religious preferences during the course of the Anlo's knowable religious history.

Finally, a note on the methodological problems associated with writing a West African social history, especially one so heavily based on oral sources. The term history in itself is used to signify two different concepts. On one hand, it refers to real events that occurred in the past, and on the other, to retrospective representations of those events. This distinction is essentially one between 'history as experience' and 'history as reflection' (Tonkin 1992: 2). 'History as reflection' is seldom a faithful and true representation of 'history as experience', given that it is reconstructed from scraps of available evidence and memories, prone to the biases of the individuals and institutions recreating it. Included in this 'history as reflection' are a number of forms of representation of the past, apart from the conventional writing of histories by historians. This study aims to combine both 'history as experience' and 'history as reflection', given the fact that it is a product of ethnographic as well as historical research. Unfortunately, the paucity of sources means that the two phenomena are represented in conversation with each other, and sometimes appear to be indistinguishable from each other in this study.

West Africanist historians have noted that it is 'difficult to combine structural analysis and narrative history' (Peel 1983: 14), and reconcil-ing the two in any West African setting, given the nature and availability of sources, is an uphill task. Peel therefore advocates a nuanced analysis of the 'past in the present' (ibid.). This study aims to address precisely this tension between structure and narrative in Anlo. Narratives of Fofie initiates (individual memories that have emerged in conversation with habit memories and tradition) are juxtaposed against a historical analysis of patterns of religious engagement in Anlo, to account for the develop-ment of the cult. While narrative is indeed the most 'spontaneous form of historical representation' (Peel 1995: 583), I attempt to stay away from the 'descriptive, extraneous orientation of much of Africanist his-tory' (McCaskie 1986: 316), which has resulted from an over-reliance on narrative sources. Instead, I attempt to combine both etic and emic per-spectives, using anthropological and historical sources in complementary fashion, in the tradition of previous historians of Anlo, such as Greene (1996a, 2002, 2011) and Akyeampong (2001b).

'Doing Fofie': Methods and Challenges

'Anthropologists who have lost their senses often write ethnographies that are disconnected from the worlds they seek to portray.'

(Paul Stoller 1995: 15)

Slavery, Religion, and Memory was initially conceived as an academic project in 2000. When I first came across Fofie worshippers in Anlo in the summer of 2000, I was unaware that they would become the focus of an academic project which lasted more than a decade. During my first visit to Ghana, I visited all the sites on the standard tourist trail. Anlo did not feature on my list of places of interest. After two months in Ghana, I met a few people from Keta, who urged me to go to Anlo upon discovering my interest in religion. Reluctantly and not quite knowing what I would find so interesting, I boarded a *tro-tro* and headed east of Accra in the direction of Anlo.

I spent a few days in the towns of Agbozume, Nogo-kpo, and Aflao. Colourful shrines with representations of other worldly creatures dotted the landscape. A number of informal discussions with people in roadside bars ('drink spots') on Anlo religion, *vodun*, and cults such as Fofie provided food for thought. My acquaintance with Adokomesi Seragagi, a *fofiesi*, provided me with a few details about Fofie worship. Just before I left Anlo, Adokomesi took me to see an Afa diviner. The diviner sat on the floor in his room, on a mat with specially decorated beads. These beads were his divining apparatus, his sacred objects with which he read into the future. After the customary offering of money and a tot of *akpetesi*, the local gin, I proceeded to ask him questions about Afa. I was not sure why I had been brought to see him: there were no pressing existential questions that I needed to have answered. 'You have been lured to Anlo by certain gods,' he told me. 'You will be back, your business here is far from finished. I believe the gods of your father's people are demanding your attention.' I smiled politely, told the diviner that I could not quite imagine what his beads might be referring to. I thanked him for his time, bade Adokomesi farewell, and left Ghana.

In 2003, I began studying anthropology. My plan was to return to Anlo and study the Fofie cult. Nothing – no amount of textbook knowledge – could have prepared me for the lived experience of ethnographic field-work. I visited Anlo-Afiadenyigba at the invitation of a friend. Although I had been to that town in 2000, nobody knew me. All the standard apprehensions of a novice anthropologist occupied my thoughts. I had a number of concerns. What if nobody spoke to me about Fofie? What if they did not allow me to witness their rituals or allow me into their shrines? After all, I am an outsider: why should they share knowledge about their ancestors and gods with me? How could I be as arrogant as to think that I – equipped with a degree in theoretical anthropology – would be able to understand the intricacies and complexities of someone else's beliefs and culture? I was determined not to let the methods associated with anthropology, an academic discipline with its origins in the colonial project and its emphasis on the systematic and somewhat clinical study of the 'other', dictate the pace of my research. Rather, I would just go with the flow, seeing what I came across, listening to stories of *fofiesiwo*, and letting them generate information about themselves, their lives, and their belief systems.

The first problem I encountered was that of access. On 12 September 2003, I attended the funeral of a Fofie initiate in Anlo-Afiadenyigba. There were a number of *fofiesiwo*, dancing to drumbeats in the mid-afternoon. Some of them entered a state of trance. There were a number of other spirit mediums, who hosted spirits from the northern savanna. The possession performance, the emergence of these spirits in their mediums, their colourful costumes and dances were an intriguing spectacle. I began chatting to a number of young people, standing some distance away from the main ceremony. I made known my intentions of studying the Fofie cult. 'You will find it difficult to learn anything about Fofie,' they insisted. 'You cannot do Fofie unless you are born into a Fofie-worshipping family,' one young man informed me. 'Fofie members will just not talk to you about their ancestors,' said another. Disheartened, I watched on, wondering what I was going to do.

A procession of Fofie worshippers walked into the bush surrounding the shrine after a possessed initiate ran in that direction. As I followed the procession to witness the spectacle, I came across a Fofie devotee, who was to play a significant part in the unravelling of my project: he is referred to simply as 'Babaa' ('father') in this ethnography. Babaa was in his early sixties, a retired army officer with a rather colourful past, who had come back to live in Anlo-Afiadenyigba, his hometown, upon his retirement. 'Fofie is my family deity,' he informed me. 'You cannot really go into these shrines unless they relate to your ancestors.' It seemed that absolutely nobody would allow me to ask them any questions about Fofie.

Babaa ran a small drink spot in Anlo-Afiadenyigba. I became a fixture in this establishment, sitting there with my notebook every morning. I asked Babaa and his visitors seemingly awkward questions about Fofie. Most of them were thoroughly irritated at my questions. 'We cannot talk about those gods without their permission,' they informed me, 'or else they will punish us severely.' Nearly a month later, I had still not managed to speak to a single Fofie initiate. I was on the verge of giving up. When I came around to realising that Fofie could be accessed only through family ties, Babaa came up with a solution to the problem – after weeks of having to endure my presence and my incessant questioning. 'I will adopt you: as my daughter, my ancestors become your ancestors; my gods will be your gods. This way you can access Fofie shrines and worshippers. You will be a daughter of my lineage.' Thus, I was adopted into a former slave-holding patrilineage, which gave me unprecedented access to the slave ancestors, as I became more and more integrated into Babaa's lineage.

The Afa diviner's rather vague prophecy in 2000 appeared to have been fulfilled. The gods of my new adopted father had desired my attention; they had made sure that I had not forgotten them over these years, and they had lured me back to Anlo. About three months after I had been 'adopted', Babaa and a number of Fofie initiates actually began encouraging me to write about Fofie. 'Fofie is how we address the wrongs of our history,' Babaa informed me. He continued: 'It is a gentle, compassionate set of ideas, by which we seek to come to terms with our own local history, in a limited way. The world would be a better place if everybody recognised the evils of their own history.' Babaa not only became my 'father', but my chief informant. Apart from the friendship he provided, he was a wealth of knowledge on religion, Anlo life, and local history. My association with Babaa, and my newly constituted social role in Anlo as his daughter, greatly facilitated my research, opening doors into a vast labyrinth of hitherto inaccessible cultural knowledge. Conventional fieldwork methodologies proved cumbersome and ineffective during the course of my research into the Fofie cult in Anlo: I quickly realised that formal interviews yielded very little information, while informal discussions and gossip, though seldom used by anthropologists in the field, were a much more significant – and effective – method of gathering information.

The other significant challenge to this study was that many of my informants were spirit mediums who frequently submitted to the act of possession. Spirit possession, central to the veneration of slave ancestors, is generally identified as a condition during which spirits or disembodied beings engage with particular human hosts, in such a way that the host is periodically absent from his or her own body, replaced by the voice and persona of the spirit (Lambek 1996: 236). *Fofiesiwo*, in the ultimate act of subordination and prayer, submit to the slave spirits and their foreign gods, by offering them their bodies to dwell in for a limited duration. Spirit possession is a complex set of multi-dimensional relationships between spirits, spirit mediums, and their audiences. The phenomenon has captured the imaginations of anthropologists, historians, and psychiatrists, mainly because of its inherently unfathomable nature. No overarching theory could describe the sheer complexity associated with the act of spirit possession. It is indeed the 'local equivalent of multiple personality disorder, Freudian sublimation, Jungian archetypes, the formation of right brain personalities, the working out of colonial and postcolonial disorders, Marxist illusions, mimetic excess and just plain good acting' (Friedson 2009: 9). Instead of using frameworks derived from North Atlantic philosophical and psychological perspectives one can, however, also try to explain what spirit possession means by studying the historical and anthropological context of those cultures in which the phenomenon appears. At other times, spirits arise to check deteriorating moral standards, as in witchcraft-plagued, conflict-ridden Uganda of the 1970s (Behrend 2000). Possession performances interrogate historical and contemporary power relations within sub-regions: Kiarabu and Kipemba spirits produce a critical commentary on the relations between the Islamised peoples of the Kenyan coast and their primitive 'other' which takes the form of the Africanised peoples of the interior (Giles 2000). The Hauka spirits, who starred in Jean Rouch's famous documentary *Les Maitres Fous* (1955), subtly challenged political order, by appropriating key personalities that symbolised authoritarian oppression (Stoller 1995). The deprivation theory put forward by Ioan Lewis suggested – albeit by being somewhat insensitive to ethnographic peculiarities – that spirit possession cults recruited from socially marginalised sections of society, such as newcomers, slave descendants, and low-status women (Lewis 1989).

The devotees of the *trowo* and *voduwo* in Anlo, especially spirit mediums, often imply that the spirits are a source of knowledge about a higher truth. The spirit mediums have absolutely no agency in choosing the ancestors, deities, and spirits that they worship. It is the spirits who identify their hosts and devotees, and proceed to ensnare them, locking the devotee into a lifelong relationship with the spirit. Spirit possession, as performance, is about a total renunciation of agency on the part of those that host the spirits. Of course, the several spirits I encountered seldom agreed to give me, an anthropologist, any formal interviews: however, I became part of what Shaw calls the 'spirit memoryscape' (Shaw 2002: 46), and the spirits, in turn, became aware of my attempts to write about them. Their utterances and interactions with their audiences were a crucial part of this research. Some of them, especially the Fofie spirits of my adopted father's patrilineage with whom I became acquainted, became my informants and critics. Some of these spirits gave me information about where their slave ancestors hailed from in the North when they emerged in their hosts. Yet others protested during an *akpedada* (Ewe: thanksgiving) that they had not been represented in my work as they would have liked, a day after I read several passages out of my thesis to members of some Fofie-worshipping families to ask for their opinions. That the Anlo hosts have assigned the spirits a more powerful agency than themselves is undeniable. To those of this mindset, spirits are active agents in the making of history, especially religious history. Spirits do indeed exhibit 'consciousness of the historical process and contentious intervention in that process' (Lambek 2002: 33). In writing this historically conscious ethnography of memories of slavery in Anlo, I have found it impossible to disregard the voices and the agency of the spirits, who are regarded as legitimate, key players in the history of Anlo religion by their devotees.[11]

Over the course of a decade, Fofie-worshipping lineages shared their family histories with me; spoke to me about their gods and slave spirits, and invited me to witness the rituals they performed in their shrine complexes. For this I am eternally in their debt. These Fofie worshippers eventually became my friends. They were always welcoming of me and my guests; generous in the time they gave me; patient in the face of my numerous questions, which must have seemed amusing and highly irritating to them. I have done my best to represent them as they would have wanted me to, often sticking to their own words. Babaa seldom left my side: interpreting, translating and making sense of countless stories and parables told to me by my many informants. He patiently corrected scripts of transcribed interviews, dealt with my poor Ewe language skills with humour, and often stood by me as he translated possessed utterances of spirit mediums. His very eventful life and the experiences associated with his many social roles had constituted his social subjectivity. Babaa had been a lifelong political activist, challenging injustice as he saw it, at the local, regional, and national level. He was a respected local figure, known for his vocal support of women's rights organisations; trade unions, and, controversially, his participation in the 'Revolution' of the 1980s. His unique subject position had constituted his – while influencing my – understanding of the raison d'être of the Fofie cult and the set of ideas associated with it. His 'Way of Seeing' became 'My Way of Seeing'. I am acutely aware of his enormous contribution to this project and his absent presence throughout this ethnography. Babaa's vision of Fofie as a set of practices which critically addressed an injustice in the past is an undertone which guided the manner in which this project came to be intellectually conceived. I made eight visits to Anlo between

---

[11] Harry West's *Ethnographic Sorcery* (2008) seeks to move beyond anthropological perspectives that read the phantoms, mythical creatures, and processes (such as sorcery) that exist in the imagined world of the Muedans of northern Mozambique as either metaphorical allegories or downright dismissals of 'primitive belief systems'. West suggests that anthropological over-interpretations often tend to miss the point: that these phenomena are rendered real by the local agents (sorcerers in this case), who project them into the invisible religious belief systems, thereby turning them into a sort of reality for the people who subscribe to them. West draws a sophisticated analogy between ethnography and sorcery, arguing that ethnographers are, in a sense, also sorcerers of a kind: their attempts to create ethnographic knowledge are akin to the sorcerer's art of sorcery. Similarly, Stephen Friedson (2009: 35–40) cautions against dismissing spirit agency in West Africanist history, arguing that they are a real presence for those that believe in them. Building upon instances and occurrences of spirit possession, Joost Fontein (2014), in a thought-provoking ethnographic vignette, presents us with a case where the phenomenon presented a legal challenge in a criminal case in the United Kingdom.

2003 and 2014: these visits ranged from a month to ten months, during which I attempted to build up a corpus of ethnographic knowledge about Fofie worship. One of my last spells of fieldwork in Anlo was conducted in December 2010, when I returned to celebrate Babaa's funeral in the company of numerous *fofiesiwo* who travelled to Anlo-Afiadenyigba from all over Anlo to bid him farewell. I would, of course, be inclined to blame all errors of judgment and interpretation on him, but I alone must take responsibility for them.

Chapter by Chapter

First and foremost, this book is an attempt to fuse two disciplines, anthropology and history. The present is the focus of the first section, in the form of Chapters 2, 3, and 4. Chapters 5–8 are historical, focusing on the period from *c.* 1850 to the present. Second, I try and juxtapose two voices through this book: the spirits, as narrators, are given equal importance as oral, archival, and other historical sources favoured by the anthropologist-historian. Chapter 2 deals with the Anlo-Ewe as a people: their location, place and role in West African history. The major religious cults and networks in Anlo are discussed in Chapter 3. Chapter 4 describes the memory practices of the Fofie cult. The period between *c.* 1780 and *c.* 1910 is the focus of Chapter 5. This period was characterised by the rise and fall of the slave trade, the end of domestic slave holding, and the introduction of Christianity, which changed the socio-religious landscape in Anlo. Chapter 6 is concerned with the period between *c.* 1910 and *c.* 1940, which is crucial to the story of slavery in the Anlo imagination. A series of religious movements that originated in the geographically distant northern savanna belt gradually came to be established in Anlo after the 1910s. The Anlo came to understand this movement of ritual resources as a direct consequence of their slave-holding past. Other social processes that were metamorphosing during this period, such as the sharpening of an Anlo identity and the development of an Ewe ethnicity, were also crucial to the reawakening of the ghosts of slavery. In Chapter 7, I chart the development of the Fofie cult against large-scale structural changes in the Anlo religious system between *c.* 1940 and the present, accounting for the intricacies in the dialogue between traditional religious practices and the strands of Christianity. Chapter 8 seeks to examine how memories of slavery, slave holding, and slave trading are being reconfigured in Anlo against the backdrop of conversations about these issues at the local, national, and global levels. Chapter 8 also concludes this study by highlighting the major structural changes that have taken place in Anlo religious history, and by examining how these affect the memory of slavery as preserved within the Fofie cult in the Anlo imagination.

2   The Anlo-Ewe: Portrait of a People

In the Ghanaian popular imagination, Anlo evokes images of desolate, sandy beaches and once-thriving trading towns in a state of decay. The Anlo themselves are regarded as an illustrious, hard-working people, keen to escape the conditions of poverty imposed upon them by a harsh natural environment. Despite their great successes in the urban centres of Ghana and West Africa, they are often unjustly accused of being inward-looking and 'tribalistic', remaining attached to their homeland and people. Anlo's location, wrapped around the Keta Lagoon, bordering Togo and the Atlantic, with several inlets and waterways cutting through the chiefdom, meant that it earned a reputation as a major hub for illicit trade and smuggling. But the Anlo are best known for their ritual landscape: they have often received unwanted – and unfair – publicity for their occult practices and apparent attachment to *juju*, which roughly translates as 'magic'.

The Anlo-Ewe are a distinctive southern branch of the larger Ewe-speaking grouping. The Ewe in turn are part of the larger Gbe-speaking ethno-linguistic cluster in West Africa. Situated roughly in the area between eastern Ghana and western Nigeria, Gbe speakers are bordered by Ga-Adangme, Akan, and Guan speakers to the west, the Yoruba to the east, and the Akpafu, Adele, Lolobi, and Aguna to the north. Gbe speakers are spread across different geographical zones: the western limit is the Volta Lake in Ghana, while the eastern boundary is the Weme River in Nigeria; the north–south border is marked roughly by the eighth parallel and the Atlantic coast respectively. They are spread across four countries: Ghana, Togo, Benin, and Nigeria. The main sub-groups of the Gbe cluster are the Ewe, Fon, Aja, Gen/Mina, and Phla-Phera, though linguists have identified as many as fifty-one distinct Gbe-speaking sub-communities in the region (Capo 1991: 2–5). The major Gbe-speaking societies have been defined by profoundly different historical experiences: the Aja people settled in and around the region of Tado in contemporary south-central Benin, which was the only organised state in the region by the fifteenth century; the Ewe people of Ghana and Togo have always been a rather fragmented group of small polities that never really merged into a single political unit; the Fon managed to organise themselves around the city of Alada in the seventeenth century, eventually forming the kingdom known to history as Dahomey; the Gen are believed to be ethnically Ga from the Accra region; the Mina of Anexo have Fanti origins; and the Phla-Phera settlements predate the arrival of the Gbe speakers. Despite the different historical trajectories of Gbe-speaking societies, they are regarded as a unit for the purposes of linguistic categorisation, and there are some striking cultural and religious traits that are common to most, if not all Gbe-speaking societies, which set them apart from the other large ethno-linguistic groups in the region, such as the neighbouring Akan and Yoruba (Capo 1991). The vast majority of Gbe speakers believe they have settled their current location in several migratory waves, between the eleventh and fifteenth centuries, from what are now modern Yoruba-speaking areas. Another distinctive Gbe societal characteristic appears to be the presence of large religious cults and networks, dedicated to deities called *vodu* amongst the Fon and Aja, and *tro* by the Ewe (Spieth 1911; Herskovits 1938, Vol. 2: 101–200; Ellis 1965: 31–90). This area witnessed intense political turmoil between the seventeenth and early nineteenth centuries, which coincided with the rise of the trans-Atlantic slave trade and the growing influence of competing European powers on the coast. Conservative estimates suggest that between 1710 and 1810 almost one million slaves – 22 per cent of the total forced exodus from West Africa – were exported from the ports of the Bight of Benin, part of coastal Gbe-speaking societies, earning this area the name 'Slave Coast' (Law 1991b; 2004: 2).

Roughly half of the eight million Gbe speakers are Ewe, who number 3.5 million across Ghana and Togo. According to the 2010 Ghana census, there were slightly under three million Ewe speakers in the country, forming a little over 11 per cent of the country's total population.[1] The corresponding figure for Togo is one million, with Ewe-speaking communities comprising 20 per cent of the total Togolese population.[2] Situated between the Volta Lake in Ghana and the Mono River in the Republic of Benin, the Ewe occupy a rather interesting geographical position in West Africa. Like all Gbe speakers, the Ewe consider their origins to have been in what is now Yorubaland (Ward 1958: 134–6; Nukunya 1969a: 1; Mamattah 1976; Amenumey 1986). They share several cultural traits with the Yoruba, the most easily identifiable being their religion, which resembles Yoruba *orisa*-type beliefs, ritual practices, and cultic organisation. Their belief in an eastern homeland has led them to promote trade and ritual links with societies located east of them, like the Aja, Fon, and Yoruba. While the Ewe have been particularly

---

[1] Source: http://www.indexmundi.com/ghana/demographics_profile.html accessed 22 January 2013.
[2] Source: http://en.wikipedia.org/wiki/Gbe_languages/ accessed 26 June 2006.

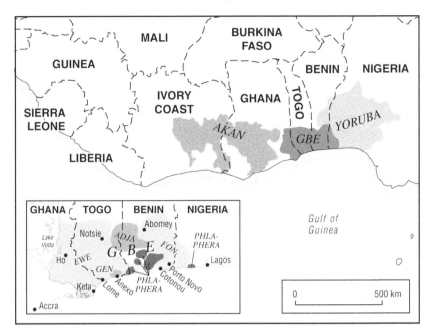

Figure 2.1. The Gbe-speaking people and their neighbours

receptive towards influences from the east, they have also been subjected to cultural and military intrusions from the Akan, who lie west of
them. The Akan belt has seen the rise and fall of many expansionist
states such as the Asante, which at its zenith in the late eighteenth and
early nineteenth century controlled large sections of Eweland. The close
proximity and influence of the Akan has resulted in the Ewe internalising
several Akan traits into their society, the most noteworthy being the Akan
system of chieftaincy and administrative organisation. Akan influence is
evident from other features, such as aspects of their material culture, like
weaving and pottery. The military, political, and cultural hegemony of
Akan in this area has meant that various Ewe groups gradually came to
define the Akan as their closest 'other', during pre-colonial, colonial, and
post-colonial phases of their history.
     Though the Ewe are identified as a modern ethnicity by the govern-
ments of Ghana and Togo, Eweland – far from being a single, uncomplic-
ated unit – is heterogeneous with respect to ecology, physical environment, and vegetation; notable differences are also exhibited in social,
cultural, and religious spheres throughout the area. Yet these Ewe-
speaking societies are united by myths of origin: traditions assert that their
original homeland was Ketu in the modern Republic of Benin (Adediran
1994: 28–9). A number of special names celebrate the centrality of Ketu

in Ewe mythology: it is often referred to as *Mawufe*, or the abode of
Mawu (God), and also as *Amedzofe*, or the cradle of mankind. Mythical
traditions – backed to a certain degree by historical evidence – suggest
that the ancestors of the Gbe-speaking peoples left Ketu in the fifteenth
century, pushed westward by the expanding Yoruba. The Aja branch of
Gbe peoples formed the kingdom of Tado, while a sub-group – later
to be known as the Fon – migrated southward from Tado. Meanwhile,
the Ewe-speaking peoples continued their journey westward from Tado,
eventually settling in the walled city of Notsie by the sixteenth century.
According to Ewe oral tradition, the reign of King Agorkoli was particularly tyrannical, and it was his oppression that drove their ancestors to
flee from Notsie into their present homeland. The commemoration of
this escape has become an important event for all groups that claim to be
Ewe: the *Hogbetsotso* festival, usually held in November, marks this mythical exodus and celebrates Ewe aversion to despotic rule (Debrunner
1965: 122–42; Greene 2002: 19–25).[3]

The Ewe believe that upon fleeing Notsie their ancestors dispersed into
three groups, accounting for the socio-cultural variations visible amongst
the sub-strands of the Ewe today (Amenumey 1986: 3–4).[4] But Eweland
can also be divided into three parts on the basis of its physical features,
and the distribution of these three groups coincides with the natural
divisions of the land. The northernmost division of Eweland is located
at the interface of the forest–savanna belts, at the northern shores of the
erstwhile Lake Volta. The inhabitants of this region are known as the Gbi
Ewe, and are associated with the settlements of Peki, Kpando, Kpalime,
Hohoe, and Alavanyo. These settlements or *dukowo* (sing. *duko*) – or
polities – probably grew from clusters of patrilineages that later came to
be administered by chiefs. No single *duko* attained any sort of dominance
over the others, and northern Eweland has always been a fragmented
cluster of such city-states. The trade routes between the societies of the
savanna in contemporary northern Ghana and the coast ran through the
major *dukowo* of northern Eweland, making the area attractive to traders.
Large communities of Hausa and Zarma peoples – mainly merchants –
settled in Hohoe and Kpando, the biggest of the northern-Ewe *dukowo*,
bringing with them their Islamised culture from the savanna and beyond.
This region was part of the Asante kingdom in the late eighteenth century,

---

[3] It is important to place these Ewe myths of origin in the context within which they
emerged: they were standardised between the 1920s and 1930s, to legitimise the movement for Ewe unity spearheaded by Christianised elites, who were in search of an
identity and history for themselves during the era of cultural nationalisms in West
Africa.

[4] This aspect of the myth, which deals with the dispersal of the Ewe, was probably retrospectively inserted into the Notsie narrative in the twentieth century, as the idea of a
single Ewe ethnicity gradually gained ground.

and it consequently became home to a large Twi-speaking community. Akan influence is profoundly felt in the nature of chieftaincy and socio-political structures: as in Akan societies, local chiefs are at the pivot of a two- or three-tiered administrative pyramid, and command a great deal of authority. Successive waves of migration from the sub-region have made the religious environment of these *dukowo* the most diverse in Eweland: Islam has been part of the landscape for over six centuries, Christianity for over two, and the region has a few 'pagan' shrines that are renowned for their prowess all over southern Ghana (Maier 1983).

The central Ewe occupy the plains immediately south of the northern Ewe. This area is often referred to as the 'Ewedome' belt, or literally, 'Ewe in the middle'. The most important *dukowo* in central Eweland are Ho, Kpetoe, Tove, Keve, Sokode, Abutia, and Adaklu. Farming is the chief occupation in this region, with maize, corn, and yams forming the backbone of the economy; agricultural productivity here is slightly higher than northern Eweland. The central Ewe have been described by the Ewe sociologist Nukunya as the most rigidly patrilineal of all Ewe sub-groups, a feature of their society which accounts for settlement patterns, occupational preferences, and inheritance (Nukunya 1969a: 2). This area was very receptive to Christianity in the past (Parsons 1963: 202). As among the northern Ewe, central Ewe chieftaincy is modelled along Akan lines. Historically, central Eweland was also characterised by the lack of a single expansionist *duko* in the past, sharing northern Eweland's political trajectory in this respect (Verdon 1983: 32).

Located in the coastal zone, southern Eweland includes the *dukowo* of Ouatchi and Lome in Togo, and Wheta, Anlo, Some, and Fenyi in Ghana. From the perspective of these coastal peoples, Eweland consists of just two zones rather than the tripartite division: the coastal belt and the inland Ewe or *Eweme*, literally 'Ewe inside', the term being used for both the central and northern Ewe.[5] Unlike central and northern Ewe societies that exhibit strong Akan influences, the southern Ewe are tied into an easterly system of exchange, maintaining closer trading and cultural links with their eastern coastal neighbours such as the Mina, Aja, and Fon. Though the southern Ewe system of chieftaincy is also modelled on Akan lines, it is not as strong an institution as it is in other parts of Eweland, as the authority of chiefs is somewhat undermined by leaders of religious cults dedicated to local deities, which often have large memberships. While the northern and central Ewe tended to be mainly patrilineal, some southern Ewe groupings practise dual descent, negotiating ties through both the matrilineal and patrilineal sides (see Lovell 1993 on the Ouatchi Ewe and Nukunya 1969a: 2, 48–53 on the

---

[5] The coastal Ewe use the term Ewedome somewhat loosely, to include not only the central Ewe belt, but all Ewe *dukowo* north of the coastal zone.

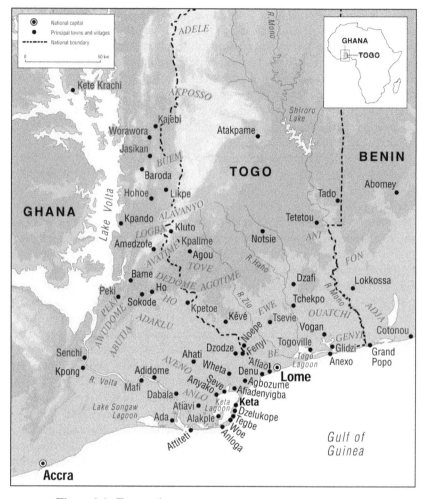

Figure 2.2. Ewe settlements

Glidzi and Anlo-Ewe). Unlike northern and central Eweland where no single *duko* ever attained a prominent position over the others, Anlo, a coastal chiefdom with its capital at Anloga, developed into a significant power in southern Eweland.

Located in the south-eastern corner of modern Ghana, the Anlo are the westernmost of the Ewe groupings on the coast. Two mythical Anlo heroes, Sri and Wenya, who are believed to have led their people westward from Notsie, are celebrated as the founders of most Anlo settlements. The very word Anlo is said to derive from Wenya's reaction to the lengthy journey in search of a new homeland: his exclamation, 'Menlo'

(Ewe: I can go no further), supposedly gave Anlo its name.[6] Modern Anlo consists of thirty-six towns (Ewe: *dutowo*, sing. *duto*). The capital of the chiefdom, Anloga, is the seat of the paramount chieftaincy. In addition to Anloga, Anlo has other important nuclei: Keta, a once-prosperous port, is still a large settlement, and Aflao, located on the border with Togo, is a thriving international centre for cross-border exchange.

The Anlo in History

Despite identifying themselves as one people by the mid-twentieth century, the various Ewe groupings have been far from united for most of their turbulent past. By virtue of their location, the northern and central Ewe were sandwiched between the kingdoms of Asante and Dahomey. The generic term for all these small city-states – peopled not only by Ewe-speaking peoples but also by Guan and Kyerepon communities – was 'Krepi' or 'Creepi' (Meyer 1999: 2). The absence of a hegemonic military power in Krepi, and its organisation into several tiny *dukowo*, made it very easy for the Asante, Dahomey, and Anlo to make regular expeditions there to acquire slaves. These intrusions left Krepi in a state of chaos during the period when slave raiding was rife in the region. Krepi was strategically located to monitor the traffic and activities on the major trade routes that stretched from the interior markets to the coastal ports. Several political entities – the tiny Krepi states, the Anlo, and the mighty Asante kingdom – constantly struggled to exercise some degree of control over these trade routes. Much of Eweland, therefore, was in turmoil between the seventeenth and nineteenth centuries, as Ewe *dukowo* were not only entangled in wars against each other, but also regularly clashed with their non-Ewe neighbours.

In addition to contributing to the chaos in northern Eweland, Anlo's ambitions on the coast led to skirmishes with other competitors, such as Akwamu, an Akan chiefdom located north-west of Anlo, and the Ge-Ewe, positioned to their east. By 1702, Akwamu had annexed most of Anlo. Though Anlo enjoyed a brief period of independence after the fall of Akwamu in 1730, it soon came under the influence of Anexo (Little Popo) for a decade until about 1750. Keta remained under the control of Anexo until the 1770s; during this period, Anlo endeavoured to expand its influence over the *dutowo* north of the Keta Lagoon by incorporating areas such as Tefle and Agave into the chiefdom (Akyeampong 2001b: 42–3). Throughout this period, the Anlo also constantly came to blows

---

[6] According to Anlo tradition, several Anlo towns were named during the search for a new homeland. The word Keta, for example, is derived from 'I have seen the Head of the Sand.' Denu gets its name from a phrase that translates into 'the beginning of palm trees', and Kedzi is a shortened version of 'I have at last arrived on the sand.' For some of the phrases associated with these names, see Akyeampong (2001b: 28).

with the Ada – their westerly Adangme neighbours – over fishing rights in the Volta Estuary (Amenumey 1986: 18–9; Akyeampong 2001b: 42–3). Until 1774 Anloga and Keta often made alliances with the Ada, Akyem, Akuapem, and Anexo against each other (Greene 1996a: 82-4). Finally, in recognising their mutual value to each other, they agreed a lasting peace that led to a loose political merger: Anloga maintained a degree of influence over *dutowo* north of the lagoon through which the internal trade routes ran, and accessing these routes was of crucial importance to Keta's trading community and mercantile elites; Keta, in addition to being a large port, was strategically located, which benefited Anloga's eastern ambitions (Akyeampong 2001b: 43). When the first European traders came into contact with the Anlo and other Ewe-speaking peoples, they encountered a shifting patchwork of warring states, frequently making and breaking alliances with and against each other, rather than a unified entity. The Danes were the first of the maritime powers to set up bases in Anlo, building Fort Prinsenstein near Keta harbour in 1784 (Norregard 1966: 146–8).[7]

By the turn of the nineteenth century, the balance of power north of Anlo had swung definitively in Asante's favour. At the zenith of the Asante power, most of northern and central Eweland formed the easternmost limits of the kingdom. Anlo remained securely outside Asante's political boundaries, but maintained friendly ties with the kingdom throughout this period. The prominence of the Asante kingdom had long-lasting effects on internal politics in Eweland, and was to rearrange political loyalties and alliances between Ewe *dukowo*.

The trade in salt, fish, and slaves formed the backbone of the Anlo economy in the eighteenth and nineteenth centuries. Slavery and pawnship were crucial to the functioning of the pre-colonial Anlo economy. Pawnship was an important means of mobilising labour and guaranteeing credit, a legal category of socio-economic dependency in Anlo customary law. The best-known system of temporary bondage was the adoption of servant-children or *kluviwo* (sing. *kluvi*).[8] Such a person, typically a child, was handed over by his or her parents as a security to a money lender against a debt incurred. Though not treated on par with the 'free' children of the household, a *kluvi* enjoyed certain limited privileges in return for performing household duties, until the debt had

---

[7] See Selena Axelrod Winsnes's translated and edited account of Paul E. Isert's diaries, written between 1783 and 1786. Isert was appointed chief surgeon to serving officials at Denmark's Gulf of Guinea establishments. His diaries contain lively descriptions of daily life and local customs in societies in close proximity to Danish settlements, including Keta in the vicinity of Fort Prinsenstein (Winsnes 1992).

[8] This was an ambiguous term which could be employed both in the context of individuals bound to religious orders as well children in temporary bondage (Westermann 1906). Terminologies shifted through the twentieth century, and by its end this term was used most often within the context of religious cultic networks.

been redeemed (Westermann 1906; Meyer 1999: 5).[9] Similar to the *kluviwo* were the *awobawo* (sing. *awoba*).[10] The creditor owned the pawning contract and not the pawn, being able to claim possession only of the services generated through the labour of such an individual. The pawning contract was often ratified by the kinsmen of the pawn and creditor in formal ceremonies.[11] Pawns were not commodities and could not be sold into outright slavery by the creditor.[12] The *awobawo* and *kluviwo* were ethnic insiders, often related to the very people who owned their labour; they were native to Anlo, rooted in the chiefdom, and existed as persons in their own right during the period of bondage, as their membership of local institutions such as patrilineages, clans, and religious networks remained unaffected (see Greene 1996b: 103). Another related practice was panyarring, which was akin to taking hostages (Akyeampong 2001b: 70–1). Upon non-payment of debts, creditors often arranged for the kidnap of an individual from the debtor's community, thus holding members of the community collectively responsible for the erasure of the debt. A panyarred individual differed from a pawn in that he was not protected by a contractual agreement; he could be sold into slavery if the debt was left unsettled for a long period.

In eighteenth and nineteenth century Anlo, there would have been a large population of foreign-born slaves. Two categories of slave in Anlo lacked all social rights, and, were in effect, the property of their owners. One such category of slave was an *amefefle* (pl. *amefeflewo*) or bought person, acquired by slave merchants from outside Anlo (Rosenthal 1998: 130), mainly through the north–south trade. The second such category included people captured in war, known as *ametsiavawo* (sing. *ametsiava*).[13] While a free individual is inserted into his social role in Anlo at birth – by virtue of kinship ties which bind him to a complex network of ancestors, deities, and future unborn descendants – these categories of slave were 'born' in Anlo – and began to exist as a social entities – only after being either bought or captured and inserted into

---

[9] Westermann used another word for such a person: he translated *home* into a pawn, though the same word is also used sometimes in the context of a bought person (Westermann 1906).

[10] *Awoba* or *woba* derives from the Twi *awowa*.

[11] Pawnship remains a complex subject when placed in the scheme of other practices of slavery. Kopytoff and Miers argue that it is an intermediate condition between slavery and full belonging, as the pawn is an ethnic insider with kinsmen present in the society. His 'rights-in-person' (Kopytoff and Miers 1977: 10–11) are temporarily transferred from one kinship group to another, making pawnship an intermediate condition of servility between slavery and full belonging.

[12] For pawnship and slavery in the neighbouring societies of the Slave Coast during the pre-colonial period, see Law 2003. While male pawns were usually relieved, female pawns could eventually be taken as wives by the creditors in the event of non-payment, with bride price being waived (Law 2003: 56).

[13] For terms employed to describe outright enslavement, see Greene 2011: 144–5.

society through their roles of servitude, coming to be identified with their owners. Lacking the elements that constituted Anlo personhood, such as *hlo* membership, kinship ties, and ritual association with local deities and ancestors, these categories of slave were objectified in Anlo, and did not have any personal or legal rights as such. Such foreign-born men were usually sold into the trans-Atlantic system, while the women were retained as slave wives to Anlo men. Slave wives, and their descendants, were gradually integrated into the patrilineages of their owner-husbands.

Denmark was the first of the European powers to abolish the slave trade in 1803, and Danish forces did their best to curtail the trade in their sphere of influence, including in Keta and its environs (Akyeampong 2001b: 52). Anlo's location between the sea and the lagoon, however, made it difficult for the Danes to regulate the activities of slave merchants. The overseas slave trade out of Anlo was to flourish for more than half a century after Denmark's official abolition, particularly between 1830 and 1860, a period that proved to be Anlo's economic golden age. Another important event changed the course of history for the Anlo: unable to maintain their possessions, the Danes sold their forts along the Slave Coast to the British in 1850 (ibid.: 57–8). By this time, the British had established a sizeable presence west of Anlo, and were seeking to expand their political influence.

The mid- and late- nineteenth century saw the Asante make desperate attempts to assert their influence over central and northern Eweland in order to secure control over the north–south trade routes. By the mid-nineteenth century, the Asante kingdom had entered a period of decline, with its military might and political domains significantly reduced, making the success of Asante's military ambitions and plans in central Eweland dependent on the active collaboration with the coastal Anlo. The Asante-Anlo coalition was mutually beneficial, as it strengthened the Anlo considerably, enabling them to exercise control over some of their northern hinterland. The skirmishes between the Asante-Anlo alliance and the northern Ewe *dukowo* became more and more extreme during the 1860s, with the most violent and sustained period of warfare – it came to be known as the 'Asante Wars' – occurring between 1869 and 1874 (Meyer 1999: 5). These wars left Eweland damaged, resulting in a great increase in the numbers of displaced and enslaved people. As part of their campaign against the Asante, the British soon attacked and defeated the Anlo in 1874 (Akyeampong 2001b: 61). This victory, however, gave the British a firm foothold only in Anloga, Keta, and *dutowo* located along the southern corridor of Anlo. While these towns were integrated into the Gold Coast colony immediately, it took the British another twenty years to secure the Anlo *dutowo* north of the Keta Lagoon (see

Crowther 1927). As the various European powers carved out spheres of influence and eventually established control over territories, Eweland came to be divided by colonial borders. Though Peki and Anlo became part of the Gold Coast colony and came under British rule from the 1890s, the other eastern Ewe had a more divided colonial experience (Welch 1966: 40; Amenumey 1989: 3–23). By 1884, Ho and most of the central Ewe belt became part of the German Protectorate of Togoland. Germany's defeat in the First World War led to the confiscation of its colonial possessions, which resulted in the division of German Togoland into British and French Mandated Territories, thereby leaving Eweland reconfigured and separated by an entirely new British–French frontier after 1916.

The Anlo economy declined steadily throughout the twentieth century, never fully recovering from the abolition of the lucrative trans-Atlantic slave trade. Most industries during the colonial period were based on primary occupations: fishing, shallot cultivation, and liquor distillation were the main contributors to colonial revenue. Anlo has also been plagued by a number of environmental problems – Keta, its economic hub, had been subjected to serious coastal erosion from the 1900s, for example. Protecting Keta and Anlo was not prioritised by the Gold Coast administration, as investment in the region was thought to outweigh its productivity (Akyeampong 2003). By the 1920s, the Anlo were forced to rethink their position within the Gold Coast colony: with the demise of Asante power, they were prompted to search out new allies. Against the backdrop of the early cultural nationalisms in West Africa, the idea of an Ewe ethnic group or Ewe 'nation' began gaining ground. By the 1940s, the Anlo Christianised elite, some traders, and chiefs threw their support behind the All Ewe Conference, a body that championed the cause of Ewe unification. For the Anlo, Ewe unification was contingent on forging strong links with northern and central Ewe groups in both British- and French-administered territories. The idea of an Ewe ethnic community or nation held little currency for the larger constituency that it was meant to represent, given the different historical trajectories of the various Ewe peoples, and was doomed to failure. Another body associated with the cause of regional unification, the Togoland Congress, was enthusiastically supported by some members of the Ewe intelligentsia in the Togolands after 1951 (see Collier 2002; Skinner[14] 2007). However, while constituencies in central and northern Eweland were in favour of Ewe and/or Togoland unity, they sought to exclude the Anlo from both movements. This inland Ewe–Anlo fault line had a long history: the Anlo had tended to align themselves with non-Ewe groups in most intra-Ewe conflicts;

[14] Née Collier.

their support for the Asante during the Asante Wars of 1869–74 was still fresh in the memories of the *Eweme* societies, and was held against them by the northern and central Ewe (Nugent 2002: 147–98). Besides, the pre-eminence of the Anlo elite in economic arenas and church affairs had come to be widely resented, which made other Ewe sub-groups fearful of Anlo domination should their efforts for a single political entity succeed. This lukewarm treatment meted out to them by the *Eweme* groups made the Anlo conscious of the unique position they had come to occupy in Eweland on account of their political and social history (Akyeampong 2001b: 196–8).

Ghana gained independence from Britain in 1957, while French Togoland became Togo in 1960. Anlo, Peki, and British Togoland (including Ho) became part of modern Ghana, while Lome and its hinterland were integrated into Togo. Anlo came to occupy an ambiguous position within the modern Ghanaian state: as the chiefdom is located in the south-eastern corner of Ghana, only a short journey from the Togolese capital Lome, the Anlo began to be perceived as a people tied into a socio-economic network that extended eastward, away from Ghana. The Anlo economy suffered greatly soon after Ghanaian independence precisely from the indifferent attitude of the state. Low levels of investment, coupled with increasing prices, soaring inflation, and declining productivity of the primary sector had a disastrous effect on Anlo (Akyeampong 2003).

Despite its small size and apparent marginalisation, Anlo has exerted a disproportionately large influence over the course of modern Ghanaian political history by producing several key statesmen. One of the founding members of the Convention Peoples' Party (CPP), along with Kwame Nkrumah, was Komla Gbedemah, an Anlo. A young professional who sympathised with the ordinary working people rather than with the United Gold Coast Congress (UGCC) and its intelligentsia, his political views appealed to the CPP's 'Verandah Boys' support base. Gbedemah emerged as one of Nkrumah's most trusted aides, first during his leadership of the CPP, and later during his presidency of independent Ghana. Nkrumah was overthrown in 1966 by what was to be the first of a series of military coups, engineered by five army officers: E. K. Kotoka (who was an Anlo), J. W. K. Harlley, A. K. Deku, A. A. Afrifa, and A. K. Ocran. Kotoka was assassinated during the next year and replaced by Afrifa as head of state. Afrifa's administration was the first Ghanaian government that was recognised as distinctively Akan (mainly Asante) in its composition, confirming that an ethno-political fault line had been developing steadily in Gold Coast and Ghanaian politics: parties that represented Asante and its hinterland were traditionally opposed by alliances of coastal peoples, such as the Nzima, Fanti (who are Akan),

Ga-Adangme, and Ewe (Akyeampong 2001b: 203).[15] Gbedemah re-
emerged in 1969, to lead the National Alliance of Liberals (NAL) in the
elections that year, though he lost to Kofi Busia of the Progress Party
(PP). Busia, an academic and politician, had been a public figure in
the Gold Coast colony and then in Ghana from 1942; the PP was a
centre-right party which was ideologically closer to the anti-Nkrumist
UCGC. Not surprisingly, Gbedemah's party was organised around an
Anlo core, and Busia's around an Asante one. Ghana was run by a series
of (inland) Akan/Asante-dominated governments after 1969: the Busia
regime between 1969 and 1972, Col. I. K. Acheampong's military dic-
tatorship from 1972 until 1976, and Lt. Gen. Akuffo's brief spell as head
of state in 1976. Anlo remained on the fringes of Ghanaian politics until
1979. Later that year, discontent in the armed forces began brewing,
which resulted in a military intervention under the leadership of Flight
Lieutenant Jerry Rawlings. Though Rawlings returned the country to
civilian rule under Hilla Limann the next year, persistent corruption led
him to intervene once more in 1981. This event is commonly referred
to as the 'Second Coming', during which three former heads of state
were executed.[16] The Second Coming, nevertheless, provided Ghana
with the longest-serving leader in its history as a nation.[17] Ghana came
under the rule of the Provisional National Defence Council (PNDC), a
body chaired by Rawlings. The revolution of 1981 was a populist one,
and Rawlings presented himself – when it suited him – as the successor to
Nkrumah's socialist policies, in opposition to the elitist politics associated
with the Danquah-Busia tradition.

Rawlings eventually implemented a structural adjustment programme
prescribed by the World Bank during the mid-1980s, and the crumbling
Ghanaian economy was gradually transformed over the course of a decade with a marked surge of petty retailing. Rawlings is closely associated
with Keta in Anlo, and his administration was perceived to be the most
Anlo-friendly of all Ghanaian governments to this point.[18] Indeed, Rawlings and his closest advisers – like his controversial security coordinator,

---

[15] One of Nkrumah's reasons for breaking away from the UGCC was his resentment of its
elitist core. His CPP was meant to be a populist party and, not surprisingly, drew most
of its supporters from Nzima (Nkrumah's homeland), Fanti, Ga-Adangme, and Ewe
regions, rather than Asante and its hinterland. The most vociferous opposition to the
CPP came in the form of an Asante nationalist party, the NLM (National Liberation
Movement), an organisation which briefly entertained the idea of an independent Asante
state, rather than assimilation into Nkrumah's Ghana (see Allman 1993).

[16] These were Acheampong, Afrifa, and Akuffo.

[17] Rawlings was popularly hailed as Ghana's 'Saviour': Biblical references were extensively
used; his initials J. J. meant that he came to be referred to as Junior Jesus. Contrary to
later representations of these events, the interventions led by Rawlings enjoyed popular
support.

[18] Part of Rawlings's ancestry is Ewe: his mother is an Anlo from Dzelukope, while his
father was a Scotsman.

Captain Kojo Tsikata – were often dubbed the 'Dzelukope mafia' by the Ghanaian press, referring to the suburb of Keta from which they hailed. Over his nineteen years as head of state, considerable investment went into Anlo: electricity became easily available, while development and construction flourished. The government managed to secure funding for the long-awaited sea-defence project, which was meant to protect Keta from erosion, reclaim land, and regulate the water level in the lagoon.[19] New roads were built across sections of the lagoon, connecting the *dutowo* north and south of the water mass, and thereby shortening journeys within Anlo considerably.

By the late 1980s, pressure began mounting steadily on the Rawlings regime from the international community and the African Union (AU) to return the country to civilian rule. The 'provisional' government of Rawlings metamorphosed into the National Democratic Congress (NDC) in 1992, on the eve of Ghana's return to multi-party democracy. The NDC won the controversial elections of 1992 and 1996, which kept Rawlings and his supporters in power.[20] The Anlo ceased to be at the centre of government after 2000, when Rawlings lost the election that year to J. A. Kufuor of the National Patriotic Party (NPP), who retained his presidential majority in the elections of 2004. Not surprisingly, the widespread perception in Anlo was that Kufour's government suffered from a severe Asante/inland Akan bias. Though the Anlo and Asante were military allies in the nineteenth century, the pattern of ethnic politics within the framework of the Ghanaian state has turned them into proponents of opposing political traditions. The Rawlings era has been crucial, therefore, in sharpening a sense of Anlo identity, culturally distinct from other Ewe groupings and politically opposed to the Asante-dominated inland Akan core (Nugent 1995: 223, 239). The elections of 2008 saw Rawlings's successor, J. E. Atta Mills of the NDC, defeat Kufour in a closely contested race. The widespread perception in Anlo is that Rawlings and his Anlo advisers continue to play a role in the running of the party, which has resulted in the Anlo remaining loyal to the NDC and the new President, despite his growing unpopularity in the rest of the country, a direct result of the steadily deteriorating economic conditions in the country caused primarily by the global recession after 2008.[21] The NDC, with John Mahama as its leader, won the elections of 2012: the party secured

---

[19] The Anlo had been petitioning the Gold Coast government for a sea defence as early as the 1920s (Akyeampong 2001b: 186). Though the work on the sea defence project started in 1999, it was completed five years later, in 2004 (Akyeampong 2003: 221–2).

[20] Critics of the regime were convinced that the elections had been rigged by the NDC.

[21] In 2011, reports in the Ghanaian media suggested that Atta Mills had lost the support of Rawlings. At party meetings to discuss the NDC leadership, Rawlings backed his wife's bid to become leader of the NDC and their presidential candidate. The death of Atta Mills in September 2012 exposed the acrimony prevailing amongst different factions of the NDC leadership. Rawlings appeared to disapprove of Acting President John

a significant portion of the vote in the southern Ewe heartland and Volta Region.

Modern Anlo: Political and Social Organisation

The highest political office in Anlo – which dates back to the early nineteenth century – is the paramount chieftaincy. Known as the *awoamefia* ('he who lives in seclusion'), the paramount chief was based in the most prominent of the Anlo *dutowo*, Anloga (Nukunya 1969a: 10). As the title suggests, the *awoamefia* was inaccessible to most of his subjects. He shared power with the chief priest of a deity known as Nyigbla, who sometimes acted as an intermediary between the paramount chief and his people (Greene 1996a: 63). Although the *awoamefia* is largely a figurehead in present day Anlo, he plays a vital ceremonial role in traditional courts and during local events. Anlo is divided into three divisions for administrative purposes: the left, centre, and right. Three war chiefs, who preside over the divisions of Anlo, are second to the *awoamefia* in importance. The *awadada* or 'war mother' formerly commanded the central section of the Anlo army. Two other war chiefs, known as *asafohenegawo*, were in charge of the right and left wings of the army, and were also chiefs of the *dutowo* of Woe and Whuti respectively.[22] Every one of Anlo's thirty-six towns has a chief, known as *dufia* (pl. *dufiawo*). Towns are further divided into several wards. Ward chiefs, known as *tokomefiawo*, are subordinate to *dufiawo*. Finally, the *hlofiawo* (clan chiefs), are the lowest tier of chieftaincy in any Anlo settlement (Nukunya 1969a: 9–15). In modern Anlo, other institutions have competed for influence, particularly over the last century; leaders of religious cults, clergy, and modern elected representatives have eroded the authority of Anlo chiefs. Village assemblies were established during the colonial period, and were usually dominated by the Christianised elite. After the second military intervention orchestrated by Rawlings in 1981, district assemblies were established to function as the lowest unit of local government: these bodies are run by a dynamic community of teachers and retired servicemen, who are elected representatives of the townspeople. Each of these towns has a local youth association, aligned with the larger regional Anlo Youth Association (AYA); these groups are important cultural institutions that disseminate information about education, entertainment, and employment prospects. Most of the groups meet fortnightly at assembly buildings in each town.

Mahama's leadership style, policies, and vision for Ghana. Nana Konadu Agyeman-Rawlings tried to float a new party with her husband's support, but was prevented from doing so by the Electoral Commission. The NDC still remains (at least in perception), despite the change in the political landscape, associated with Ewe interests.

[22] This title is the Eweised version of an original Akan term (Nukunya 1997: 47–72).

The fundamental unit of organisation in modern Anlo is the clan or *hlo* (pl. *hlowo*), of which there are fifteen. Every Anlo individual belongs to one such *hlo*. Members of a *hlo* are believed to have descended patrilineally from a common putative ancestor, thereby sharing the totemic observances and common taboos (Nukunya 1969a: 21). These *hlowo* are distributed all over Anlo, with members of almost every *hlo* being represented in each large settlement. Because they are so big, the *hlowo* are not exclusively exogamous. All of these fifteen *hlowo* (apart from one) have ancestral houses at Anloga, called *hlokponuwo*.[23] In modern Anlo, these *hlokponuwo* are monitored by the clan head, who is usually the custodian of sacred relics of sentimental value to the clan. A group of councillors, who work for the general welfare of the clan, are subordinate to the clan head. All clans are equal in status, and traditionally have been assigned different ceremonial roles and functions within the context of the Anlo state. For instance, the paramount chieftaincy alternates between the Adzovia and the Bate clans, the Lafe are the kingmakers, the Amlade and the Lafe provide ritual specialists in every Anlo settlement, while the Dzevi clan produces the chief priest of Nyigbla, Anlo's patron deity. In every village or settlement, the clan with the largest population provides the chief. For example, the Alakple stool currently belongs to the Ame clan, while the Woe stool is usually occupied by a member of the Blu clan (Nukunya 1969a: 23–4).

It is the local patrilineage which is the most significant institution in every settlement. This unit is termed the *afedo*, which is generally a subbranch of a *hlo* that consists of people in any given settlement who can trace their genealogy to a common male ancestor through the male line (Westermann 1935; Manoukian 1952; Nukunya 1969a: 25).[24] An *afedo* is usually exogamous, as the genealogical depth of this unit is usually eight to ten generations. The head of the *afedo* is either the oldest member of the oldest generation in the ward, or is elected by members of the *afedo* (Nukunya 1969a: 26). Membership of an *afedo* is likely to influence factors as diverse as livelihood, residence, and worship of certain deities. Land, palm groves, and fishing creeks are owned by such *afedowo*, and members may exploit such resources together for their mutual benefit. In the past, members of an *afedo* usually resided in the same ward of a settlement, as they were concentrated around the ancestral house (*afedo-me*). Not all members of the *afedo* lived in the *afedo-me*, as they dispersed through marriage, or were forced to leave on account of overcrowding. The new location that they establish is called a *kope*, which maintains

---

[23] The only exception is the Getsofe clan, which does not have a representation in Anloga. The reasons for this are speculative (see Greene 1996a: 61–3).

[24] Ethnographers that studied the Ewe in the twentieth century, from Westermann (1935) to Manoukian (1952), have used a range of terminologies – *fome*, *afeme*, *kponu*, and *afedo* – each with slightly different definitions for the local patrilineage.

strong ties with the *afedo-me*. The original *afedo-me* is an important symbolic location for all members of the lineage, irrespective of whether they live in it. Shrines within these *afedo-me* are dedicated to the memory of common patrilineal ancestors. The worship and reverence of ancestors is expressed by the creation of a *togbui zikpi* (*togbui* = grandfather, *zikpi* = stool). A caretaker (stool father) is appointed by every *afedo* to look after the stool house. These stool houses are usually located at the *togbuifeme*, or the home of the apical ancestor of the *afedo*, synonymous with the *afedo-me*.[25] In addition to determining residence and ancestor worship, in present-day Anlo the *afedo* may also influence an individual's participation in religious cults.

It has been argued that although the Anlo appear to be chiefly patrilineal, they cultivate strong ties with their matrilineal kin, and bilateral kinship is practised in religious and social spheres. For instance, the Anlo believe in a process akin to reincarnation, where ancestors are reproduced in their descendants. Ancestors from either side of the family may demand an individual's attention and the process is not restricted to patrilineal ancestors (Nukunya 1969a: 47–8). Patriliny is thought to influence inheritance patterns, and personal property is usually passed on from individuals to their sons. However, when this emphasis on patriliny evolved is in doubt. Westermann and Ward, writing about the Anlo during the 1890s and 1920s respectively, suggest that property was often passed on matrilineally, and inheritance from one's mother's brother (the Akan model) was not uncommon (Westermann 1935; Ward 1958: 3–5). Matrilineal descent groups do not exist in Anlo, and there were no official social and religious institutions organised along these lines, leaving us to conclude that matrilineal ties were – and still are – developed and maintained informally (Nukunya 1969a: 46; 1997: 52).[26]

'Somewhere Land', 'On Top of the Sand' and Beyond

Anlo is roughly a three-hour journey from the Ghanaian capital Accra on the Aflao–Accra road, one of southern Ghana's main arteries of transport. The northern rim of the lagoon is connected to the southern coastal towns by a circular road network, completed in 2004, known as the 'Sea Defence Road'. An intricate network of mud paths also connects most Anlo towns, some of which run parallel to the major Accra–Aflao road. These mud paths (popularly known as 'smugglers' roads') are in reality the main arteries of trade, with most informal and semi-legal trade

---

[25] In central Eweland, stools move with the stool fathers, frequently changing location. On the Abutia Ewe, see Verdon (1983: 91–2).

[26] Lovell's study of the Ouatchi Ewe of southern Togo, a group sharing historical and cultural similarities with the Anlo, confirms this trend: a significant emphasis is placed on matrilineal ties for participation in religious networks (Lovell 1993).

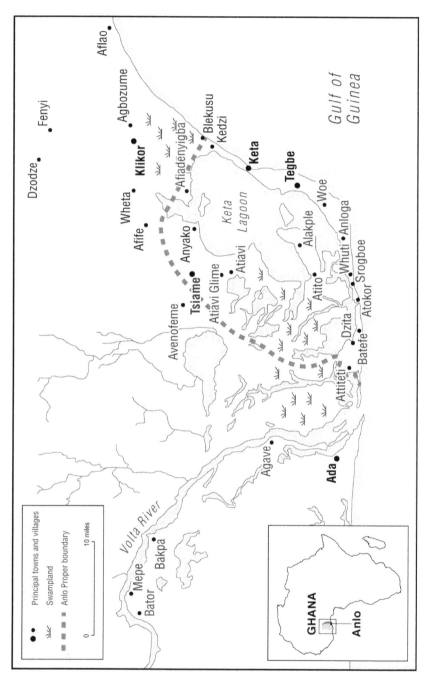

Figure 2.3. Anlo

being conducted through them. Much of the fieldwork for this research was based in and around three Anlo towns: Anlo-Afiadenyigba, Keta, and Anloga. Anlo-Afiadenyigba is located at the north-east of the Keta Lagoon, while both Anloga and Keta are positioned at the seafront on the southern rim. Aflao and the Togolese capital, Lome, are within easy reach of all three locations, and accessible by two sets of roadways. Anlo still has a very high rate of out-migration, with young people seeking education and employment in other parts of Ghana, Togo, and Nigeria. Several Anlo towns have hometown associations in Accra, each with thousands of registered members, most of whom have very strong links with their towns of origin.

Afiadenyigba may be translated as 'Somewhere Land',[27] reflecting its isolation between creeks of the Keta Lagoon. Afiadenyigba is also the shortened version of a lengthy exclamation which proclaims the town as 'the place where the land must be worked very hard in exchange for money' – a sentiment with which most residents would heartily agree. Local traditions assert that this inhospitable piece of land grew into a settlement when a prestigious slave dealer based his operations on it several generations ago. It is located just off the main Accra–Aflao road. Several *tro-tros*, shared taxis, and buses ply their routes through the Afiadenyigba junction. From the junction the town is a ten-minute car journey. One sees the marketplace first – a rather large, crowded cluster of shops selling daily commodities: raw foodstuffs, soap, school books, groceries, and other provisions. There are three drink spots around the market place, in which people frequently congregate to celebrate special occasions. A number of 'chop bars' (makeshift restaurants) provide food throughout the day – cocoa and milk in the morning, rice and stew at noon, and local delicacies like *akple* (a local dish prepared out of maize) and meat soup in the evening. In and around the market area in 2003, prior to the widespread availability of mobile phones, there were several communication centres, where people could make and receive calls.

When I began my research over a decade ago, Anlo-Afiadenyigba had a population of about twelve thousand.[28] The most important landmark in Anlo-Afiadenyigba is the Evangelical Presbyterian (EP) church. Church services are held every Sunday for the small community of Christians based in the town. The EP church is an epicentre of activity and runs the largest primary school in the town from the neighbouring compound. There are two other primary schools in the town, one run by the Roman

---

[27] The term bears strong connotations of remoteness, referring to the location and the inaccessibility of the village in the past.
[28] Information provided by Anlo-Afiadenyigba village council.

Catholic Mission, and the other by the local government. The town also has one Junior Secondary School (JSS). A small police station has four officers permanently stationed in it: petty crime, theft, and land disputes are the most common complaints referred to the police. There are also a number of pharmacies and one clinic that provide basic first-aid treatment. Walking away from the marketplace takes one into the residential alleyways of the village. Dense settlement characterises the tiny village streets of Anlo-Afiadenyigba, with large and little shrines located at almost every corner, dedicated to *alegbawo* (sing. *alegba*, protective household gods), anti-witchcraft deities, or the ancestors.

The word Keta is derived from the Anlo phrase 'on top of the sand', which refers to its location on the seafront. Keta used to be much larger than it is now, on account of decades of ferocious coastal erosion. The watermark in Keta has steadily encroached into the town since the 1920s, and estimates in 1980 suggested that two-thirds of the town lay under water (Akyeampong 2001b: 206–7). Settlement patterns have been altered drastically as there has been considerable damage to private dwellings and public buildings alike, and the population has witnessed a sharp decline over the past seven decades. An air of decline now characterises the town, formerly a bustling port and the economic hub of Anlo. Large houses and ornately decorated buildings bear testimony to exactly what sort of place Keta was at its zenith during the mid-nineteenth century. Its position of eminence in the past, however, means that the town has better facilities than most others in Anlo: it boasts about four schools and a well-equipped hospital. Keta comes to life at weekends, when funerals are held: people flood in from Accra and neighbouring villages, and the town livens up considerably. The population of Keta was estimated at roughly sixteen thousand in 2004.[29]

The most important landmark in neighbouring Anloga is the *awoamefia* secretariat, a large two-storey building, the official headquarters of the paramount chief. There are a number of small Pentecostal churches and one large Roman Catholic church in the town. The population of Anloga was roughly ten thousand in 2004.[30] The stool of the paramount chief remained vacant for thirteen years after the death of Togbi Adelaza II in 1998. Between 2007 and 2011, Anloga was the site of an acrimonious dispute related to the installation of the *awoamefia* as two rival candidates from the Adzovia clan (backed by rival parties), sought to ascend the the most important stool in Anlo. Togbi Sri III was duly installed as *awoamefia* of Anlo in 2011.

Economic activity in most Anlo towns is very strongly influenced by their inconvenient positioning between the 'sea and the lagoon' (Akyeampong

---

[29] These are estimates obtained from the AYA.
[30] Ibid.

2001b). Most people settled in Anlo-Afiadenyigba, Keta, and Anloga are engaged in either fishing and/or salt collection, depending on the time of year. Fishing takes place in the rainy season between July and November, during which the lagoon fills up. Between ten and fifteen men come together to form cooperatives, and they usually own the fishing equipment and the canoe (Manoukian 1952; Hill 1986).[31] Salt collection involves such cooperation too: cooperatives are usually formed along kinship or residential patterns, with members often being closely related. Every cooperative negotiates the right to access a patch of land with the owners, sharing the salt collected and profits from the sale.[32] The lands between the settlement and lagoon are dotted with large heaps of salt, collected from the salt pans. The trade in salt is a thriving part of Anlo's economy, which in March attracts buyers from as far away as the Northern Region of Ghana and Burkina Faso. Among the other occupations that men take up are taxi driving and retailing; their average wages range between ¢10,000 and ¢40,000 per day.[33] Most women are traders and retailers, selling their goods (fish, cooked food, etc.) for anything between ¢500 and ¢3,000 either at local markets or in neighbouring towns. Women also work as seamstresses and hairdressers, sometimes conducting their business at home for a small charge.

Shallot cultivation is also one of the most important sources of livelihood for people in Anlo, with trucks piled high with shallots a familiar sight, usually part of the export trade out of Anlo. Most shallot farmers are involved in small-scale farming, usually cultivating lands belonging to their families, to which they are granted access through kinship ties (Hill 1986). Women sometimes grow cassava, tomatoes, aubergines, and maize on family land, though only at the subsistence level. Anlo-Afiadenyigba in particular is also well known as a town of *kente* weavers: men usually weave, while other, less-experienced members of the family market the cloth in various towns, mainly Agbozume, the largest *kente* market in Anlo. Most weavers work on a commission basis, and have customers from other towns, as *kente* is in demand for ceremonial occasions. Several looms are spread out in family compounds, and outside houses. Weaving is a skill which is often passed on within families, and children, almost always boys, are taken on as apprentices from an early age (Kraamer 2005). The industry has been in decline; weaving is not as lucrative as it was about four decades ago. No description of Anlo – and

---

[31] The 'fishing companies' first described by Ward (1958) still exist, though in a very informal set-up (Manoukian 1952: 16). Polly Hill also details such cooperation amongst fishermen and shallot farmers (Hill 1986).

[32] Land is mainly accessed through kinship connections, as in the case of shallot farming.

[33] *Cedi* (pl. *cedis*); (symbol ¢, international abbreviation GhC) the Ghanaian currency, was valued at 16,600 to the British pound sterling in June 2004. The redenomination of the cedi in 2007 meant that four zeros were struck off, and a new currency – the new Ghana cedi (GhS) – was introduced. As of the first quarter of 2014, GhS4.0001 = GBP1.

Afiadenyigba in particular – is complete without reference to its pig rearing, one of the region's most lucrative industries. There are a number of piggeries in the town, owned by both individuals and families, sometimes organised into cooperatives. One of the most striking features of Anlo-Afiadenyigba is that pigs roam freely in the town. Fowls, ducks, and sheep are also raised in Anlo-Afiadenyigba, as in other Anlo villages, though only for domestic consumption. Cats are often kept in household compounds, and are considered to be a delicacy, consumed on special occasions.

Markers of religious activity appear to be everywhere in Anlo, and religion is intimately fused with aspects of everyday life. While using terms such as 'Anlo belief system', 'Anlo religion', and 'Anlo culture', I am indeed reducing an extremely complex set of phenomena into convenient definitional shorthand. These are, in fact, 'communities of interpretation' (Fardon 1990: 9). As Fardon observes, what is often described as 'Chamba culture' – that is, what he assumes to be complex institutional contexts 'of clans, cults, localities, gender prerogatives and so on' – seldom coincides with what is assumed to be a Chamba ethnic boundary. These 'communities of interpretation' are not uniformly accessed in all Chamba places, and 'matrices of knowledge' are not produced consistently throughout Chamba territory. Like Anlo 'culture', Anlo 'religion' is not a static, taken-for-granted entity, which coincides with an ethnic Anlo boundary, but a dynamic, layered, lived institution, comprising cults, deities, and shrines, held together by ancestral networks and living human ties, a complicated jigsaw of village, kinship, and familial loyalties. It is to these layered 'matrices of knowledge', some of which may be categorised as Anlo religion, that I now turn.

3 The Dance of Alegba: Anlo-Ewe Religion

Visitors to Anlo towns are struck by the all-pervasiveness of religious activity. Deafening drumming ceremonies organised by members of *trowo* cults and numerous services conducted by churches of several denominations bear testimony to the constant religious performances so characteristic of Anlo towns. Initiates of local religious cultic networks, known as 'wives of the gods', are immediately recognisable from their dress, scarifications, and beads. Brightly painted shrines dedicated to the different *trowo*, *voduwo*, and ancestral spirits are visible almost everywhere: Hevieso, the fiery thunder god, is depicted presiding over nature spirits, which include Avleketi, the pretty goddess of the sea, and Mami Wata, the seductive mermaid; Kunde, a hunting spirit from the savanna, is often seated alongside his wife Abrewa and her leopard companion, while ancestral shrines celebrate the accomplishments of individuals in the past, such as successes in war and the capture of slaves. The most frequently occurring deity, worshipped at entrances and crossroads, is Alegba (Figure 3.1). There are hundreds of Alegbas (Ewe: *alegbawo*) in any Anlo town, constructed in front of houses, shrines, at street corners, and, indeed, in places of no particular importance: offerings of food and drink are usually placed before the rounded, sometimes decorative, mounds of earth representing the deity. For Alegba is the gatekeeper and the trickster of the Anlo pantheon: his blessings are sought before any significant ritual, journey, or undertaking, as Alegba has the power to clarify and confuse in equal measure.

Ethnographers of the Ewe take Alegba's role just as seriously as their anthropologised subjects. It has become customary to invoke Alegba at the beginning of ethnographies on Ewe religion, a precautionary measure to avoid confusion and incoherence (Rosenthal 1998: 9; Friedson 2009: 1–5). There is, also, a deep analogy between Alegba and Anlo religion, for Alegba has been transformed into a metaphor for the latter's structured chaos. There are several stories told about Alegba: that he has a peculiar sense of humour; that he is a prankster, a practical joker; that his victims range from the hot-headed Hevieso to the devious Mami Wata and the all-knowing Mawu. Alegba is reportedly not a pretty sight: he is stout and ugly, making him the object of curiosity for other spirits and deities; he has

Figure 3.1. Alegba, the trickster of the pantheon and deity of crossroads, outside the Fofie shrine in Ablesikope, Anlo-Afiadenyigba, flanked by Fofie devotees, including a *fofiesi* (in white), August 2005

an unquenchable sexual appetite, which results in his leading both gods and mortals astray. He can change form at will, turning into a woman, animal, or any another being. Alegba is also the guardian of the body of extremely complex ritual knowledge that is Anlo religion. Ethnographers of Ewe religion have noted the enormous complexity of the spiritual world: like Alegba, it defies definition and structure; it is probably best conceptualised as a (non)-system in a constant state of disorder, flux, and disequilibrium (de Surgy 1988; Rosenthal 1998; Lovell 2002; Friedson 2009). The Anlo, however, are well adapted to this divine chaos, and are sensitive to the uncertainties of their spirit world.

Like most other West African peoples, the Anlo simply did not have a word for religion in their pre-Christian past (Spieth 2011: 48). Religious activity was – and still is – described as *subosubo* or the act of service to various unseen forces, the most common among these being *trowo*, *voduwo*, and deceased ancestors.[1] Christianity is an integral part of Anlo

---

[1] Closely related West African peoples, such as the Yoruba, also conceptualised religion as 'service' to spiritual beings. The modern Yoruba word for religion is *esin*, which is derived from *sin* (to serve) or *isin* (service). It was originally applied only to Christianity and Islam, and not to the indigenous belief system (see Peel 2000: 89).

life, having been embedded into the religious system for over a hundred and fifty years, and is older than some of the most successful networks dedicated to the *trowo* in Anlo today. Missionary discourse created a fundamental divide between Christianity and 'heathenism', with Christianity cast as the realm of the virtuous, and 'heathen' non-Christian practices relegated to the realm of the Devil (Meyer 1999). Christianity, with its emphasis on God and the afterlife, was considered other-worldly, while 'non-Christian' religious agents were constructed as its diametric opposite, addressing 'this worldly' afflictions in the here and now. In theory the idea that Christianity and non-Christian practices are mutually incompatible traditions is entrenched in Anlo thought, and most Anlo people are able to divide practitioners of 'religion' into these two camps. But upon closer inspection, and in practice, the dividing line between the Christian and non-Christian realm is far from impermeable: Christians often leave their churches and join *trowo* cults, while weary devotees of the *trowo* convert to Christianity if they are unable to satisfy their *trowo*. Depending on the nature of the existential problems they have to resolve, practitioners of either tradition are sometimes able to access services provided by the other camp without changing their primary religious identities, 'dual worshipping' with ease. It is difficult, therefore, to sketch a picture of a 'non-Christian' or a Christian set of practices in contemporary Anlo in isolation from each other.[2] Anlo cosmology owes a great deal to both worldviews.[3] The non-Christian spiritual agents did not vanish from the Christian Anlo mindset upon conversion: the *trowo, voduwo,* and the ancestors continue to torment Christians. In my description of the Anlo religious terrain, I have attempted to treat both Christianity and non-Christian practices as part of the same Anlo tradition, fused in both the ritual sphere and the religious imaginations of the Anlo.[4] What

---

[2] I refrain from using the term 'syncretism' when describing any of the forms that result from the interplay of the two religious traditions in Anlo. The issues raised by Stephan Palmié (2003), in his study of North American *orisa* worship are very relevant to the study of Anlo's religious history. Peel (1968a), in his study of Aladura churches in Nigeria, tells us that what is relevant in the case of a 'syncretic' religious tradition is not the details of the level of cultural debt to heterogeneous sources associated with the tradition in consideration, but the practitioners' understandings of their traditions and the labels they apply to themselves – making self-identification important, another idea applicable to Anlo. During my fieldwork, in the case of dual-worshipping informants I took their religious self-identification at face value.

[3] As Meyer notes, previous ethnographic works on the Ewe, such as those of Rivière (1981) and de Surgy (1988), which have attempted to draw a picture of the pre-Christian tradition, have produced 'blueprints of traditional religion rather than delving into people's actual religious praxis' (Meyer 1999: 226, fn 10).

[4] Non-Christian practices are often referred to by the Anlo, and indeed other African peoples, as 'traditional' religion, implying that they are understood to be at odds with modernity at some level. As Baum points out, within a socio-historical context, it is useful to think of traditional religion, as 'not quite a contrast with modernity' but as 'religion

follows is a description of the various forces that the Anlo encounter most frequently in their religious system.

Anlo-Ewe Cosmology

The Ancestors

The ancestors are believed to be the most accessible of all spiritual forces, as they have the closest connections with their living descendants, having just parted from them. Several authors of Anlo religion suggest that there is a widespread belief in what can loosely be termed reincarnation (Nukunya 1969b: 2; Blier 1995: 178; Geurts 2002: 174–7). Reincarnation is not akin to rebirth of an individual who once lived; instead, in Anlo, each person is believed to be a 'unique combination of ancestral parts, energy, and individuality that come together in a certain way only once' (Friedson 2009: 104). An individual is thought to consist of four elements: *aklama, gbogbe, luvo,* and *dzogbe. Aklama* may be defined as the substance that determines an individual's character and unique distinguishing traits. *Gbogbe* refers to breath, or the force that keeps the body alive. *Luvo,* loosely translated as shadow, consists of two parts: *luvoagbeto,* the soul of life, and *luvokuto,* the soul of death. *Luvo* also refers to the physical elements of a person, such as hair and nails, elements which were believed to contain the essence of an individual. After death, the *luvo* proceeds to *tsiefe,* the world of the dead, but sometimes continues to haunt the living until the appropriate ceremonies have been performed. The *luvo* also consists of mother and father parts, ancestor souls (*dzoto*), and signs of non-kin determinations or life signs (*kpoli*). *Dzogbe* is the mechanism that charts out the specific path the individual has to follow; it is the individual's destiny, to which he or she has to aspire. An individual is meant to live in accordance with *dzogbe,* the unique path which has been predetermined for him or her. If this plan has been challenged, an individual's *dzogbe* continues to live on as a discontented presence in the world. These *dzogbewo* are capable of altering their descendants' destinies to the detriment of the latter. Rosenthal tells us that her informants suggest that an individual can withhold his *dzoto* after death, which will then cease to exist; *gbogbe* goes on, especially in the case of a traumatic death. *Gbogbewo* remember how they lived and how they died (Rosenthal 1997: 188). Sometimes, an ancestor has a great degree of agency in determining his or her descendants' characteristics and life chances. A particular ancestor can bestow on a newborn a part of who they were when they were alive. This is possible as various parts that make up an ancestor

developed by a particular people closely associated with their sense of ethnic identity' (Baum 1999: 3, fn 1).

(benevolent or malevolent) can be in *tsiefe*, *kodzogbe*, and *bome* (the place where souls wait to be born) at the same time (Friedson 2009: 105). The process of sponsoring a descendant in this way is called *amedzodzo*;[5] the ancestral sponsor is an *amedzoto*. Often, individuals take to worshipping certain *trowo* or *voduwo* because of the relationship their *amedzotowo* had with the entities in question, a move which is believed to complete their social personhood.

The Anlo have two basic categories of ancestor, one benevolent and the other malign. The *togbuiwo* (sing. *togbui*) or the grandfathers, and *mamawo* (sing. *mama*) or the grandmothers, are the more established category of ancestor, believed to have led long and virtuous lives. They have successfully made the transition from the world of the living or *kodzogbe*, to *tsiefe*, the resting abode of the deceased (Meyer 1999: 63). While the influence of the *togbuiwo* and *mamawo* on the living is profound, they are almost always benign, with the well-being of their descendants their paramount concern. The worship and reverence of the *togbuiwo* and *mamawo* is expressed by the creation of *togbui zikpi* (*togbui* = grandfather, *zikpi* = stool). These *togbuiwo* and *mamawo* are frequently honoured in ancestral *zikpi* houses, which are the property of the *afedowo*, the local patrilineage. A caretaker (stool father) is appointed by every *afedo* to look after the stool house (Verdon 1983: 91–2).

Other categories of ancestral spirit, who have lived unfulfilled lives or have died traumatic deaths, are capable of harming their descendants. Known as the *togbuiwofenoliwo* (Ewe: souls of bad ancestors), these ancestors are believed to have led dissatisfied lives, and continue to project their disappointment on the living. One of the main reasons is that they are thought to be unhappy with the manner in which their funerals have been performed (de Surgy 1988: 129; Meyer 1999: 64). More malicious than the *togbuiwofenoliwo* are the *ametsiavawo*. These *ametsiavawo* have died premature deaths, generally attributed to human agency, caused by accident or murder. They manifest themselves constantly, by activities such as causing untimely deaths of their descendants or contributing to their economic downfall. Like the *togbuiwofenoliwo*, the chief reason for the anger of the *ametsiavawo* derives from the fact that their funerals were haphazardly performed, either by genuine error or wilfully to disgrace them. They were also buried outside the realms of the village, usually in the forest, in an attempt to erase them from social memory. Convicts banished from society, ill-treated slaves, and murdered people usually return as *ametsiavawo*. While the benign *togbuiwo* and *mamawo* are revered in stool houses which are clan property, special provisions are made for the *dzogbewo*, *tobguiwofenoliwo*, and *ametsiavawo*, as the latter require different forms of worship and ritual tactics for their pacification.

---

[5] (Ewe: *ame* = person; *dzo* = born; *dzo* = born).

Of Witchcraft and Sorcery

Witchcraft (Ewe: *adze*) is believed to be a human force, produced by tensions within a patrilineage or matrilineage.[6] Witchcraft is generally acknowledged as the cause of a wide variety of problems, from persistent, incurable sicknesses to the inability to create wealth, and the loss of reproductive fertility. *Adze* is generally thought to be the by-product of conflicting familial relationships, usually generated by jealousy: siblings seeking each other's downfall, co-wives competing for their husband's attention, and poorer relations envious of richer family members are all situations which potentially could generate *adze*. Women and old people are potential *adzeto*, or owners of witchcraft (Meyer 1999: 91). A decade's fieldwork in Anlo suggested that *adze* was a widespread spiritual problem: unlike the wrath of particular *trowo*, *voduwo*, and ancestors, which was relatively easy to diagnose and address, *adze* attacks were steady and relentless. Protective medicines were employed on a trial and error basis, until one of them actually worked to protect the victim from the effects of *adze*. Both Christians and non-Christians devoted considerable resources to combating *adze*. Most Pentecostal Christian churches conduct frequent 'deliverance sessions' aimed at expelling *adze* and potential witches from congregations; these take the form of intensive prayer sessions and exorcisms (Gifford 1997: 97; Larbi 2001: 301–5). The other popular prophylactic measure employed to deal with *adze* is *dzo*. The term *dzo* usually refers to a physical object, generally a string of beads, made by specialist *dzotowo* (*dzo* owner) for individual protection. The more colloquial *juju* is often used to denote not only both *adze* and *dzo*, but also the cause, process, and effects of witchcraft.

Gods and God: Trowo, Voduwo, *and Mawu*

There are two words that the Anlo use most often in the context of 'deity': *trowo* and *voduwo*. *Tro* – when used as a verb – means to change, or to modify in Anlo-Ewe. But a *tro* (noun. pl. *trowo*) is used to describe a deity, which has some recognisable form, attribute, function, and personality, as well as a specific place in the Anlo pantheon. As the etymology of the

---

[6] In his epic study of the Azande, Evans-Pritchard (1937) distinguished between 'witchcraft' and 'sorcery'. Witchcraft was the inherent ability to cause harm, generated unknowingly, while sorcery, performed deliberately, involved a series of acquired techniques. Witchcraft (Ewe: *adze*; Twi: *bayi*) has been analysed so extensively in the context of lived and historical religion and social practice in Eweland and southern Ghana that it merits a thorough investigation of its own: the phenomenological usages differ greatly from study to study. (For witchcraft and envy [Ewe: *n'bia*], see Rosenthal 1998: 228–33; for witchcraft [*adze*] and other protective measures [*dzo*] used to combat such phenomena, see Meyer 1999: 90–4). During my fieldwork, informants appeared to be using *adze* rather loosely to imply both an unconsciously generated force as well as the by-product of a deliberately orchestrated ritual.

word *tro* suggests, the *trowo* are generally moody and unpredictable; their actions are inconsistent, and do not always mirror the conduct of their devotees. They are aptly described by people as confusers who make unreasonable demands on their devotees, sometimes unfairly meting out punishments for non-compliance.

Isolating the conceptual differences between the *trowo* and *voduwo* has preoccupied several ethnographers of the Ewe. According to Rosenthal, who worked east of Anlo in southern Togo, *tro* is the term used more commonly amongst the western Anlo-Ewe, for what the eastern Ouatchi (Watchi) Ewe and Fon call *vodu* (Rosenthal 1998: 60). So not only do *tro*, *vodu*, and the more colloquial 'fetish' refer to a deity, but the terms are also used to denote 'the spirit and host during possession ceremonies', as well as the 'nature-spirit, divinised ancestor, slave-spirit or guardian divinities of other kinds'. In addition, the term usually included 'the god-object that is never entirely separable from the spirits themselves, the "made thing" without which the spirits are not divinised' (Rosenthal 1998: 61). While Rosenthal implies that the difference between the *trowo* and *voduwo* is virtually non-existent, Kathryn Geurts, who conducted her fieldwork in Anlo, claims that the two have very different ontologies. For her, *vodu* symbolises the totality of practices, which include ceremonies and performative aspects of *trowo* worship. While a *tro* had a personality and often anthropomorphic attributes, *vodu* falls more in the realm of metaphysics, described by Geurts as a 'power, philosophy or state-of-being'. So *vodu* is a system of knowledge, of which the *trowo* are just one aspect. *Vodu* in its entirety included various practical aspects of worship, so '*vodu* was drawn on in constructing [a]*legba* figures; *vodu* was drawn on in communicating or interacting with a *tro*; *vodu* was drawn on for empowerment within the context of various religious sects' (Geurts 2002: 193).

There appear to be other key differences between the *trowo* and *voduwo*, which I became aware of through an analysis of the manner in which my Anlo informants spoke of religious entities. Indeed, as Geurts suggests, at a non-specialised level, *vodu/n* is often used to refer to various aspects of religious practice in Anlo. For instance, the term 'Gorovodu' referred to the entire corpus of northern ritual knowledge associated with certain *voduwo* from the savanna, such as Kunde, Abrewa, and Tigare. As most ethnographers have noted, Anlo people do indeed use religious terminology loosely, which makes it difficult to assess whether a conceptual distinction is being made at all when these words are employed. Michelle Gilbert tells us the Anlo substituted the terms *alegba* (protective deity), *vodu*, and *atike* (medicine) for each other, whilst asserting that they were completely different things (Gilbert 1982: 62). The most emphatic distinction that I came across in Anlo is that association with the *trowo* was normally inherited, while the relationships with the *voduwo* were contracted on a more casual basis. *Voduwo* could be bought, or be made by anyone, who could then make his services (and those of the *vodu*) available to potential supplicants. *Voduwo* are believed to have entered the religious system from outside Anlo, while *trowo* are thought to be either native to Anlo, or so thoroughly naturalised after a long passage of time that their foreign origins are no longer common knowledge.

Of the *trowo* and *voduwo*, Mawu has been accorded a privileged position. He has also become synonymous with the Christian God. Herskovits claimed that Mawu and his spouse Lisa were at the heart of the religion of the Gbe-speaking peoples, and hence have always occupied the pivotal position in the Ewe pantheon. Creation myths recorded in Dahomey present Mawu and Lisa as the original cosmic couple, the mother and father of mankind and all other divinities respectively (Herskovits 1938, Vol. 2: 101–2). Scholars of the western Ewe and Anlo, however, maintain that Mawu was a rather distant deity in pre-Christian times, and it was missionary discourse that created the Mawu as the Ewe recognise him now, with his unique, God-like attributes (Meyer 1999: 65–6; Greene 2002: 16).[7] British colonial official A. B. Ellis observed this transformation when he was based in Anlo in 1874: Mawu's position as the head of the Anlo pantheon was being created and reinforced by Christian discourse, while the *voduwo* and *trowo* were coming to be represented as lesser deities (Ellis 1965: 32–3).[8] As Mawu assumed the pivotal position in the Ewe pantheon, Christianity came to be known as *Mawusubosubo* or service to Mawu. Characteristically, Mawu differs greatly from the whimsical *trowo* and *voduwo*: he is endowed with a strong sense of justice, in addition to qualities such as compassion and forgiveness. Unlike the *trowo* and *voduwo* whose realm of operation is restricted to petty problems that concern their devotees' well-being, Mawu was believed to be responsible for the macrocosmic tasks such as the preservation of the universe and mankind. Despite professed non-adherence to Christianity, many non-Christians acknowledge Mawu's position as the most important god, and consider all other deities to be subordinate to Him: the many Anlo gods are believed to be intermediaries between humans and Mawu (see Nukunya 1969b: 1–7). For some Christianised Anlo, the *trowo* are

---

[7] Greene claims that Mawu was worshipped in Anlo as the Supreme Deity until the eighteenth century, after which it was deposed from its position of pre-eminence by Se, a divinity associated with the Ifa system of the Yoruba, that was gradually becoming a cornerstone of Anlo religion (Greene 2002: 16–7). Rosenthal observed that Mawu is a local *vodu* or *tro* in non-Christian Ewe ritual cultures, sometimes revered as a female creator god (Rosenthal 1998: 61, 265), which I also found to be true during the course of my fieldwork. See also Gaba (1969) and Greene (1996c) for further contributions to the debate on the Supreme Being in the Anlo-Ewe ritual cosmos.

[8] Spieth (2011: 53–4) suggested that, in some parts of Eweland, a pre-eminent divine cosmic couple – Sodza (m) and Sogble (f), who took the form of thunder and lightning (ibid. 48–9) – were revered instead of a Supreme Being.

regarded as the children of Mawu, or *Mawuviwo*, and are believed to be more easily approachable than the rather distant Supreme Being. The customary pouring of libation is often integrated into Christian services to honour the *trowo* of the community.

Modern Anlo is characterised by several distinct religious networks, organised around distinct clusters of *trowo*, *voduwo*, and ancestors. Each of these networks has a number of shrines dedicated to various combinations of entities, and associated with them are a large number of devotees at various stages of submission. Unlike the clear-cut descriptions presented above, the *trowo*, *voduwo*, ancestors, and *adze* are not well-defined and neatly compartmentalised forces. Transformations from one category to another occur frequently. For instance, *tro* and ancestral cult groups 'coincided' over time as they both addressed the same functions of reinforcing lineage solidarity through worship of common deities and ancestors (Gilbert 1982: 64). Meyer writes about *dzo* that could be transformed by worshippers into new *trowo* and then be known as *dzozutro* (*dzo* that became *tro*) (Meyer 1999: 67). Gilbert observes that an entity exhibiting all the characteristics of a *tro* was described as a *vodu* by Fiawoo three decades prior to her fieldwork (Gilbert 1982: 66). Anlo cultic networks could be organised around *trowo*, *voduwo*, and ancestors. An individual could 'marry' a *tro* or *vodu* for a number of reasons: on account of his or her *amedzoto*, or for protection against witchcraft. Rosenthal calls such formations 'orders', 'because they create law and organise meaning, ritual, and relationships between humans, as well as between humans and deities' (Rosenthal 1998: 1). Elsewhere, they are referred to as 'cults' (Greene 1996a; Akyeampong 2001b), on account of their hierarchical organisation and possession of esoteric knowledge. But they are several things at once: they are belief systems that cement relationships between the living and spirit world, creating moral and spiritual order; they are a bridge between the past and the present, between history as it is locally construed and contemporary memory; they are social networks that are hierarchal in nature, that create and sustain power structures in Anlo communities, through ritual performance and a veneer of secrecy. Generally, I refer to such formations as cultic networks, or simply as religious cults. What follows is a description of most of the major religious cults in Anlo, the deities around which they are organised, their functions, structure, and recruitment patterns.

The Religious Field

Yewe: Of Thunder and the Sea

Of the colourfully painted shrines in Anlo villages, the vast majority will have depictions of Hevieso, the thunder god. Hevieso, an imposing figure, looming across shrine walls, is sometimes seated beside his wife,

Avleketi, who controls the seas and serpents. Avleketi's favourite serpent, Voduda, is never far away from them. These three deities are most commonly referred to as Yewe in Anlo.[9] A selection of nature spirits, including the famous mermaid Mami Wata, is also worshipped alongside Yewe deities.[10] The three core Yewe deities – Hevieso, Avleketi, and Voduda – were brought to Anlo from the former Dahomey during the first half of the nineteenth century (Akyeampong 2001b: 107–11).[11] At the heart of this gradual westward diffusion from Dahomey were enthusiastic Anlo worshippers enamoured by the prowess of these Yewe deities. In due course, shrines grew around them, whose reputations led to an increase in the numbers of worshippers. Yewe shrines metamorphosed into trading houses in the mid-nineteenth century, an adaptation to Anlo's competitive export-based economy, where individuals sought to broaden their networks of influence by controlling people (see Greene 1996a: 96–8).

There are about eight or nine major Yewe shrine houses in Anlo-Afiadenyigba, and several minor ones.[12] In size, these range from small box-like cubicles to large houses built around courtyards with several rooms. Two of Anlo-Afiadenyigba's biggest Yewe shrines, with which I became well acquainted, are known as the Gbanyaga and the Goku shrines (Figure 3.2).[13] The Goku shrine is one of the larger and more popular Yewe houses in the town. The shrine has four rooms, dedicated to different deities, from Hevieso to Voduda and Mami Wata. The Goku shrine, like all Yewe shrines, is 'owned' by an individual, known as *hubono* (pl. *hubonowo*). This shrine was established about six generations ago, in

---

[9] Some of the other minor deities worshipped in Yewe shrines in Anlo-Afiadenyigba are Ada, Amaka, and Eda (see Kraamer 2005).

[10] On Mami Wata, see H. J. Drewal (1988a, 1988b, 2008). According to Drewal, Mami Wata, the seductress and mermaid, (often depicted as a Hindu deity), is believed to be capable of bestowing upon worshippers great wealth suddenly, while simultaneously bringing about their downfall in equally spectacular fashion. Widely regarded as a symbol of copious consumption and unrestricted excesses, the deity entered the visual and ritual vocabulary of Slave Coast religion *c.* 1885, probably inspired by images that reached the then Gold Coast from British India as a result of colonial trading networks.

[11] Herskovits notes that different cultic networks developed in Dahomey around the Earth, Sky, and Thunder deities. Yewe was synonymous with the term *vodu* in Dahomey. Dahomean informants of Herskovits were puzzled by Yewe's western manifestations amongst the Anlo (Herskovits 1938: 189–90). I have come across Yewe shrines in Anexo and Pahou, which vary greatly from their Anlo-Ewe counterparts in organisation, structure, and the deities worshipped by initiates.

[12] Nadia Lovell (2002) analyses in detail the initiation rituals, spirit possession ceremonies, and making of *vodhun* shrines in Watchi-Ewe settlements in southeastern Togo. The *vodhun* shrines of the southeastern Ewe closely resemble the shrines of the Yewe cult in Anlo. *Vodhun* spirits were taken to Anlo from Dahomey, and were reconfigured into Yewe *voduwo*.

[13] While Gbanyaga is derived from a set of words which means 'to engulf', Goku is the given name of the individual who first established that shrine.

Figure 3.2. Outer walls of the Goku shrine, depicting Hevieso, the god of thunder, Anlo-Afiadenyigba, August 2005

the middle of the nineteenth century.[14] Artefacts used to create the Yewe god-objects were brought to Afiadenyigba from the village of Ketakore in Togo. Goku's shrine is known simply as Goku *afeme*, or Goku's house. Goku is the owner of the shrine and the descendant of the man credited with establishing that particular shrine, also known as Goku. While Goku is not a Yewe initiate himself, he is intimately involved with the running of the shrine. A number of ancestral deities (*togbuiwo*) of Goku's patrilineage are also revered in the shrine. This shrine also serves as a residential dwelling for about eight members of Goku's family. A small drink spot, selling a selection of beverages, operates out of the outer enclosure of the shrine.

Full-fledged Yewe initiates, who are mainly women,[15] are generically known as *yewesiwo* (sing. *yewesi*) or *vodusiwo* (sing. *vodusi*), meaning 'wives of Yewe' or 'wives of the *voduwo*'.[16] They dress in cloth and are almost always bare-shouldered. They usually have scarifications on their faces, in the form of three short parallel lines on both cheeks and forehead, as well as several short lines on their arms, back, and legs. These are symbols

[14] Interview with Togbi Goku, Anlo-Afiadenyigba, 31 October 2003.
[15] Anthropologists have long pondered the question of why women outnumber men in their membership of possession cults in West African vodun (see Lovell 2002: 72–99).
[16] Male initiates are known as *husunuwo* (sing. *husunu*). *Vodusiwo* greatly outnumber *husunuwo*.

associated with Hevieso and Voduda.[17] Wives of Hevieso in particular are usually men and are specifically known as *sosiwo* (sing. *sosi*); wives of Avleketi are mainly women and are known as *avlesiwo* (sing. *avlesi*); while wives of Voduda, again generally women, are called *dasiwo* (sing. *dasi*). All these *vodusiwo* have their own special ritual regalia and dance styles, reflecting the personalities of the deities to which they are pledged (see Rosenthal 2005: 186). Each Yewe shrine is controlled by a chief priest or priestess, known as a *midao* (pl. *midawo*) or *minao* (pl. *minawo*).[18] The process of becoming a *vodusi* is a lengthy, expensive one. *Vodusiwo* join the shrine as the result of an affliction, illness, or other troubled circumstances.

Vodusi Dadziezor's story is typical of why an individual would commit to the worship of Yewe gods. She was born in Nigeria, the daughter of Anlo migrants to Badagry. She was married, had two children, and ran a successful grocery store. However, events conspired against her in her early thirties. An inexplicable recurring illness plagued her. Her husband, a Yoruba Muslim, took a new wife, and stopped supporting her. He became abusive towards her, and did not allow her to see their children. By her own accounts, she became depressed. She returned to Anlo-Afiadenyigba, the hometown of her parents, to stay with extended family. There, she was drawn to Yewe worship. Several of her patrilineal and matrilineal ancestors were *vodusiwo* who belonged to the Goku shrine. She believes that one of them, in particular, who was 'married to Voduda', was her ancestral sponsor, or *amedzoto*.[19] *Vodusiwo* take on new names upon initiation into the cult, which are reminiscent of Dahomean names, a vestige of the cult's easterly origins (Nukunya 1969b: 5). Dadziezor went through a lengthy period of initiation into the cult, staying in the Goku shrine for several months, learning rituals associated with the worship of the Yewe deities. Usually clad in white, such novice initiates are known as *husikpokpowo* (sing. *husikpokpo*) or simply *kpokpowo* (sing. *kpokpo*).[20] She was finally transformed into a *vodusi*. She attributes her past sufferings to ignoring the Yewe deities, who had desired her attention ever since her birth.

Midawo and *minawo* are recruited through the same process as *vodusiwo*: they are replaced within patrilineages or matrilineages, depending on the identity of the ancestral sponsor and his or her relationship

---

[17] Markings associated with the Yewe cult are known as *dakpla*, *kpemeblinui*, and *nyadui* (see Spieth 2011: 280).

[18] The Yewe elders are different from the *hubonowo*. *Midawo* and *minawo* do not hail from the patrilineages of the *hubonowo*; the former are more involved in the spiritual matters of the cult, while the latter are more concerned with the logistical operations.

[19] Interview with *Vodusi* Dadziezor, Anlo-Afiadenyigba, 19 February 2004.

[20] *Kpokpo* = (*Yewegbe*) looking; searching; (see also Kraamer 2005: 291).

with the potential Yewe *midao* or *minao*. The chief priestess of the Gbanyaga shrine, simply known as *Minao* Gbanyaga, assumed her position
on account of her paternal grandmother, whom she is meant to replace
within the Yewe shrine. Her story is similar to that of Dadziezor's: her
misfortunes ended upon the realisation that she was meant to follow her
grandmother's path, and assume her role in the Gbanyaga shrine.[21] A
number of other casual supplicants, known as *ahewo* (sing. *ahe*)[22] are also
associated with each Yewe shrine. *Ahewo* will tell you that they 'belong'
to a Yewe shrine in question, because members of their patrilineage or
matrilineage are initiates of the shrine in question. For example, Christian Seeku, a retired school teacher who describes himself as a committed
member of the EP church, is associated with the Gbanyaga shrine in such
a capacity. Members of his *afedo*, including his sisters, were *vodusiwo*.
Seeku occasionally petitions the Yewe deities at the Gbanyaga shrine for
spiritual favours; he attends funerals and festivals associated with the
shrine as an observer. He also considers some deities in the shrine to be
divinised ancestors.[23] The *ahewo* form a pool of casual, non-committal
associates or worshippers, who identify with various shrines, usually in
close proximity to their ancestral homes or the *afedo-me*.[24] Yewe *ahewo*,
vodusiwo, and *midawo* come together during 'outdoorings'[25] and funerals
of other cult members. Funerals of Yewe cult members are extremely
elaborate ceremonies (see Kraamer 2005: 688–90), usually transacted in
three stages: the burial, *adadada*,[26] and *tsyoga* or 'grand funeral'.

Much of the academic literature on Yewe refers to it as a 'cult' or 'secret
society', a reference to the hierarchical membership structure, and the
ethos of secrecy (Spieth 1911: 163–80; Nukunya 1969b: 1). *Vodusiwo*
speak a ritual language, known as *Yewegbe*, understood only by them.
Yewegbe has words from Fon, AJA, and Mina, reflecting the gradual
westward diffusion of Yewe deities from Dahomey. All Yewe initiates
observe certain food taboos: barracuda and dolphin are out of bounds for
them. Yewe initiates have a special ritual privilege of falling into a state
known as *alaga*, or 'going wild'. This is a mechanism which probably
made joining a Yewe shrine so attractive to people in different periods
in Anlo's history. The initiate may go *alaga* when insulted by another
individual. The initiate fallen into this state usually wanders about the
village lamenting his insulter. An *alagadzedze* has to be 'caught' by other

---

[21] Interview with *Minao* Gbanyaga, Anlo-Afiadenyigba, 4 November 2003.
[22] *Ahewo* (sing. *ahe*) is a generic term used across the Anlo religious landscape to refer to
uninitiated followers and casual worshippers of most cults.
[23] Interview with Christian Seeku, Anlo-Afiadenyigba, 6 March 2004.
[24] The term is used to refer to uninitiated members of any Anlo cult.
[25] Ceremonies where new initiates are introduced to members of the public for the first
time after spending months within the confines of the shrine.
[26] Ada = deity; dada = cooking (cooking for Ada, part of Yewe initiates' funeral rites, see
Kraamer 2005: 281).

members of the cult, and the dispute between the violator and the person has to be resolved.

Yewe is the most popular religious network in Anlo. By Nukunya's accounts, in 1969, in Woe, a town with a population of 3,450, there were four Yewe 'lodges' or shrines. On the basis of estimates, the total number of cult members was five hundred, which was about 15 per cent of the town's population. He also estimates that *vodusiwo* comprise about 10 per cent of Anlo's entire population (Nukunya 1969b: 1). My research in Anlo-Afiadenyigba suggested that the Goku and Gbanyaga shrines had a combined membership of a hundred and fifty *vodusiwo*, on the basis of the records maintained by the elders of those shrines. (There are at least eleven other Yewe shrines in Anlo-Afiadenyigba, each with at least thirty *vodusiwo* attached to them.) The *husunowo* and *midawo* of some shrines are so influential that there are a fixed number of seats reserved for them at the village council in Anlo-Afiadenyigba.

Rituals aimed at the appeasement of the sea are entrusted to devotees of Yewe. For example, a procedure known as *agbodedefu* is deemed crucial to the success of fishing in Anlo. *Agbodedefu* literally means 'sacrificing a ram to the sea', where a ram is offered to Avleketi by cult members.[27] Dispute resolution, usually involving theft and petty crime, is carried out by members of the Yewe cult in Anlo villages today. Yewe deities are renowned for their spiritual punishments, meted out to enemies of the cult – in the most severe case, death by lightning (Akyeampong 2001b: 225).

Gods of the North: Gorovodu/Atikevodu

There are a cluster of deities in Anlo that are known as Gorovodu. Named after the kola nut, or *goro*, these deities are believed to originate in the northern savanna. The kola nut, a gentle stimulant, is strongly associated with the Islamised peoples of the savanna, who used it in the face of the alcohol prohibition imposed by their faith: it was a prized commodity, exchanged along the north–south trade routes. Gorovodu is also known as Atikevodu in Anlo, which translates into 'religion of medicine.'[28] These

---

[27] Several Yewe initiates and elders paddle into the ocean in a canoe with a ram on board, which is then given to the sea as an offering. Akyeampong notes that this ritual was carried out once in three years by Anlo fishing communities (Akyeampong 2001b: 120–1). Even Anlo Christians knew what it entailed, which means the ritual was an integral part of 'secular' Anlo culture.

[28] While the Gorovodu deities have their origins in the northern savanna, they have undergone a structural and functional metamorphosis in the southern Ewe littoral, and are virtually unrecognisable in form compared with their original manifestations (Rosenthal 1998: 36–99; Venkatachalam 2012: 55–9). Most of these deities are better known in the academic literature as anti-witchcraft movements that swept through the Akan forest

deities are also known as the Blekete or Brekete gods, referring to the drum beats and melodies that are associated with their manifestation in their devotees through possession.

Kunde, a hunter spirit, is the head of the Gorovodu pantheon. His wife, Abrewa, is revered as the patron of market women. They have several children: Sacrebode, their first son, is believed to be a horse by some Gorovodu worshippers; by others he was revered as the god of land. Banguele, sometimes known as Ketesi, a fierce hunter spirit, has several manifestations in the form of figures of authority: Tsenge is the god of knives; Gediya is a policeman, and Surugu is a lieutenant. Banguele represents all those who have died violent deaths. Senyakupo, the youngest offspring of Kunde and Abrewa, was a chameleon, represented as a beautiful Islamised woman. Wango, a crocodile spirit, is associated with water and the natural elements.[29] Those that submitted to the worship of these deities are known as *trosiwo* (sing. *trosi*).[30] Gorovodu worship and ritual knowledge go hand in hand with spirit possession. *Trosiwo* are individuals who have surrendered themselves to the Gorovodu spirits. When they appear through their mediums, these spirits offer advice and opinions on a great range of concerns from social problems to local politics – or, simply, the health of their worshippers.

Like the Yewe cult, there are several Gorovodu shrines in Anlo villages, which range from small structures (see Figure 3.4, for example) to rooms in family compounds (Figure 3.3). Owners of shrines are called *sofo* (pl. *sofowo*), from the Akanised *osofo* (priest). Some members of the network have ritual functions during ceremonies: known as *senterwawo* (sing. *senterwa*),[31] they attend to the mediums when the spirits come to possess them. Uninitiated members are known as *adehawo* (sing. *adeha*), literally 'hunting group', who partake in Gorovodu worship and organise important ritual events. *Fetatrotro* (which translates into 'the turning around of the year'), is a triennial cow sacrifice, which brings together all Gorovodu initiates in communities, climaxing in a display of spirit possession (Friedson 2009: 27). Sacrifices can take place on a number of other occasions like thanksgivings and to make amends to the *trowo* for the violation of Gorovodu taboos.

During my time in Anlo, I came across several *trosiwo*. I became acquainted with Wango Adzinu of Blekusu (a town near Keta). Wango

---

belt between *c*. 1890 and *c*. 1920 (Parker 2004, 2006; Allman and Parker 2005: 106–42).

[29] Rosenthal describes the attributes and sacrificial preferences of closely related Gorovodu spirits in southern Togo; they vary in slightly in attributes and preferences from those in Anlo (Rosenthal 1998: 60–70).

[30] *Tro* = deity; *si* = pledged. *Goro*= kola; *vodu*= religion.

[31] *Senterwa* is, according to Friedson, a cognate of the English word sentry (Friedson 2009: 32).

Figure 3.3. Gorovodu shrine, depicting various northern deities, a Muslim *mallam*, a crocodile spirit, Kunde, and a three-headed Indian deity, Anlo-Afiadenyigba, December 2010

Adzinu was a former secondary school teacher who had submitted to Wango, a crocodile spirit. I also knew several *trosiwo* married to Ketesi and Banguele, the violent slave spirits. They were referred to by their ritual names when in possession. Apart from Wango, none of these spirit mediums had any family or ancestral connections to Gorovodu: they were simply 'caught' by the spirits in question, and had come to serve them. While each of these spirit mediums kept personal household shrines, there were several large shrines in Anlo-Afiadenyigba where Gorovodu devotees could congregate. *Sofo* 'Slender''s shrine, with representations of snakes, kola nuts, northern deities, and crocodiles, was particularly well known (Figure 3.3). Inside was an enclosure devoted to Kunde. *Sofo* Slender's position as a Gorovodu priest was hereditary: his family had a long history of engagement with Gorovodu, and this shrine had been managed by his father and grandfather before him.[32] A number of people approached it for advice on how to cure low-key illnesses. *Sofowo* are uninitiated devotees of Gorovodu: the spirits do not come to possess them; they are, however, conversant in the ritual and medicinal lore of

---

[32] Interview with *Sofo* Slender, Anlo-Afiadenyigba, 19 September 2005.

Figure 3.4. Household Gorovodu shrine, depicting Banguele, Kunde, and Abrewa, Anlo-Afiadenyigba, May 2013

Gorovodu. Anybody could approach a Gorovodu *sofo* for advice. Potential devotees are not tied to a particular shrine (as in the case of Yewe), and membership was not transmitted through patrilineal or matrilineal ties. I have seen Wango, Ketesi, and Banguele get possessed individually at the behest of clients in search of spiritual advice, which ranged from remedies for minor health problems to queries about their life chances; I have also witnessed them all getting possessed simultaneously at large communal gatherings to honour the *trowo*.

Gods of the North: In the shadow of slavery

Another cluster of spirits, said to have come from the north of Anlo, are known collectively as Fofie or Krachi Dente. These are umbrella terms to refer to a corpus of practices dedicated to the veneration of the slave ancestors of some Anlo, and the gods of these slaves. Like the other Anlo ritual networks, a number of women, known as *fofiesiwo*, are pledged to Fofie worship. The *fofiesiwo* believe that their patrilineal Anlo ancestors enslaved non-Anlo peoples, mainly women, in the past. Most of these women were integrated into Anlo society by marriage to their Anlo masters. *Fofiesiwo* are descended from these mixed unions. My research indicated that there were about eighty slave-owning lineages in the town of Anlo-Afiadenyigba; 56 of them were actively involved in Fofie worship in 2010. Each slave-owning lineage has a shrine dedicated

Figure 3.5. Fofie shrine at Nyerwese, Anlo-Afiadenyigba, September 2003

to their particular slave ancestors. These shrines house objects such as personal belongings of the slaves, relics carried away in war, and the gods of the slaves. A *fofiesi*, upon death, is replaced by a member of the successive generation of her patrilineage. In addition to the *fofiesiwo*, other members of the lineage are also intimately involved with the slave ancestors. A category of persons known as *fiamanyawo* (sing. *fiamanya*), are not quite aware of what their association with Fofie is, and how exactly they ought to serve the slave ancestors: they are awaiting divine indications that will make this clear to them. There are men known as *agbotawo*[33] (sing. *agbota*), who are responsible for making sacrifices to the slave ancestors. An *agbota* is usually a close male relation of a *fofiesi*, usually a son or a nephew.

While every Fofie-worshipping lineage keeps a shrine which relates to their own slave ancestors and their family's experience of slavery, there is a large shrine in the Nyerwese division of Anlo-Afiadenyigba where *fofiesiwo* congregate to perform rituals for all the slave ancestors of the community (Figure 3.5). This shrine is a very ordinary room in a standard rectangular household compound, one of several cubicles facing inward onto a central courtyard. Two fading images – a regal figure seated on a

---

[33] *Agbo* = ram; *ta* = head. This is not a Fofie-specific position: ram sacrifice is practised by members of other Anlo cults, and men responsible for this role within the context of other cults are also addressed by the same title.

stool and a crocodile – adorn the outer façade of the shrine. The contents
of the shrine are seldom displayed publicly: these are believed to include
the remains of a stool carried away by local warriors in the aftermath of
a military campaign against an inland Ewe city-state during the Asante
Wars of the mid-1860s. The compound in which the shrine is located
houses a large extended family of at least thirty people. A fisherman in his
mid-fifties, known as Ajakoku, is the patriarch of this family. He lives in
this shrine complex with his two wives, children, and some grandchildren.
Ajakoku is a very important member in the cultic hierarchy, as his family
is believed to have a long history of engagement with these Fofie deities:
his patrilineal ancestors were known to have enslaved several Ewedome
slave women in the past; one of these slave women was Ajakoku's great-
grandmother, Ablesi, who is believed to have introduced the worship of
the slave ancestors and their deities into the town, during the 1940s.

Fofie is a possession cult. Exactly what or who comes to possess the
fofiesiwo is not as clear-cut as in the case of the Gorovodu *trosiwo*. Some
fofiesiwo say their northern slave ancestors, who died in Anlo, speak
through them. When possessed, they speak to their audiences in a mixture of broken Hausa, Twi, and the northern Ewe dialect, depending
on from where the slaves originally hailed. Some of them say they are
possessed by the gods of these northern slave women, as well as a few of
the Gorovodu deities. Sometimes, when the Gorovodu deities come to
possess their devotees, the several slave spirits associated with Fofie soon
follow, coming to control the bodies of *fofiesiwo*. Some Anlo insist that the
Gorovodu deities are in fact gods of the slave ancestors, which is what
explains their intimate association with Fofie. Family shrines of slave-
holding patrilineages often have ritual objects or depictions of Brekete,
Tigare, Kunde, and Abrewa in them, to be revered alongside the actual
slave ancestors. Fofie initiates claim that Gorovodu is a type of esoteric
medicinal knowledge, initially known only to the peoples in the slaves'
homelands; it has travelled, along with the slave spirits, to the southern
lands. Not all Gorovodu spirit mediums are from Fofie-worshipping lineages. While Gorovodu is recognised as a 'northern religion' of savanna
peoples in particular, one does not have to be of slave descent to learn
about it or practise it. The entire community, even those not descended from slaves, may practise it. When I asked why the Anlo practise
the religion of their slaves, the answer I received, over and over again,
was, simply, that 'the religion and the medicine of the slaves are good
for us'.[34]

---

[34] Interview with Wango Adzinu, Blekusu, 15 June 2004; Interview with Sacrebode, Anlo-
Afiadenyigba, 18 September 2005; Interview with *Sofo* Slender, Anlo-Afiadenyigba, 19
September 2005.

Figure 3.6. Adzevodu shrine in Anlo-Afiadenyigba; seated by the door is the owner and founder, June 2004

Anti-Witchcraft and Protection

Adzevodu, Mamma, and Koku are a number of ritual networks associated with protection from witchcraft (*adze*). Witchcraft manifests itself through the loss of wealth and fertility, through recurring failure in the financial and personal sphere. Witchcraft is generally believed to be generated within the structures of the family and, in southern Ghana in particular, to be transmitted within the matrilineage, caused by a 'breakdown of long-term moral commitments between close kin' (Daswani 2010: 450); it is aggravated by jealousy and envy, representing 'the dark side of kinship' (Geschiere 1997: 11). Adzevodu and Mamma are anti-witchcraft deities that entered the village in the1940s and the 1980s respectively. Both the owners of these shrines were also the founders of the networks, and both deities supposedly originated in Nigeria. Adzevodu is fairly successful in Anlo-Afiadenyigba: Sogolum Kwasiga, the founder of Adzevodu, estimates that he has about five clients during the average day (see Figure 3.6). Mamma is an anti-witchcraft deity whose fortunes were linked to its charismatic founder; the network had about a hundred followers, drawn from all over the town. Adzevodu and Mamma, two relatively young networks in Afiadenyigba with their hubs in Benin and Nigeria respectively, could potentially signal the beginnings of a new trend in Anlo: the search for spiritual resources, which traditionally has been focused in a northern direction, may be in the process of shifting eastward.[35] Koku is an older, less-studied protective medicine, which offers supplicants protection against physical harm. Adepts display the potency of their medicine by attempting to cut themselves with knives, a feat which is unsuccessful on account of the protective powers of Koku. Protection cults differ from the other networks in that they can attract several followers at any given moment; these followers may have other religious affiliations, but may associate with these networks only until their needs are met, using them as a means to an end. Priests of these networks set themselves up as leaders with specialist ritual knowledge, which they use to the benefit of their paying clients.

A typical shrine in Anlo is a rather complicated institution. Cultic networks are never strictly dedicated to one set of deities only. While shrine owners may primarily identify with one religious network, a myriad of deities associated with different cultic networks may be accommodated within a single shrine. Anlo-Ewe shrines are ever-changing: god-objects are constantly being added by worshippers in stages, while deities are being transformed in their functions over periods of time. A Fofie priest invited me to visit his shrine in December 2013. At the altar were placed a few Gorovodu god-objects, recognisable by the references made to the Islamic north. In crowning position was a crucifix, a common feature in Gorovodu shrines. The owner, however, insisted that his Fofie deities were disconnected from the far north. He informed me that Mami Wata had married these particular spirits one day without his knowledge and now slept under his bed, usually with them in an elaborately decorated shrine. Her luxury-loving ways meant that she only drank imported Schnapps or Bombay Sapphire; she had bestowed upon him great wealth, which he had lost on account of not knowing how to appease her and the slave spirits that kept her company. Kunde and Abrewa, he proceeded to tell me, were servants of Mami Wata. A number of other slave ancestors of his family also live in his shrine.

Yet another shrine that I began to frequent in 2013 identified firstly with the Yewe network, but in fact accommodated a number of oceanic water spirits in addition to northern Gorovodu deities; there were also representations of Indian gods, and other oriental deities collected over time by the shrine owners, simply described in Anlo-Afiadenyigba as 'Buddhas'. Indeed, Anlo's location, between the Gold Coast and Slave Coast, and between two major ethno-cultural zones (the Akan and the Gbe-speaking peoples) meant that the region acted as a religico-cultural 'vortex', incorporating influences from all directions, creating a 'fertile

---

[35] See Axel Klein (1998) for an anthropological study of Ewe fishing communities in eastern Nigeria, especially the Lagos-Badagry area. In recent years, this region has received migrants from Anlo-Afiadenyigba, and the resulting ritual traffic between settlements like Lagos-Badagry and the village has been substantial.

mosaic of international, transcontinental, and transoceanic peoples, histories, commodities, and spirits' (Rush 2008: 150). Anlo religion and
religious imagery is very much a product of this vortextual phenomenon,
owing much to migrations, wars, slavery, travel, individual creativity,
and more recently, exposure to the modern mass media, evident from
the material and visual culture of shrines associated with the numerous
cultic networks.

Afa Divination

Central to the working of the religious system is Afa, a divination method,
present throughout the Gbe-speaking and Yoruba belt. Known as Fa by
the Fon of Benin and Ifa by the Yoruba and Edo, the divination system
is, as Bascom's pioneering work suggested, a form of communication
between gods and man in several West African cultures, an indispensable
element of religious practice (Bascom: 1969). Afa is the term used to
refer to an oracular divinity as well as a practice. Afa in itself is a reservoir
of stories, myths, and legends, a knowledge which is accessible only to
Afa diviners, known as *bokowo* (sing. *boko*).[36] *Bokowo* undergo a lengthy
period of initiation and rigorous training, studying the various codes and
myths associated with divinatory knowledge. They usually do not participate in the activities of any other cultic network. A *boko*'s divinatory
apparatus (*agumaga*) consists of either sacred palm nuts (*hunkuwo*) or
divining beads (*kpele*), attached to a few strings. A client of a *boko* typically approaches him in times of need, after suffering practical problems
such as loss of wealth, persistent illness, or the loss of fertility. The consultation with the *boko* focuses on the exact causes of such problems and
on possible remedies.

Each time the *boko* casts his string of divining beads, the seed pods
attached to them land in a particular position, which resembles one of the
sixteen combinations that the *agumaga* makes as it hits the ground, known
as Afa signs (*medzi*) (see Figure 3.7). On identifying the *medzi* in question,
the *boko* continues to cast his divinatory apparatus until he has isolated
the client's *kpoli*, or life sign. The two hundred and fifty-six *kpoliwo* are
combinations of the sixteen major *medziwo*. Isolating a client's *kpoli* is
the key to dispensing any advice. Every *kpoli* is associated with stories
of *voduwo*, *trowo*, the ancestors, plants, and animals (Maupoil 1943).[37]
Both Rosenthal (1998: 157) and de Surgy (1981: 146) emphasise the
importance of the concept of destiny (*se*)[38] for the Afa system. Each

---

[36] The Yoruba term for an Ifa diviner is *babalawo*, which translates into 'father of secrets'.
For Ifa and *babalawo*, see Peel (2000: 114–15).

[37] Maupoil records the stories associated with every *kpoli*, though most of his fieldwork
was carried out in Fon areas (Maupoil 1943).

[38] Se is also a deity, sometimes associated with the Afa divination system itself (Greene
2002: 16).

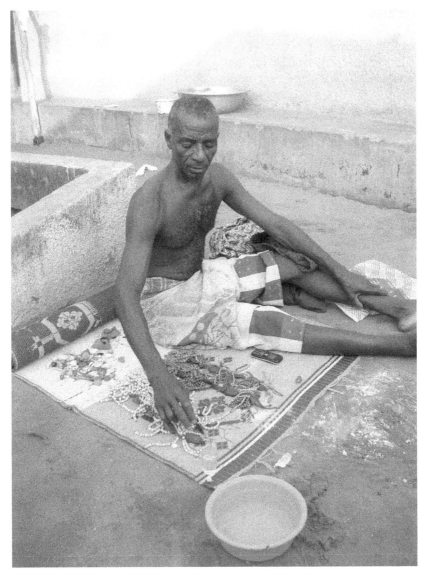

Figure 3.7. Afa *boko* with divinatory apparatus, Anlo-Afiadenyigba, December 2010

kpoli also has encoded within it guidelines on exactly how the individual should live, what profession he is suited for, which ancestors he must revere, and what dietary taboos he must observe. Deviating from the course of destiny is thought to have dangerous repercussions for the individual and his or her descendants. Afa diviners are usually consulted at the discretion of the client.

Afa diviners determine the remedies to individuals' problems through a combination of careful counselling and religious functions. First, *bokowo* have to determine the nature of the agency acting upon their clients, and if it is to be interpreted in terms of good or evil, and whether the problem is caused by individual or familial neglect of particular *voduwo*, *trowo*, or ancestors. The various Anlo *trowo* and *voduwo*, such as Nyigbla, the Yewe deities, the Gorovodu and Fofie spirits, appear in the stories associated with the *kpoliwo*, and probably entered the Afa vocabulary in Anlo after they became established presences in the religious system. Therefore, a *boko* is able to tell a client exactly which *tro* or *vodu* is exercising its influence, and how he should respond to it. An Afa *boko* would arrive at his conclusion by analysing his client's *kpoli* against the *medzi* made by the pattern cast, as well as isolating the exact problem by relating it to the religious history of the client's family. For example, certain Afa *medzi* are associated with stories about slavery and how slaves should be treated, and if a client's *kpoli* and *medzi* point towards these stories about slavery, Fofie worship is pronounced to be the logical solution. In most cases, the measures required to pacify deities may not warrant steps as severe as complete submission to a cult: measures may range from relatively trivial solutions such as offering small sacrifices or pouring a libation; more lengthy and expensive measures may be prescribed by the *boko* depending on the gravity of the problem experienced by the client.

Patterns of Religious Engagement

Anlo cultic networks are organised around entities in the religious system that are constantly mutating in form: the dividing line between *trowo*, *voduwo*, ancestors, and other forces is not clear-cut. The nature and form of Anlo deities change not only at a macro but also at a micro level – from village to village, street to street, and shrine to shrine, mirroring the preferences of the worshippers. Deities in Anlo that enter the religious system as *voduwo*, upon getting established in Anlo, begin acquiring characteristics of the *trowo* as they come to be associated with Anlo worshippers and lineages. It would be right to assume that Anlo deities that enter the religious system are constantly altering, from a state of *voduwo*-ness to a state of *trowo*-ness, gradually shedding their alien traits and forming ties with Anlo lineages and people. Some deities may never acquire such ties and may survive, rather successfully for a limited period, in a state of kinlessness, before they finally fade away.

This distinction that the Anlo appear to acknowledge – between autochthonous and immigrant gods – is common to other West African societies, and is crucial to mapping religious change in the chiefdom.[39] Jakob Spieth, one of the first missionary-ethnographers of the Ewe, classified Anlo beliefs into two categories: he identified what he considered authentic or native Anlo gods, in opposition to the new deities at that time, which probably entered Anlo just before the arrival of the Bremen missionaries in the 1850s (Spieth 1911: 11, 172–88, 2011: 48–50; Meyer 1999: 61). Michel Verdon, who studied the Abutia Ewe, located north of Anlo, develops this classification system further, and attributes key differences to the two categories. Autochthonous gods in Abutia were 'earth deities', associated with the land, referred to as the *togbui trowo* or simply *trowo*.[40] The *togbui trowo* were usually worshipped by those who claimed to be original inhabitants, or at least the first to arrive in the area. The clan elders elected priests of the *trowo*. The priesthood of such autochthonous cults was passed on through the clan system, generally through the patrilineage. There was no possession involved, and the *trowo* were usually benign. Celestial gods, on the contrary, were imported from outside. The priesthood and membership of cults of celestial gods were passed on through the female line, from mother to daughter. The celestial gods were called *mama trowo*, and their devotees known as *trosiwo*.[41] As the celestial gods were not clan property, patriliny was not the preferred means of transmission. Worship of celestial gods included possession, and their influence was malign, with acts such as murders and sickness attributed to their agency. Such immigrant gods in Abutia were represented by stools and usually did not touch the ground (Verdon 1983: 87–8). In Anlo, immigrant *voduwo*, in time, after becoming established assumed the attributes of *trowo*: as they gradually indigenised, their external origins were forgotten by their worshippers. For example, Nyigbla, now regarded as the patron deity of Anlo, was originally an immigrant god or *vodu*, brought into the chiefdom in the seventeenth century by new arrivals from the Adangbe area, who would configure themselves into the Dzevi clan (Greene 1997: 49). As Nyigbla became integral to the functioning of the Anlo polity, the deity assumed the function of the war god. If one were to slot Anlo deities into Verdon's classificatory system, deities such as Nyigbla, Yewe, and Fofie, despite having external origins at various points in time, exhibit all the characteristics of autochthonous gods in contemporary Anlo. Gods associated with cultic networks such as Gorovodu, which entered the religious system more recently from the northern savanna belt in the 1920s, qualify as *voduwo*, corresponding to Verdon's celestial gods or *mama trowo*. Anlo cultic networks may

---

[39] See for example Spieth (1911; 2011) on the Anlo; Rattray (1959) on the Akan; Verdon (1983) on the Abutia Ewe; Gilbert (1988, 1989) on the Akan, and Peel (2000) on the Yoruba.

[40] *Togbui* = male ancestor; *Togbi* = elder; honorific title for a respected or elderly man.

[41] *Tro* = deity, *si* = pledged, *wo* = plural.

therefore be divided into those that are more established (Nyigbla, Yewe, and Fofie), and those that are less established (Gorovodu, Mamma, Adzevodu, and the newer anti-witchcraft cultic networks).

Structurally, all Anlo cults may be divided into inner and outer circles of memberships. A number of people – casual supplicants and committed followers – are associated with these cultic networks in various capacities; those in the inner circles of cultic membership are the most committed worshippers. They have formed life-long relationships with the deities in question, and, in the case of possession cults, may also be spirit mediums. Yewe *vodusiwo*, *fofiesiwo*, and Gorovodu *trosiwo* fall into this category. The priests of these religious networks, Yewe *midawo* and *minawo*, Gorovodu *sofowo*, Adzevodu *dzotowo*, and Afa *bokowo* are inner-circle members of their respective cults. Inner-circle members usually inherit their positions vis-à-vis the cultic hierarchy on account of familial or ancestral ties: replacement of dead ancestors is a recurring theme. Yewe *ahewo*, Gorovodu *adehawo* members of Fofie-worshipping lineages, and clients of anti-witchcraft practitioners form an outer circle of worshippers. These are less committed worshippers, who are usually casual supplicants; they do not form committed relationships with the deities at the centre of these cults. They use the services of these deities – and their priests – as a means to achieving an end, and then, after attaining the spiritual favours they sought, they dissociate from the cult in question. Often members of outer circles can be associated with one or more cult: an individual may be a Yewe *ahe*, a Gorovodu *adeha* and an occasional user of the services of other protective deities. Less frequently, members of inner circles can be associated with one or more cults in a more committed capacity: Yewe *vodusiwo* may sometimes also be *fofiesiwo*; Gorovodu *trosiwo* may also be Yewe *vodusiwo* or *fofiesiwo*.

Anlo cultic networks may also be divided, on the basis of how they recruit their inner- and outer-circle members, into closed and open cults. In the case of some cultic networks, like Yewe and Fofie, inner-circle members have to be replaced within lineages; outer-circle members must also be drawn from the same lineages as the inner-circle members. Yewe *ahewo* and *vodusiwo* only associate with the particular Yewe shrine of their ancestors and families; casual Fofie worshippers and *fofiesiwo* hail only from former slave-owning lineages. The deities associated with these cultic networks function like *trowo*. Other cults, such as Gorovodu, Adzevodu, and Koku, have very large outer-circle memberships. Generally, outer-circle members come to be attached to most *voduwo* out of personal choice, in an attempt to sample the nature and quality of the religious services provided by these entities. They are more open than closed cults, where replacement of devotees does not play a significant role in the recruitment process. Membership of the cults organised around the *voduwo* is less restrictive than in the case of cults organised around *trowo*. Any individual, irrespective of Anlo clan or lineage identity, may approach an 'open' cult for spiritual services. Although a minority of inner-circle supplicants transmit positions on a hereditary basis, anyone may join the more open *voduwo* cults, in both inner and outer circles. While the priesthood of *vduwo* cults is usually hereditary, priests and spirit mediums associated with these open networks do not need to have prior familial connections in order to assume their positions.

Therefore, the major differences between the more restrictive (closed) and the less restrictive (open) cults in Anlo could be understood as conceptualised below.

Cults where recruitment patterns that are more 'closed' than 'open'	Cults where recruitment patterns are more 'open' than 'closed'
Hereditary ties significant to recruitment	Hereditary ties not necessarily needed
Inner and outer circles drawn from selected lineages	Inner circle members replaced by lineage members; majority of outer circle members mainly join out of choice
Older cults such as Yewe, Fofie, and clan deities (Adzima, Nyigbla, Vena)	Newer cults such as Adzevodu, Koku, and Gorovodu
Not generally associated with spirit possession (apart from Fofie)	Usually (but not necessarily) associated with spirit possession

The devotees of the *trowo* and *voduwo* engage with Anlo Christianities to varying degrees depending on how committed they are to cultic worship. There are many strands of Christianity in Anlo, making it increasingly difficult to talk about an Anlo Christianity as an undifferentiated concept. What makes these Christianities different is their stances on 'traditional religion'. Mainline Christians – the denominations established during the colonial period – appear to be more tolerant towards their members engaging in 'fetish' worship. Engaging with these 'traditional' practices, which are largely believed to appease the ancestors, is deemed crucial for peoples' identities and subjectivities as Anlo, Ghanaian, and African. There is another Christianity in Anlo, Pentecostal in its orientation, which has arisen over the last twenty years. These Christians are more intolerant towards non-Christian practices, which for them are the root cause of all evil, including their lack of material progress. Outer circle devotees of cults often attend church services, as Christianity is associated with concerns of the afterlife, unattainable by engaging with worldly African religious practices. However, members of the inner circle of cultic worship are less likely to attend church: inner-circle members of the Yewe, Fofie, and various anti-witchcraft cults rarely engage with Christianity in contemporary Anlo, as they are locked into life-long relationships with the deities around which their cults are organised. Nor do church attendance figures reflect the numbers of strictly committed Christians either, as most church goers appear to have had some contact with non-Christian practices in the past, or continue to make use of the services provided by Anlo cults, either openly or surreptitiously.

I must now return to Alegba. Some may read the above description and analysis with a degree of scepticism, and may ask if I have been misled or have misunderstood what I encountered in Anlo. Perhaps Alegba was at work, helping me define the indefinable, causing boundaries that do not exist to appear, simplifying things for the benefit of one untrained in the ways of Anlo culture. After all, West Africanists know that religious cultures in that region are never static – they have always been dynamic, thriving, energetic traditions, which have incorporated visual, ritual, and performative aspects of all the local, regional, and global cultures that they have come into contact with over their existence. West African religious experience does not lend itself easily to description or analysis. It may be said that Alegba is always playing tricks in Anlo country, creating illusions, causing things to appear and disappear before the ethnographer can actually grasp the complexities of the cultural processes in play.

The divine dance of Alegba means that Anlo-Ewe religion persists in this state of chaos; however, it is the ethnographer's job to confront Alegba, to seek out order in chaos. In the absence of any statistics that reflect patterns of religious adherence, I have sought to capture the dynamics of the religious system in Anlo by discussing some of the underlying principles of participation within the cultic environment in an attempt to illustrate the structural and functional similarities and differences between cults. I have suggested that the religious terrain is characterised by open and closed cults; initiates may be associated with one or more of these cults as inner- or outer-circle members, depending on the nature of their existential problems. Some cults are more open than closed; others more closed than open. Anlo people may be members of both types of cults simultaneously in various capacities. But more often than not they maintain a primary religious identity along with several secondary ones: for example, inner-circle members of one cult may join another cult as outer-circle members. Some cults recruit members involuntarily through replacement via lineage structures, while others recruit members voluntarily. The practices associated with Fofie are entangled with a larger mass of esoteric knowledge, deities, and rituals, derived from the geographical north. In the next chapter, I attempt to define the structure and memory practices of this cultic network, and account for the ways in which the Anlo appease their slave ancestors.

4   Slavery in the Anlo Imagination

Womeflea kluvi kple efe dzi o
You can buy a slave, but not his heart.
(Ewe proverb, in Dzobo 975: 54)

Grace Becomes Metumisi

On 23 November 2003, a flurry of activity descended upon Ablesikope, which is part of Nyerwese, one of the constituent divisions of the town of Anlo-Afiadenyigba. Much of this activity was centred on the largest Fofie shrine, located in a rather remote corner of the town, which has traditionally served as a convergence point for all *fofiesiwo* during communal rituals held to honour the slave ancestors. Ajakoku, the head of the cult, had been officiating over a series of ceremonies that would oversee the initiation of another *fofiesi*. A young woman, who was being referred to as Dzogbesi, had been living in the sacred enclosure of the shrine, known as *dzogbe*, usually kept secret from the public gaze. Ajakoku informed me that spirits associated with Fofie had chosen to 'follow' her. She was to undergo a crucial series of rituals known as *tro wowo* (Ewe: 'gods doing for person'), which would turn her into a *fofiesi*. One of these rituals was known as *nuvuvu* (Ewe: 'mouth opening') after which the spirits would finally be able to speak freely through her. Not everybody chosen by the spirits has their mouths opened: the costs of a mouth-opening ceremony, including the sacrificial animals, schnapps, and other necessary items, are beyond the reach of many of those that the spirits have chosen. (If the spirits continue to torment a person who has not yet become a full-fledged medium, family members do eventually contribute to the *tro wowo*, being fully aware of the implications of having voiceless spirits within the bodies of their kinfolk. Such a situation could have implications for all lineage members, including the ancestors and the future unborn.) Sometimes, the spirits may themselves prefer to come to a person without actually speaking through them. Such individuals who 'have' the spirits, share their bodies with them, but never fully surrender to them in the act of possession. In the context of the Fofie cult, there are a number of names to refer to such devotees, who 'sleep with the spirits', but never marry them with ritual pomp and splendour: they are called *fiamanyawo* (sing. *fiamanya*).[1]

Dzogbesi had been living in Ajakoku's shrine for a fortnight, in preparation of her 'spiritual marriage' to Fofie, or the process of becoming a *fofiesi*. She was also, as her family explained, 'opening herself with truth' (*dome kokoe*), which involved confessing all the evil (*nuvo*) she had done, and acknowledging all the people she had wronged during the course of her life. Her head had been shaved (hair is thought to contain impure qualities), and she had been bathed in specially prepared herbs (*amatsi*) every day. She had come to be known as Dzogbesi over these few weeks, as she was living in the enclosure known as *dzogbe*, the liminal part of the shrine associated with all kinds of in-between-ness. *Dzogbe* is that part of a shrine where the living and the ancestors meet; where transformations occur, and where ordinary people without any extraordinary spiritual qualities are turned into 'wives' of spirits.

According to her family, Dzogbesi's submission to Fofie was totally unexpected at the outset. Born Grace Amavedzi in Anlo-Afiadenyigba in 1975, she was baptised and sent to school. She came from a family of nominal Christians, though it seemed to me in 2003 that most of the members of her immediate family had returned, as she was about to do, to the worship of the *trowo* in various capacities. She had had several male suitors over the course of her adult life, but had been unable to conceive any children. Infertility is considered to be a great misfortune, often associated with being either the victim or perpetrator of *adze*, or in some cases with the neglect of certain *trowo*. Grace had accepted that she was not destined to give birth, resigning herself to looking after her brother's children, who had been left motherless. Her life, however, became unbearable over the two years preceding her 'mouth opening'. Her business in Lome collapsed. She was unable to make ends meet, often being prevented from working by a mysterious illness, which medics at her local hospital were unable to cure. Because of her inability to have children, her husband had taken another wife, who had borne him children. As a result, he had started spending more and more time away from Grace, and with his second wife. Grace turned to ritual specialists in the hope that they would shed light on her predicament. Believing she was the victim of *adze* – witchcraft typically caused by envy or jealousy generated from within the ranks of one's kin – she first consulted priests of Kunde, Abrewa, and other witch-finding deities, as amongst her patrilineage there were several Gorovodu *sofowo* and *trosiwo*. They gave her

---

[1] *Fia* = queen; *manya* = unknown.

a medicine and offered to look after her until she recovered. She felt slightly better initially, but fell back into a depression after a few months. She then travelled as far as the Republic of Benin to seek the opinion of an anti-witchcraft specialist who was held in high esteem by her father. Her quest to identify the spiritual causes behind her illness led her to guardians of Mami Wata shrines in Ouidah, as sudden monetary successes – and failures – are associated with this deity's whims. According to Grace's brother, she believed at this stage that her inability to conceive children was caused by her husband 'sleeping with Mami Wata', who had then proceeded to 'eat her womb' following the persuasions of the rival wife.[2] Costly sacrifices to Mami Wata yielded nothing. Penniless and weakened by ill-health, a despondent Grace returned to her native Anlo-Afiadenyigba.

In her hometown, a number of Afa diviners were presented with Grace's case. She often complained of persistent dreams, in which several women spoke to her, sometimes menacingly and sometimes soothingly, in strange foreign languages that she did not understand. Dreams in Anlo cannot be analysed as products of overactive minds and anxieties; rather, they are transcendent manifestations of alternative realities, all of which impinge on the Anlo world. For the Anlo who invest importance in the spirit world, dreams are believed to come to the dreamer as opposed to being produced by her or him. Dreams are not creative acts performed by autonomous individual subjects, but dreaming is more akin to 'tuning in' to the affairs of the real world and deeper realities of the imaginary spirit world as they are culturally construed (Mittermaier 2011: 19).[3] This imagined spirit world, of course, is rendered 'real' by belief in it.[4] The women who visited Grace's dreams – and whom she was able to describe in such vivid detail, from their dress to mannerisms – had to be intimately intertwined with her sense of self, personhood, and her own destiny. The Afa *agumaga* always fell to the ground in the same *medzi* whenever Grace sought the opinions of *bokowo* on her predicament. All these *bokowo* came to the same conclusion after analysing her dreams and life story against her *kpoli*: the slave ancestors of her patrilineage were seeking her

---

[2] Interview with Kwaku Amevedzi, Anlo-Afiadenyigba, 23 November 2003.

[3] Ethnographers have long neglected the 'very processes through which dreamers and interpreters endow dreams with meaning' within religious contexts, preferring to concentrate on subject matter of such dreams and providing explanations for the process of dreaming itself (Mittermaier 2011: 15). It is unhelpful to employ Jungian and Freudian models, which suggest that dreams are all about the dreamer, in contexts where dreams are intertwined with complex belief systems and conceptions of personhood. Mittermaier convincingly makes a case for recognising the complexities of the 'dream cultures' and socio-historical contexts which give rise to them (ibid.: 13–4).

[4] It is the unbeliever who fails to recognise the true order of reality, also failing to recognise the relationship between dreams and religious practice (Mittermaier 2011: 19).

attention.[5] The women who spoke to her when she was asleep were the slave ancestors of her patrilineage. The revelation that she was under the influence of the slave ancestors was not entirely unexpected: her fore-fathers were known to have enslaved Akan and Ewedome women in the past. Grace hailed from a Fofie-worshipping patrilineage: her paternal aunt, Nyomi, and her great aunt, Metumisi, were both *fofiesiwo* during their lifetimes. At Grace's birth in 1975, the then-deceased Metumisi was identified as her *amedzoto* or ancestral sponsor, but as Fofie already had one 'wife' in the form of Nyomi within the lineage at the time, this rev-elation was not acted upon. In 2003, Grace and her parents approached Ajakoku and his entourage of Fofie worshippers in Ablesikope for advice. Grace lived with other Fofie devotees for a few months, during which time she was taught the ways of the cult: she was briefed about the various slave ancestors, their origins and how they came to Anlo, the food taboos that cult members observe (sheep must never be consumed), and the medicinal and ritual knowledge associated with the veneration of these foreign deities. During this period in *dzogbe*, the physical enclosure of the shrine associated with that state of divine liminality, Grace was known simply as Dzogbesi, or 'the one in *dzogbe*'.

Around 10 a.m. on 23 November 2003, at the climax of the mouth-opening ceremony, Dzogbesi emerged from the shrine, amid the presence of at least about a hundred *fofiesiwo* from Anlo-Afiadenyigba and bey-ond. Frantic drumming erupted from the shrine compound. Foaming heavily through her mouth, Dzogbesi was possessed by the slave spir-its immediately. The spirits uttered a few words triumphantly in Ewe-ised Twi (for the benefit of the audience), which translated into 'We have returned . . . to the patrilineage, and the *duto*.' They continued: 'We are *fofie* [house people], not outsiders.'[6] *Fofiesiwo* seldom become pos-sessed, apart from during initiation ceremonies and funerals. Dzogbesi ran out of the compound, away from the limits of the settlement into 'the bush', or the dense secondary forest located some distance away from the cluster of compounds that formed the settlement of Ablesikope. She was followed by an entourage of *fofiesiwo*. The bush is associated with all things unclean: it is where dangerous talismans are cast aside; where corpses of diseased animals are discarded, where sewerage and house-hold wastes are dumped. Traditionally, slaves were buried in areas such as these, beyond the habitable limits of the village. Dzogbesi's disap-pearance into the bush was meant to emphasise this conceptual divide the Anlo had created between habited and uninhabited spaces, between

---

[5] Several Afa notions are associated with stories of slavery. If these notions are produced during spiritual consultations, the family's slave-holding past is usually interrogated against the client's problems.

[6] Dzogbesi (in trance), Anlo-Afiadenyigba, 23 November 2003.

things clean and unclean, and between legitimate ancestors buried in the village (with monuments erected to their memory) and the slave ancestors who were buried outside the village (erased from public memory). Dzogbesi returned to the shrine compound, repeating this sequence of events three times, vanishing into the bush for several minutes on every occasion. She gradually turned into a medium for the slave spirits: the long-ignored slave ancestors, whom the Anlo had tried to distance from their society by purging into the bush, had returned to the realm of civilisation by inhabiting the bodies of one of their Anlo descendants through possession. Thus incorporation, the opposite of expulsion, occurs during spirit possession ceremonies, as the slave ancestors re-enter Anlo society (triumphantly, while in control of the bodies of their descendants), eventually gaining the acceptance and attention of their former masters.

As the ceremony progressed, the other *fofiesiwo* began singing praises of their slave ancestors, the gods of these slaves, and descriptions of their distant homes. These songs were in Twi, Hausa, and Dagbani, the languages of the slaves. Entranced, Dzogbesi danced along. The spirits that spoke through her stopped to greet members of her patrilineage, posing a number of questions. These included questions about the health of ailing members of the family, and demands for new rituals to be instituted for the slave ancestors. One chant became louder and louder: the crowd began asking the slave spirits to rename Dzogbesi, in recognition of her newly constituted status as a *fofiesi*. Dzogbesi's dancing turned more confident, synchronising better with the drumming rhythms. The beats became faster, as the drummers, fuelled by tots of *akpetesi*, proceeded to beat their drums more vigorously. Dzogbesi started spinning uncontrollably, before collapsing into the crowd. The drums then fell silent. Dzogbesi sprung to her feet as suddenly as she had fallen to the ground, announcing to the gathering that she was henceforth to be known as Dzakpasi Metumisi. She approached members of her patrilineage again, telling them about the Ewedome and Ashanti slave women they once owned. The spirit of a formerly enslaved woman called Mama Adzo spoke through her, identifying herself as an Ewedome ancestor of the lineage. Mama Adzo threateningly told her descendants that they must worship her favourite crocodile spirit (Ewe: Dzakpa), if they were to keep her happy; she informed them to make pilgrimages to her natal village, near Peki, for their peace of mind, to pay respects to her Ewedome ancestors and gods. Members of Grace's lineage greeted the spirit, telling her that they would support Dzakpasi Metumisi in her quest to please the slave ancestors. Another spirit, called Metumi, also surfaced soon after that, within the person of Dzakpasi Metumisi. Metumi identified herself as an Akan divinity and the guardian of an Akan slave woman whom Grace's patrilineage had once enslaved. Sternly, Metumi instructed her audience that she must be worshipped for their well-being, to prevent the slave spirits from disrupting their lives. Lineage members bowed to Dzakpasi Metumisi in an act of subordination, and agreed to the spirits' demands.[7]

Several Gorovodu priests, priestesses, and all the *fofiesiwo* present gathered around Dzakpasi Metumisi that evening. Ajakoku poured a libation of imported schnapps over the Alegba by the ritual enclosure, inviting all the slave ancestors, spirits, and deities to grace the evening with their presence. The drummers began playing a gentle Ewedome rhythm, which resulted in Dzakpasi getting possessed. Several other *fofiesiwo*, by the names of Mamedu Badesi, Nyomi, and Salamatu, also relinquished their bodies to the slave spirits, who danced alongside Dzakpasi Metumisi in the ritual enclosure. As the drumbeats changed to Brekete, the northern rhythm associated with Gorovodu, several northern spirits from the savanna – Banguele, Sacrebode, Mossi, and Wango – came to possess the bodies of *trosiwo*. They were led away by the *senterwawo*, the young women who attend to the needs of the possessed, and were helped into their ceremonial attire. Sacrebode, the horse, galloped into the enclosure amid shrill whistling noises in the frail body of a 78-year-old fishmonger known out of trance as Mama Abena. Mossi, dressed in a *batakari* and fez-like headgear, bearing strong resemblance to an Islamised trader, surfaced in the body of a 30-year-old woman.[8] The spirit proceeded to greet the new *fofiesi* with excitement before it launched into its characteristic twirling dance. Wango, a crocodile spirit, dressed in black, came to control the body of a 40-year-old secondary school teaching assistant. Wango embraced Metumisi, telling her that he knew the water bodies where Dzakpa, the crocodile spirit, is worshipped in the Ewe north. Dzakpasi Metumisi's family members listened to Wango's words of advice on how to appease the foreign crocodile spirit. About twenty other spirits emerged in their mediums during this ceremony, each responding to their favourite drumbeats or melodies. Occasionally, spirits singled out members of the crowd, giving them advice on a range of issues, from health to money making to family relationships. The spirits danced on for several hours and into the night, in a display of perfect musical harmony and feverish ecstasy, while the crowd watched mesmerised.

Weary members of the audience gradually deserted the enclosure at dawn, as the spirits left their mediums. The mediums were returned from the state of being in trance with absolutely no recollection of how the spirits had controlled them. Even the aging Mama Abena displayed all the signs of a well-rested person, apart from a few complaints related

---

[7] Dzakpa and Metumi are the principal divinities to which this *fofiesi* is pledged; hence the name and prefix *si* at the end, which indicates the relationship of submission to the deities in question.

[8] *Batakari* is used to refer to the tunics worn by northern people.

to minor aches and pains in her back, the result of 'when Sacrebode rode in her'.[9] Fofie and Gorovodu devotees congregated once more the next morning, to offer a ram to the slave ancestors and their gods. The crucial player during this ritual is an individual known as an *agbota* (Ewe: *agbo*: ram, *ta*: head). Every Fofie-worshipping lineage has, pledged along with a *fofiesi*, an *agbota* who is responsible for arranging the customary ram sacrifice during ceremonies. Apart from his ritual functions, the *agbota* is also pledged to Fofie in his capacity as a free-born Anlo man. The *fofiesi*, upon initiation, represents the several slave women owned by Anlo lineages. The pledging of a free Anlo man to the service of non-Anlo gods is a symbolic act which reverses the relationship between master and slave, as the *fofiesi* (representing the slave) introduces an Anlo man (the *agbota*) to the worship of foreign, non-Anlo slave gods. The *agbota* of Dzakpasi Metumisi's lineage leads the ram into the enclosure, after which it is bled with a special ritual knife. At this moment, Fofie and Gorovodu spirits return to the bodies of their hosts. Some spirits smear the blood of the ram onto their faces, while others drink straight from the jugular vein. The ram is cooked and served to *fofiesiwo* (in and out of trance), members of their lineages, *trosiwo, sofowo*, and all others present at the occasion. The Fofie slave spirits (and some Gorovodu spirits), after enjoying the hospitality of their descendant-hosts, retreat once more, content in the knowledge that their descendants still revere, respect, and fear them.

Dzakpasi Metumisi did not return to Lome after her initiation ceremony, preferring instead to stay on in Blekusu, a town near Anlo-Afiadenyigba. She was able to reconstruct her life. She began selling rice and stew by a large junction near the town. In due course, she met the man who became her second husband. I met her in 2010, seven years after her transformation into a *fofiesi*. She had had two children of her own with her new husband. I continue to remain in touch with her as of 2014. She still worships the slave spirits, and is an enthusiastic member of the Fofie cult. The slave spirits, she tells me, are part of her, and were her salvation. She is happy now, and is thankful that order has been restored to her life.[10]

Descended from the Spirits: A Slave-Holding Patrilineage

The term Fofie takes the form of a Twi word (Twi: *fo* = people; *fie* = house). In the Akan calendar, the term is associated with the fourth Friday of a month, during which libations and prayers are offered to

---

[9] Interview with Mama Abena, Anlo-Afiadenyigba, 24 November 2003.
[10] Interview with Dzakpasi Metumisi, Blekusu, 5 December 2010.

deities or *abosom*. Fofie is a stratified set of practices, which probably first made an appearance in Anlo as early as the beginning of the nine-teenth century, to address the spiritual repercussions of turning foreign slaves into assimilated members of Anlo lineages.[11] The traditions asso-ciated with Fofie today evolved over a period of time, as practitioners associated with the cultic network absorbed ritual influences from a wide range of geographical sources, which they found relevant to the artic-ulation of their concerns about the slave-holding past. Acculturation was an important part of enslavement. Slaves, devoid of kinship ties in their host societies, and lacking knowledge of local culture and norms, were thought to lack attributes of civilisation and humanity as they were locally perceived. There were several words used in Anlo to describe such kinless outsiders with 'slave' status, most of whom were acquired through warfare and trade. A prisoner of war was known as *ametsiava* (pl. *ametsiavawo*) and generally enslaved in the chiefdom with little hope of release. An *amefefle* (pl. *amefeflewo*) was a bought person. A *dzikpleadu* (pl. *dzikpleaduwo*) was 'one who was born with teeth', referring to a per-son acquired not at birth but later in life, especially during late childhood. *Nkekevi* (pl. *nkekeviwo*) and *dogbevi* (pl. *dogbeviwo*), both referred to chil-dren obtained during the day, when most trade is conducted, instead of the night. All these words create an analogy between being 'born' and being 'bought'.[12] While a free individual was inserted into his social role in Anlo at birth by virtue of his kinship ties which bound him to a complex network of ancestors, deities, and would-be descendants, a slave is 'born' in Anlo – and begins to exist as a social entity – only after being bought or captured and inserted into society through his role of servitude, coming to be identified with his owners. Enslaved people gradually attained some degree of social personhood in Anlo over the passage of time, typically by measures such as forging kinship ties to their masters' families, by participating in social institutions such as the patrilineage and clan, and by learning Anlo norms, customs, and the language.

I estimate that there are about eighty former slave-owning patrilineages in Anlo-Afiadenyigba. Fifty-six of these lineages are actively involved in Fofie worship, and had pledged *fofiesiwo*, like Dzakpasi Metumisi, to the cult as of 2010. Most slave-owning lineages have only one *fofiesi* at any given time in contemporary Anlo.[13] Upon the death of a *fofiesi*, a new

---

[11] Greene's work indicates that Fofie has been a part of the religious landscape in Anlo since at least the early nineteenth century, though she provides us with little detailed information about the mechanics and nature of Fofie worship (Greene 1996a: 67). Her information is based on interviews with Anlo elders.

[12] These terms for enslaved people were used interchangeably by my informants.

[13] In previous generations, more than one *fofiesi* were initiated into the cult in most slave-holding lineages. At present, about thirty-four lineages do not have a *fofiesi* pledged to

initiate is sought out in the next successive generation of the same patri-lineage. Only people from former slave-owning patrilineages get involved with Fofie, as it is a corpus of ritual practices aimed at correcting the imbalances created by the incorporation of enslaved peoples into local patrilineages through marriage; products of master–slave unions will be found only in former slave-holding lineages.

Ideas of continuity, replacement, and personhood play an import-ant role in who becomes a *fofiesi*, determined largely by an individual's *amedzoto* or ancestral sponsor. Every Anlo person is believed to have some traits or characteristics of at least one particular ancestor, and this ancestor is responsible for guiding them into the world of the living. An individual is destined to resemble his or her *amedzoto*, with his or her life chances being predetermined by that ancestor to a large extent. There does not have to be a one-to-one correlation between the *amedzoto* and the individual: two people in one generation can have the same *amedzoto* and hence the personality traits of a single ancestor. Similarly, one indi-vidual may have had two ancestors guiding him or her into the world of the living, and therefore two *amedzotowo*. Anlo conceptions of 'reincarn-ation', while acknowledging ancestral agency, also subscribe to extreme individuality: while the ancestor plays an important role in determining a descendant's life chances, that descendant is a unique individual. It is up to individuals to discover who their ancestral sponsors were – as Dzakpasi Metumisi did – and how best to imitate them for their own success and well-being.

Dzakpasi Metumisi's family history showcases the degree and nature of engagement with the Fofie cult in a typical former slave-holding patrilin-eage. The active *fofiesiwo* that I encountered also presented very similar case histories of their families in relation to Fofie worship. Dzakpasi Metumisi, who became a *fofiesi* in November 2003, is a third-generation Fofie initiate. She became a medium for the slave spirits on account of several complex multidimensional relationships with deceased slave ancestors and their gods, all of which have exercised a degree of agency upon her, turning her into a *fofiesi*. Members of her family possess limited information about their slave-owning past, a history which is largely based on retrieved fragments of information from some slave descendants of the lineage. The genealogical information about the ancestors of this fam-ily extends about seven generations into the past. Dzakpasi Metumisi's great-great-grandfather Kwasi (born *c*. 1850) had a slave wife, who was carried away as a child from the Peki region during the late 1860s. With no prospect of returning to her homeland, she married her owner, and lived in Anlo until her death. According to her descendants, she bore her

the worship of the slave ancestors. Most of these lineages are waiting for replacements of deceased *fofiesiwo* to be identified.

husband several children, though only one of them, a boy called Kwami, survived into adulthood. Kwami in turn had three children of his own: two daughters and one son. Metumisi, his eldest daughter, was a Fofie initiate until her death in 1965. Metumisi's ancestral sponsor was believed to be her Ewedome slave grandmother. At her death – she died a few years before her sixtieth birthday – Metumisi was thought to have been involved in the cult for over thirty years, which suggests that she was born *c.* 1910. Metumisi had a shrine which she maintained in her house: it contained a small stool representing the slave trade; three idols of Ewedome gods, and some of her slave grandmother's personal belongings, such as amulets, clothing, and earrings. Her son Kwaku has been the caretaker of his mother's god-objects since her death; the Fofie deities are credited with aiding his mother at his birth in 1941, and he therefore has a natural affinity for them. Metumisi had to be replaced by another member of her family, more specifically by a woman from her father's patrilineage only. Kinship rules come into force here: her children, including Kwaku, belong to *their* father's non slave-holding patrilineage and are therefore not appropriate candidates to inherit her position vis-à-vis the Fofie cult; Kwaku's patrilineage is not responsible for the enslavement of his Ewedome great-grandmother. The most appropriate candidates to replace Metumisi were her brother's daughters, as they belong to her patrilineage, the patrilineage of the original slave master, the man who married the Ewedome slave woman. Metumisi's brother's daughter, Nyomi, became a *fofiesi* in the 1970s, just before the birth of Grace (Dzakpasi Metumisi). While Metumisi was identified as Grace's *amedzoto* – ancestral sponsors usually skip a generation or two – there was little need to pledge Grace to Fofie worship immediately, as Nyomi had already replaced Metumisi. Nyomi died in 2000. Grace's dreams of slave women (accompanied by her personal and financial troubles) began around then, and within three years, she had been transformed into a *fofiesi* (see Figure 4.1).

I encountered about thirty *fofiesiwo* in and around Anlo-Afiadenyigba during the course of my fieldwork, and a smaller number in the towns of Keta, Anloga, Whuti, and Aflao. Their accounts of their family histories proved crucial to building a generalised picture of when Fofie worship became institutionalised. Most of these women asserted that the first generation of *fofiesiwo* from their patrilineage were initiated into the cult during the 1940s, which suggested that the first initiates were born around the 1910s. The women I came across during the course of my fieldwork were either second- or, in some cases, third-generation initiates. As the first full-fledged initiations date from the 1940s, it seems appropriate to conclude that the Anlo were plagued by the realisation that there were 'ghost women' – slave ancestors – in slave-holding patrilineages that they had little or no knowledge about during this period. Fofie worship was meant to be a practical exercise in rewriting slave

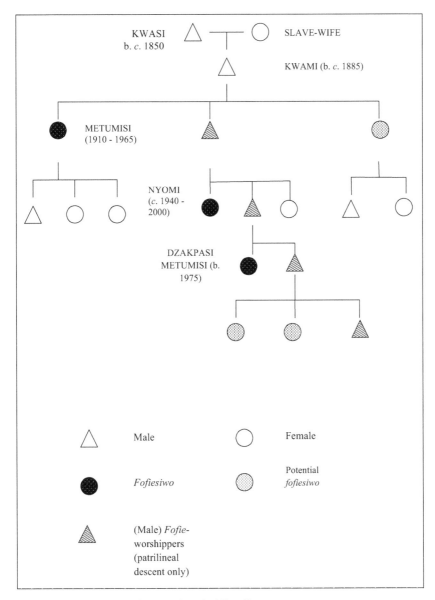

Figure 4.1. A former slave-holding lineage

women and their gods into Anlo slave-holding lineages and family trees. In principle, to an outsider, the idea of Fofie worship suggests that there are several blanks in Anlo family trees, and that these blanks represent the many slave women that the Anlo enslaved in the past. In reality, how-ever, most Anlo families lack the genealogical resources to trace their slave ancestors as well as their legitimate Anlo-born patrilineal ancestors beyond the six-generation mark. The event that took precedence in the accounts that emerged out of the historical reconstruction process undertaken by Fofie-worshipping lineages was the enslavement of Ewedome slaves during the Asante Wars, which was still fresh in the memories of the Anlo. Some of the slave women carried away during these wars were still alive in Anlo at this point. Many of the first-generation *fofiesiwo* – those initiated during this period, when Fofie worship was being moulded into its current form – may have known their paternal Ewedome (slave) grandmothers at some point in their lives. Their memories of these slave women came to inform their ideas and perceptions of their Ewedome neighbours. While the Anlo enslaved a number of peoples of Asante, Hausa, Tchamba, and Ewedome extraction, the details and the cultural contributions of the non-Ewedome slaves to the corpus of Fofie worship were largely imagined by the Anlo themselves, as there were few such first-generation slaves present in Anlo during this period to help with the reconstruction process. Ewedome slaves, carried away during the Asante Wars of 1869–74 (conflated in oral sources with the Peki Wars of 1831–3), therefore naturally feature in the knowable genealogical history of most families, given the relative historical proximity of the event, and stories about them take pre-eminence in narratives of the slave-holding past.[14] The Ewedome belt and the high north are configured differently in the imaginations of Fofie worshippers, the former being more accessible and immediate, while the later is more distant, inaccessible, and mysterious.

Shrines to Slavery

Every patrilineage (*afedo;* pl. *afedowo)* in Anlo has a shrine dedicated to its ancestors. These shrines are known as stool houses (*zikpifemewo*; sing. *zikpifeme*; Ewe: *zikpi* = stool, *afeme* = house) (see Figure 4.2). These shrines usually house objects known as *tobgui zikpi*. Two objects became important symbols of wealth and prestige in Anlo society: the *hozi*, a wealth-creating stool, and an *avadzi*, a war stool. When a lineage engaged in the slave trade, members usually established a stool known as a *hozi*, to mark out their special slave-owning status. *Hozi*-owning lineages were relatively wealthy, and owned various categories of bought people (Fiawoo 1976: 274–6). Certain lineages were wealthy enough to establish armies of mercenaries, and in addition to acquiring

---

[14] The Peki Wars occurred in the 1830s, when the Anlo were allied with the Asante against the Peki. The Asante Wars took place between 1869 and 1874. The two episodes are conflated in narratives of *fofiesiwo*, but the episode they are usually referring to is the Asante Wars, the most recent sustained period of warfare in recent Anlo history.

Figure 4.2. Stool house, Anlo-Afiadenyigba, June 2004

slaves through trade, they were able to capture slaves by warfare. These lineages possessed another category of stool, known as *avadziwo* (sing. *avadzi*). Owners of *avadzi* stools are few in Anlo in comparison to those who own *hozi* stools.[15] Slave-owning lineages usually have shrines that contained both these objects (in addition to their ancestral *togbui zikpi*), as early as the eighteenth century (Akyeampong 2001b: 47). In Anlo-Afiadenyigba, there are about eighty stool houses, dedicated to ancestors of slave-owning lineages.[16] Typically, the sacred spaces of the interior of such a shrine contain a *hozi* and an *avadzi* (see Figure 4.3). Knives, gags, and equipment that aided in the capture of slaves are displayed alongside boxes of cowrie shells. Cowries were money in the past (as slaves were), and have come to be revered along with the relics of the slave trade. Money making is a positive and life-enhancing activity: cowrie shells and weapons which enabled the capture of slaves are symbols of ritual potency (Piot 1999: 73). Cowries also make a statement on the predicament of the Anlo after slavery: the Anlo believe that they have actually declined from a more prosperous period to the state of poverty that they

---

[15] Fofie-worshipping families in the town of Anlo-Afiadenyigba and Keta appear to have *hoziwo* in stool houses, and seldom had *avadziwo*, an indication that slaves were overwhelmingly purchased through trade rather than acquired through war. Interview with Quasi Nyamesi, Anlo-Afiadenyigba, 19 May 2013.

[16] Non-slave owning lineages may also have such *zikpifemewo* to honour their ancestors, though the ritual paraphernalia inside these houses will not bear references to the slave trade.

Figure 4.3. *Hozi* and *Avadzi*, inside a stool house, Agbozume, August 2000

experience now. Most Fofie-worshipping lineages have such stool houses in their custody. They are typically tended by a 'stool father' – usually the head of a patrilineage – and are associated with the worship of slave owners. Through such shrines slavery and slave holding are constructed as positive, lucrative activities, which benefited lineages and bestowed wealth upon them.

Fofiesiwo are not usually involved in the worship of the *togbuiwo*, but are associated with the worship of the unknown matrilineal ancestors of slave-owning patrilineages. The slave spirits are the *togbuiwofenoliwo* and the *ametsiavawo*, discontented ancestors who are incomplete in death. The two sets of ancestors are therefore incompatible with each other, and cannot coexist in the same ritual space. Another category of shrine dedicated to the slave ancestors is usually built at a different location, as the Anlo ancestors and slave ancestors are different and, in Anlo parlance, 'do not mix'.[17]

Dzakpasi Metumisi's personal Fofie shrine, dedicated to several slave ancestors from inland Eweland and the northern savanna, stands a few blocks away from her family's *zikpifeme*. The contents of this Fofie shrine were initially assembled by Dzakpasi Metumisi's great aunt (the first *fofiesi* from this *patrilineage*) and her family during the 1940s, though sacred

---

[17] Interview with Dzakpasi Metumisi, Anlo-Afiadenyigba, 30 November 2003.

objects have since been added by various members of the patrilineage. As one approaches the shrine, a large *alegba*-like figure, resembling a mound of earth, is visible by the door. This figure is meant to represent the first slave woman that Dzakpasi Metumisi's family ever owned, simply known as Mamma, a Hausa woman bought from a northern market. Mamma is believed to have first come to Whuti – where Dzakpasi Metumisi's patrilineage was originally based – when she was very young. Mamma died at a ripe old age, after bearing her owner-husband many children. Her appeasement is considered vital, as her enslavement marked the patrilineage's transition from poverty to a prosperous, slave-owning patrilineage. When members of the patrilineage moved from Whuti to Anlo-Afiadenyigba during the 1930s, they took Mamma's belongings with them. The relics associated with her were then installed outside the first compound the family settled in, and subsequently outside the shrine they created for all their slave ancestors a decade later.

As one enters the shrine, three large idols are placed on the left. I am informed that the first is an Ewedome woman, the second is a Hausa man, and the third a Tchamba man. Both the Hausa and Tchamba men have several scarifications on their faces. Though the southern Ewe and Akan practise cicatrification to an extent, they consider excessive markings to be a distinguishing feature of peoples from the northern savanna, and the facial markings on these idols are meant to signify the patterns with which the former slaves might have adorned themselves. The Hausa man is dressed in colonial military uniform: when Anlo came under British rule in 1895, the colonial authorities aggressively policed the chiefdom with the help of a Hausa constabulary, which was installed at Keta. The activities of the Hausa constabulary have been recorded in Anlo folk tradition (Akyeampong 2001b: 63–4).

Another set of idols is placed across the room. The central figure is Mamma, the first Hausa slave that the patrilineage ever owned. Mamma is depicted with her children (several smaller idols representing Anlo men), in order to remind her descendants of her contribution, in the form of human capital, to the patrilineage. Her northern gods, dressed in the flowing robes characteristic of the savanna states, are placed beside her. Other statues – meant to symbolise the slaves who died accidental, traumatic deaths in Anlo – are placed beside Mamma. I have visited this shrine several times over my association with this patrilineage in Anlo. Its caretaker, Kwadwo Tamakloe, an *agbota*, often petitioned the deities on my behalf for permission to photograph them. If the sacred cowrie shells, used for communication with the ancestors, had fallen flat, it would have meant that the slave spirits had granted my request. Over the course of about seven visits to this shrine, between 2003 and 2006, the cowrie shells indicated that the camera-shy deities simply did not want to be photographed.

Several conflicting stories are told about these figures by members of Dzakpasi Metumisi's patrilineage. In one version, the Ewedome woman is believed to have married the Hausa man, and all their children continued to serve her ancestors as slaves. These children eventually married other members of their master's lineage, and gradually became inseparable from their owner-hosts. In yet other versions, the Hausa and Tchamba men were northern gods who came looking for the enslaved Ewedome woman. They were sometimes believed to have been her sons, who left Anlo in search of their distant northern homes, and captured other Hausa and Tchamba slaves on their journey back to the coast from the North. There is little consensus on such stories, and the details vary constantly. Individual memories – and individual narrations about the patrilineage's slave-holding past – are fluid, changing constantly according to who is describing aspects of the slave-holding past.

Senchisro, a *fofiesi* whom I first met in 2003, boasted to me that she was a hundred and fifty years old. (I had not realised at the time that I was speaking to a collection of slave spirits, for Senchisro was possessed, perched on the balcony of her cement-reinforced dwelling in Nyerwese, smoking the spirits' favourite brand of imported cigarettes, where she was surrounded by family members eager to seek the advice of the slave spirits). In reality, Senchisro was in her late eighties. Her frail body could not serve as a vehicle for the spirits as it once did. When the spirits surface in her, they usually summon family members to her house. They do, however, dance vigorously on a few selected occasions. The contents of Senchisro's shrine have been assembled over three generations, collected by her or by other members of her patrilineage. Some of her deities were acquired from an Ewedome village, believed to be the birthplace of Senchisro's slave grandmother, who was brought to Anlo-Afiadenyigba soon after the Asante Wars. Several other slaves were incorporated into her family during various stages prior to these wars. This *afedo* also owned Dagomba and Hausa women, bought from Kete Krachi and beyond. Senchisro's idols bear interesting names: Moses, Joshua, Monica, and Felicia, her most important deities, are described by her as gods of the Book. Senchisro believes all four deities were revered by her Dagomba and Hausa ancestors, who were Muslims. Placed beside them is Ameeria, a Hausa divinity, seated on a horse (see Figure 4.4). Shells and cowries are scattered on the altar: the currency of the slave trade, the most easily identifiable marker of the slaving era. On another altar, a little stool, miniatures of the *hozi* and *avadzi* are placed beside another set of deities. Strings of cowries are tied to the base of the stools: each shell represents one slave owned by the family. Quranic amulets with Arabic writing are placed at the altar. An iron bracelet, associated with the divinity Tchamba, is placed on the stool. The significance of the bracelet is

Figure 4.4. Fofie shrine of Senchisro's household, depicting the northern gods of the women enslaved by her patrilineage [L-R: Moses, Joshua,
Monica, Felicia, Ameeria], Anlo- Afiadenyigba, August 2005

twofold: on one hand, it is believed that slaves wore a certain type of
bracelet to mark their status in southern Eweland, and, on the other, the
descendants of these slaves associated this bracelet-like object with the
chains that were used to enslave people (Rosenthal 1998: 111–12; see
Rush 2011) (see Figure 4.5).

There are many household shrines dedicated to non-Anlo deities all
over Anlo, owned by Fofie-worshipping lineages. The deities in the
shrines I have visited differ greatly, reflecting the diverse nature, personalities, and religious inclinations of the slave ancestors of different
Fofie initiates. Belief systems, visual cultures, and performance cultures
of Fofie and Gorovodu networks fuse in idiosyncratic ways in personal
and public spaces in Anlo to produce this dynamic documentary dedicated to the remembrance of slavery and the worship of the slave ancestors.
The Anlo Gorovodu deities – Kunde, Abrewa, and Sacrebode – are very
real, and continue to have parallels in the societies of the savanna and the
forest belt. However, the Fofie deities and ancestors encountered in personal shrines do not actually exist outside Anlo; they are purely products
of the Anlo imagination, invented almost two or three generations

Figure 4.5. Fofie shrine of Senchisro's household, depicting her patrilineage's slave ancestors, Anlo-Afiadenyigba, August 2005

after large-scale slave holding – and slavery – had been brought to an
end. Each patrilineage, and indeed every person, appears to narrate a
different version of the stories concerning their slave ancestors, how they
came to Anlo, and what their northern ancestors' deities must have been
like. This Anlo history of slavery is therefore additive: accounts of later
generations do not displace earlier ones, but coexist unproblematically
alongside them; the truth in the factual details is of little value (Lambek
2002: 51). This multiplicity of points of views is the norm, and several
opinions are expressed, all of which are equally valid. While these narratives about the slave ancestors are profoundly historical in themselves, in
that they refer to a past, the details change from person to person, from
generation to generation; they cannot be analysed in terms of a detailed
chronological or discursive account of the past. These narratives are not
arranged in chronological order by the narrators, and their historical
sequencing is unimportant.

Thus while the Anlo have valid information about the last generation of Ewedome slave ancestors on account of the relative historical
proximity of the event, they know little about the slave women from the
high north, the faraway area that the Asante called the *Sarem*. They have

failed to detect exactly where their northern slaves came from, a situation which continues to generate great anxiety in Fofie-worshipping circles. The reasons for this are obvious: the high north is a significant distance from Anlo, and could not be accessed as easily as the Ewedome belt. Besides, most slaves from the high north were bought people, acquired at slave markets such as Salaga and Kete Krachi over a period of three centuries. Therefore, the only point of contact for the Anlo slave merchants would have been the slave markets, rather than the villages from which the slaves came. Salaga and Kete Krachi consequently occupy a special place in the Anlo ritual imagination, often represented in Fofie worshippers' discourse as the 'homes' of the northern slaves. Knowledge about these slave ancestors survives only in fragments: they are remembered in myth and re-imagined in stories told by older members of a patrilineage to the younger generations. Details about these slave women are also largely revealed and retrieved through divination, and through the spirits themselves. On at least two occasions, a *fofiesi* called Nanunsi sought me out from the audience upon getting possessed: two spirits speaking through her proceeded to identify themselves as 'Ayesha and Habiba, twin daughters of Prince Ibrahim Mahama of Navrongo, devotees of the Prophet Mohammed and of his horse al-Buraq'.[18] They then told me about their place of origin, describing in great detail a compound in a village near Navrongo in the north, supposedly guarded by crocodiles, serpents, and panthers. (The reference was, of course, to the famous crocodiles at Paga, north of Navrongo, on the Ghana–Burkina Faso border.) They had been bought from Salaga by an Anlo merchant 'thirteen generations ago' and had married into his family. The spirits then requested my help in finding their natal village and their northern kin. The members of Nanunsi's patrilineage were aware that they had Dagomba and Hausa Muslim ancestry in the distant past.[19] Ayesha and Habiba, however, do not surface in Nanunsi as often as the best-known slave of the family: an Ewedome woman who died as recently as the 1940s, and is still remembered by older members of the lineage. Also, the two sisters had never described their northern home in detail to their Anlo descendants; instead, whenever they surface, they prefer to advise their descendants on how to offer Islamic prayer for their own salvation. Ayesha and Habiba must have detected some scepticism on my part: to dispel my doubts about the validity of their accounts, they suggested taking me to the north to show me where they originated – a journey that I am yet to undertake.

[18] Nanunsi (in trance), Anlo-Afiadenyigba, 3 June 2004.
[19] The lineage has no recorded information about these ancestors. Dagomba and Hausa were used rather vaguely to denote forms of northernness.

Imagining the North

It is useful to think of Fofie and Gorovodu worship as an elaborate display of non-Anlo-ness: non-Anlo slaves are commemorated, non-Anlo imagery is used, and possession – during which the Anlo spirit medium actually 'becomes' a non-Anlo slave ancestor or a non-Anlo deity – are all part of an elaborate discourse of foreignness (see Figure 4.6). Dual processes of incorporation and separation occur simultaneously at several different levels of Fofie worship. The Anlo were created out of their encounter with slavery, and through Fofie worship, they acknowledge their debt to their foreign slave ancestors. Fofie and Gorovodu initiates are possessed by slave spirits and northern gods, who are finally incorporated into Anlo religion and society, after generations of being ignored and written out of the historical record (Wendl 1999). By possessing Anlo spirit mediums, these slave spirits re-enter Anlo society, after decades of existing outside Anlo consciousness. Northern gods are finally revered in shrines of their own, just as legitimate Anlo ancestral deities are. However, despite the fact that they have been incorporated into society, these northern deities are still regarded as foreign and they are thought to differ greatly from indigenous Anlo deities. Therefore the worship of these foreign deities warrants different forms of expression, different rituals and practices (see Kramer 1993). The kola nut – or *goro* – is an inseparable part of the worship of these northern gods in Anlo, used before any religious ceremony or performance. The north–south system of exchange was integral to bringing these deities into southern societies of the Akan forest belt, and, subsequently, Anlo (Allman and Parker 2005). Kola nuts and the internal slave trade were constituent parts of this exchange, as southern coastal peoples – like the Anlo – traded these cherished commodities from the north, in exchange for salt. Gorovodu spirit mediums speak Ewe-ised versions of Hausa, Twi, and other non-Anlo languages when possessed. Drumbeats imitate foreign rhythms, and mediums usually become possessed only when these non-Anlo rhythms are played.

As eloquently argued by Taussig, the process of mimesis – the act of mimicking aspects of northern culture – occurs in different arenas, and is often simultaneously accompanied by alterity, the act of distancing one-self from it (Taussig 1993). Through aspects of Fofie and Gorovodu wor-ship, the Anlo believe they are adopting certain aspects of other cultures, whilst simultaneously distancing themselves from them. In an attempt to honour these foreign non-Anlo deities of their slaves, the Anlo are in fact producing a cultural commentary on the customs and traditions of their northern slaves, especially aspects of northern culture that appear strange and exotic to them. Several idols and statues on display in Fofie shrines bear testimony to exactly how the Anlo imagine their non-Anlo

Figure 4.6. *Fofiesi* in trance, Anlo-Afiadenyigba, December 2010

neighbours (see Figure 4.7). The idols I have encountered are meant to represent Ewedome, Akan, and northern – Dagomba, Hausa, Tchamba, and Mossi – slave ancestors. Akan slave ancestors are often dressed in fabric that resembles bright patterns of Asante *kente*. The statues meant to represent northern slave ancestors are dressed in *batakaris*, turbans or

Figure 4.7. Gorovodu shrine depicting Wango, a crocodile spirit. Among Wango's devotees are the European trader (depicted on the right) and the *sofo* in red cloth and Islamic prayer cap, Agbozume, August 2000

flowing robes associated with the northerners. These northern ancestors in shrines reflect the stereotypes the Anlo have created about various non-Anlo peoples: Akan women are depicted as short and petite, while northern slave ancestors are taller in stature. Possession performances are also a cultural commentary, and spirit mediums adorn themselves with 'dramatic northern garb' (Kramer 1993: 46–7). Spirit mediums mark their faces with particular patterns, which they imagine signify the scarifications that their northern slaves may have sported in the past.

Household shrines contain objects associated with the north: Islamic amulets, imagery, Arabic inscriptions, Akan charms are all part of the display, meant to signify the religious preferences of the northern slave ancestors. These shrines contains what Tobias Wendl calls 'northern ethnographica', a collection of northern 'kitsch' objects, which the Anlo have invested with ritual potency (Wendl 1999: 116). Muslim and Catholic rosaries are often used in Gorovodu ceremonies, and they are sometimes revered as god-objects themselves (Rosenthal 1997: 113). Christianity and Islam were closely associated with each other in Anlo historical imagination, even though the Anlo encountered the two world religions during different periods of their history and through different circumstances. Horses, associated with the northern savanna peoples, often feature as puppets in these performances. The sacrificial animal for Kunde, Abrewa, and the Gorovodu deities is the dog: this refers to the southern perception that northerners reared dogs for domestic consumption.[20] More recently, Indian and Oriental deities – images derived from Vedic gods, characteristically depicted with several heads and limbs – have found their way into shrines throughout the Slave Coast (Rush 2008), including Anlo Gorovodu shrines, as a result of centuries of thriving intercontinental trade, adding to the international flavour of West African religion.

Performative features resembling Islamic ritual activity have become an integral part of Fofie possession ceremonies: some *fofiesiwo*, who believe their slaves were Muslims, imitate such gestures as the call to prayer, reciting impromptu verses from the Qur'an while possessed. *Salah*, a proliferating practice amongst Gorovodu initiates, which began in the 1950s, incorporates many orthodox Islamic features, such as the *adhan* (call to prayer), *shahada* (profession of faith), *basmalah* (recitation spoken before parts of the Qur'an) and parts of the *al-Fatihah* (opening *surat*) of seven verses of the Qur'an (Friedson 2009: 43–68). During *Salah* ceremonies, Gorovodu *trosiwo* dress in white. As Friedson points out, there is absolutely no attempt to syncretise Islam and Gorovodu through *Salah*, but an attempt to introduce a veneer of a world religion to make Gorovodu rituals more acceptable, as a response to an environment characterised by proliferating Pentecostalism (ibid.: 49). The constant incorporation of new artistic, visual, and conceptual forms of northernness is an indication of how such mimetic practices are constantly changing, as conceptions of the north evolve in the Anlo imagination, against the backdrop of changing relationships that the Anlo have and continue to build with these northern ethnic groups within the frameworks of the post-colonial state. Spirit mediums in Anlo often use imagery associated with the NPP, a political party associated with the Ashanti and (erroneously) with the north in the Anlo imagination. The NPP is regarded as the arch-rival of the formerly Anlo-dominated NDC. I have witnessed ceremonies in which the elephant, the symbol of the NPP, was part of the visual paraphernalia of a Gorovodu performance, immediately drawing associations for the Anlo audience with the peoples of the Akan forest belt and the northern savanna. Thus the ethnic politics of the Ghanaian state influences southern perceptions and prejudices of northernness, which

---

[20] The dog is the symbol for transgression and otherness on many levels: it stood as a metaphor for the otherness of the savanna world, which appeared strange to peoples of the south; for the ethnic northernness of the *Sarem*, and the 'spiritual otherness' of Gorovodu and Fofie ritual networks.

in turn are reflected in visual and performative aspects of mimetic ritual practices that make references to the north (Venkatachalam 2011).

Ritual Consciousness and Counter Publics

Other anthropological studies indicate that other southern Ewe peoples have a range of provisions – not unlike the Fofie cult of the Anlo – that address the consequences of integrating people into their society through slavery (Rosenthal 1998; Wendl 1999). The Tchamba cult of the Mina is a case in point. The Mina withheld social rights from their slaves, did not acknowledge their contribution or presence in the historical record, and, attempting to erase them from social memory, buried them outside the habitable realm of the village. As a result, the slaves of the Mina have traditionally been outside the mainstream historical consciousness of the community. Tchamba is a possession cult, and supplicants that submit to the spirits associated with this cult believe that they are indeed these forgotten slaves, who have returned to remind their living descendants of their agency in history. While the Mina expelled the memory of slavery into the silent realm, they could not keep these memories permanently repressed, and they return to a society's consciousness through the medium of ritual and spirit possession. Wendl reads the Tchamba cult as an attempt to correct the 'mainstream' version of Mina history, in which slaves were deliberately marginalised, excluded, and eventually forgotten. He argues that this discourse on slavery, developed in the 'ritual consciousness', runs parallel to the historical tradition, serving to correct it and fill the void (Wendl 1999: 119–22).

Two official discourses suppress the memory of slave holding in Mina society. One is a discourse internal to the Mina and constructed by them in relation to the position of socially marginalised descendants of slaves. It was taboo to talk about slavery openly in many West African cultures, as it exposed an individual's slave origins, leaving him or her vulnerable in society. Another powerful discourse is fashioned by the machinery of the Togolese state. The fact that Togo is dominated by the Kabye – one of the peoples that the southern Mina enslaved – makes any open discussion of slavery potentially explosive, especially as the Ewe- and Mina-dominated south is viewed by the ruling northern elites with great suspicion (see Rosenthal 2002).[21] For Wendl, the Tchamba cult is, therefore, a 'counter public', an encoded discourse that survives in a relatively hostile environment, dominated by two other analogous

---

[21] The Kabye are one of northern Togo's ethnic groups, to which President Gnassingbé Eyadema and his son and successor Faure Eyadema – and most members of their governments – have belonged.

discourses that attempt to repress that version of history (Wendl 1999: 121).

But did slave descendants in Anlo find it easy to deal with their slave origins outside the context of the Fofie cult? Sandra Greene argues that the Anlo were quite Akanised in this respect, and condemned the disclosure of peoples' slave origins in the public and political spheres (Greene 2003, 2011). In the Akan belt, the subject of slave origins cropped up during succession disputes: chiefs, office bearers, and indeed most Asante used the issue of slave ancestry, where they could, to discredit their competitors. Disclosing another's origins publicly was considered a punishable offence under Asante customary law (Wilks 1975: 86). In Anlo, the silence about slave origins in the political sphere goes hand in hand with public proclamations of slave descent in the ritual sphere.

Anlo was, in the words of one of my chiefly informants, a 'society full of strangers'.[22] The chiefdom had been settled in waves by migrants in different stages. Internal wrangling amongst Anlo clans often revolved around how long they had been settled in the chiefdom, with the oldest clans claiming more importance than the newer ones (see Greene 1996a: 49–50, 65–8). Greene's attempts to construct the origins of Anlo's clan system indicate that there is indeed a tension in society between (free) newcomers and earlier settlers. Some of Anlo's clans were associated with the former, others with the latter; while all clans were equal in theory, the membership of the older clans carried more prestige in the case of certain ritual and ceremonial functions. Anlo is a patrilineal society, and membership of key social institutions was inherited through a person's father's status. In pre-colonial and colonial Anlo, there would have been a number of male strangers in the chiefdom, who would have lacked membership of an Anlo clan. While some of them were enslaved, others would have settled in Anlo voluntarily. Greene's work suggests that Anlo society had developed various mechanisms to disguise the foreign patrilineal antecedents of highly assimilated strangers – both free and enslaved – over time.

There were provisions within the clan system for the integration of descendants of non-Anlo men: the Blu clan, one of Anlo's fifteen clans, consisted of highly assimilated newcomers to Anlo, who founded patrilineages at the point of their incorporation into Anlo society. Over the last century and a half, the free individuals who settled in Anlo from Ga-Adangme, Akan, and other more distant areas, were incorporated into this clan. Membership of the Blu clan conferred legitimate status in Anlo society, even though it failed to disguise the origins of its members completely. There was little correlation between marginalisation and membership of this clan. Key figures in Anlo history were members:

---

[22] Interview with Togbi Akpate Akrobotu, Whuti, 17 September 2003.

Elias Quist, a successful merchant-priest, was the son of an Afro-Danish officer and an Anloga woman; Gbadzo, an Anlo commander during the Peki Wars of the 1830s, was descended from an Adangbe man and an Anloga priestess (Greene 1996b).

In her study of land ownership and the clan system, Greene also suggests that clan membership was relatively open until the twentieth century. Prior to the establishment of the Blu clan in the late nineteenth century, people of non-Anlo ancestry simply had to make sacrifices, and pledged to serve the deities of the clans they wished to join. So descendants of male slaves, foreigners, and later, members of the Blu clan, could claim membership of the more 'authentic' Anlo clans, if they wished to shed their association with the newest clan of the chiefdom.[23] Anlo history is dotted with such figures (Greene 1996b).[24] The best example is that of Geraldo de Lima, the domestic slave of the Portuguese slave merchant Cesar Cerquira de Lima. Upon his master's death, Geraldo is believed to have inherited all his assets, including his wives and property. He is said to have become so powerful that the *awoamefia* admitted him as a member of the ruling Adzovia clan. Although it seemed that male slaves and both low- and high-status foreigners were thoroughly Anloised in patrilineal Anlo, and had metamorphosed into Anlo people with all the requisite markers of Anlo-ness, their outsider status remained visible despite high levels of assimilation. Therefore, foreign patrilineal origins are never discussed in Anlo, seeing that non-Anlo men could have founded patrilineages in the chiefdom in the recent past, attaining membership of Anlo society through the Blu clan, and by integration as junior kinsmen through the clans of their slave owners.[25]

On the other hand, though female slaves were as thoroughly Anloised as their male counterparts, the elaborate discussion and commemoration of

---

[23] The situation was very different amongst the neighbouring Mina, where Wendl argues that descendants of male slaves, the *dzidzidome* ('born betweens'), never attained full status: they were permitted to cohabit, but not to marry legally; they could procreate but could not establish their own descent groups; they could worship their (non-Mina) forefathers, who never really attained the status of other legitimate ancestors of the community (Wendl 1999: 112).

[24] Greene presents us with two life stories of influential foreigners who lived in Anlo, based on oral traditions, in order to examine the politics of assimilation in nineteenth-century Anlo. Her findings reveal that assimilation was a relatively easy process in Anlo when compared with the neighbouring Akan (Greene 1996b).

[25] In the late nineteenth century, men descended from slaves used Christianity and colonial education to further their acceptability in Anlo after domestic slave holding was abolished in the Gold Coast colony (Greene 2011: 139–57). Many such men came to be incorporated into Anlo society through membership of the Blu clan. Membership of this clan was, however, not entirely unproblematic: as recently as the 1980s, certain Blu elders protested their marginality vis-à-vis the running of Anlo affairs, complaining that they are still occasionally treated as 'outsiders' by members of other clans – a reflection of their ancestors' status as recent migrants to the chiefdom (Greene 1997: 18).

their foreign origins in the ritual and public sphere causes little disadvantage to their descendants. The Fofie cult is a channel for commemorating mainly female slaves of Anlo slave-holding families within the structure of the patrilineage. As the cult became institutionalised in the chiefdom during the 1940s, it is apparent that hidden matriliny became a problem for the Anlo only as recently as this period. This also demonstrates that admissions of matrilineal slave ancestry were not disadvantageous, an indicator that the Anlo had already begun laying emphasis on patriliny as a prerequisite marker of an Anlo identity by the 1940s. Anlo-ness was, by the mid-twentieth century, essentially an identity inherited by an individual, through membership of an Anlo patrilineage. Not coincidentally, Fofie worship, that commemorated female slaves who were incorporated into Anlo patrilineage, became firmly established in the chiefdom soon after this cultural renegotiation of an Anlo identity, to which legitimate patrilineal antecedents had become central. Fofie initiates – who are descended from non-Anlo slave women who married Anlo men – are therefore spread across all Anlo clans, from the Adzovia and Bate clans (the kingmakers), to the Amlade (the warriors), the Like, and even the Blu clans. Therefore, in patrilineal Anlo of the 1940s – characterised by impoverishment and economic decline – the admission of matrilineal slave antecedents actually worked to an individual's advantage, as it suggested that their ancestors had possessed considerable wealth in the past, of which their slave-owning status was an indication. Unlike the case of the Tchamba cult amongst the Mina as detailed by Wendl (1999), memories of slave ancestry in Anlo are neither restricted to ritual consciousness, nor are they aspects of the slave-holding past manifested as counter publics. Discourses about slavery and slave holding intrude from the ritual consciousness into the realm of mainstream historical consciousness. Some Anlo are not reluctant to acknowledge the agency and contribution of slaves to the making of both their chiefdom and themselves as a people. The issue of slave descent, which arises through the Fofie cult, touches on ethically problematic issues such as slavery, servitude, and (damaged or incomplete) personhood. Why and how these anxieties have come to be dealt with in this manner, and at what juncture in Anlo's history concerns about slave holding have crossed over from the realm of ritual consciousness to the realm of historical consciousness, will form the subject of the next four chapters.

5 Religion and Society in Early Modern Anlo, *c.* 1750–*c.* 1910

One of the first attempts at the systematic study of Anlo religion stems from the evangelical project: the most significant written accounts of religious practice emerge within the context of the dialogue between Christianity and 'heathenism'. Given the conspicuous lack of historical sources prior to the arrival of Christian missions, the knowable history of Anlo religion is largely the history of the interactions between various African religious traditions and Christianity. Arguably, missionaries of the Norddeutsche Missionsgesellschaft (NMG) have been among the most important players in Anlo religious history, because Anlo religion is viewed by later historians through the lens of the missionary encounter, and because that encounter has profoundly altered the nature of the religious terrain. The NMG was founded by Lutheran and Reformed Protestants in 1836 (Meyer 1999: 28).[1] In 1847, four missionaries of the NMG arrived on the Slave Coast. Their search for a mission field took them to northern Eweland, and Lorenz Wolf became the first missionary to operate in Peki later that year (Debrunner 1965: 68). As Peki was on the brink of war with the Asante in the early 1850s, the second group of missionaries who arrived from Bremen in 1852 abandoned the mission station there. Encouraged to look for a new base on the coast, they chose the port city of Keta, which was not only the gateway to Anlo, but also the most cosmopolitan of the constituent *dutowo*. In addition to Keta, another mission station was founded in the heart of Anlo in 1857, at Anyako. Two other stations were built in central Eweland: Waya in 1855 and Ho in 1859 (ibid.: 78–9). What sort of society did the first missionaries encounter in Anlo?

Anlo had been well integrated into the trading networks that existed along the West African coast from the 1650s. The Danes, Dutch, and British had frequented Keta harbour as early as the 1710s. Anlo was also the abode of several wealthy traders, who amassed their fortunes by trading in salt, fisheries, and textiles. The slave trade had been the backbone

---

[1] A rift between the Lutheran and Reformed Protestants led to the Mission reorganising itself as the Reformed Protestant Mission in 1851, with Bremen as its headquarters (Meyer 1999: 28).

of the Anlo economy until the 1860s, and several Anlo ports, including Atorkor, Woe, Adina, Blekusu, and Keta, had been important slave markets (Akyeampong 2001b: 45). The most prominent power in pre-1850s Anlo was Denmark, which owned Keta's Fort Prinsenstein. The Danes outlawed the slave trade as early as 1792, and made a number of feeble attempts to abolish it in Anlo in the first half of the nineteenth century. However, rather than marking a decline, the six decades that followed the abolition – between 1800 and 1860 – proved to be the golden age of the slave trade in Anlo.[2] Several Afro-Portuguese, Brazilian, and Cuban slave merchants had made Anlo their home by the 1840s. Of these foreign slave traders, Bahian Gonzalves Baëta at Keta, Spaniard Don José Mora based in Woe, and the Afro-Portuguese Francis Olympio of Blekusu were the most prominent. In their service were a number of 'returnees' from Latin America. Such returnees, including Baëta and Olympio, belonged to a category of people who evolved into a heterogeneous community that came to be known all over the Slave Coast as 'Brazilians'. They bore Portuguese names and were usually descended from mixed unions. Most of these returnees had made their way to West Africa from Brazil in stages during the 1830s – firstly after a law which freed all non-native Brazilian slaves came into effect in 1831, and, secondly, after the Bahia Uprising of 1835.[3] They settled along the coast, created a distinct Brazilian subculture, and married into prominent African families (see Debrunner 1965: 35–8). The word 'Brazilian' in Slave Coast societies referred to any Lusophone trader or Brazilian returnee, from not only Brazil but also Angola and other Portuguese-speaking domains. Eventually, the term Brazilian was extended to include not only the direct descendants of the first-generation returnees, but also their entire entourages: locals in service of these Brazilian households took on their masters' names, gradually coming to identify themselves as Brazilians (Law 2001: 23).[4]

---

[2] Descriptions of this period in Anlo history appear in Fofie worshipping lineages' accounts of their past. This period is regarded as a prosperous one, during which the Anlo were rich and owned slaves, the most precious commodity of that era.

[3] A law that championed the freedom of all 'non-native' slaves came into effect in Brazil in 1831 (Debrunner 1965: 37). This law was rather ambiguous, and several different categories of people applied it to themselves to gain their personal freedom. A few slaves trickled back to West Africa after 1831. However, after the Bahia Uprising in Brazil in 1835, numerous ex-slaves were deported to West Africa, and large communities of Brazilian returnees sprang up on the West African coast after this date (Law 2001: 27; Strickrodt 2008). The Bahia Uprising is also known as the Male Revolt. It derives that name from 'Imale', which is what Yoruba Muslims were known as in most societies in the Atlantic World. The leadership of the movement was largely Muslim, and the Uprising took place during the holy month of Ramadan, which is what linked the event to Islam in the Brazilian popular imagination (see Lovejoy 1994: 151).

[4] The best-known Brazilians in Anlo history were the Portuguese trader Cesar Cerquira de Lima of Keta, and his domestic servant Geraldo de Lima, who was a native of Anlo (Greene 1997: 127–34). Bruce Chatwin's famous historical novel, *The Viceroy of Ouidah* (1980), is loosely based on the life of a Brazilian merchant, Francisco Felix de Sousa.

The Brazilians of the Slave Coast set themselves up as merchants, engaging in trade with Brazil, as Brazilian produce like rum and tobacco was in great demand in West Africa. Most of these returnees also became active agents in the slave trade upon their arrival in Anlo, thereby giving it a boost.[5]

By the 1840s, Anlo slave markets – and in particular the largest port, Keta – were busier than ever. As Accra had come under close scrutiny from the British, slave merchants based there relocated east of the Volta and were forced to collaborate with the Anlo (Dumett and Johnson 1988: 73). By the 1850s, the influence of the foreign slave merchants had waned, and most prestigious traders were Anlo: some of these included Tamakloe at Whuti, Bomiklo at Alakple, Ajorlolo and Dokutsu at Atorkor (Akyeampong 2001b: 58). Tensions were building up between the Anlo and their neighbours, and by the 1850s the Anlo often clashed with the Ada to the west, while slave raids into central and northern Eweland became frequent. In 1850, the British took over Fort Prinsenstein from the Danes, which marked the beginning of the steady growth of British influence.

Into the 'Bastion of Heathenism'[6]

To the first missionaries who arrived in Anloga, the Anlo capital was a rather forbidding town: it was clearly everything they dreaded. As their focus was religious conversion, the Bremen missionaries noted one striking fact: the chief priest of a deity known as Nyigbla was the unrivalled spiritual leader and exercised considerable control over the town. The Nyigbla cult had a large following, drawn from diverse sections of society, and had some rigorously observed taboos. On his first visit to Anloga in 1854, missionary Plessing noted that as he 'mounted the horse and rode through a few streets . . . the inhabitants started a terrible clamour' (Plessing, quoted in Greene 1996a: 94). He soon realised that 'nobody may ride a horse in Awuna-ga [Anloga], not even the king, for the fetish would kill him'.

---

[5] Elsewhere in West Africa, such returnees from the Americas were incorporated into the local coastal African intelligentsia, and, in Akurang-Parry's words, became 'agents of creolisation, social and economic change, cultural transmission, Euro-Christianity, and political transformation' (2004: 27). From Cape Coast to Yorubaland, it was members of this new social group that developed and espoused the strong anti-slavery ideologies that helped colonial authorities implement abolition (Falola 1999; Gocking 1999; Parker 2000; Sanneh 2001). This was unlike the situation in Slave Coast societies such as Anlo, where the arrival of returnees initially reinvigorated the slave trade.

[6] 'Anloga: Eine Hochburg des Heidentums' was a phrase used by E. Salkowski in 1907 in a Bremen Mission periodical, *Bremer Missionschriften* (1907, No. 20: 25, cited in Greene 2002: 149).

This deity captured the missionary imagination, evidenced in several excerpts from diaries:

The priest of Nyigbla wears white clothes like the white people and he cannot tolerate a black or half white entering the town in European clothes, although the whites may appear in his clothes. . . .

In his honour children from neighbouring families were caught and killed. It is said that they were then roasted and pulverised and that their ashes were thrown by the chiefs into drinking water (the spring) of the population. Some captured children were brought up in the Nyigbla precincts for his service.

(Spieth, quoted in Debrunner 1965: 62).

What exactly was this deity? Nyigbla was identified as the war god of Anloga, and was the most powerful Anlo deity until the decline of his cult during the 1850s (Greene 1996a). On how exactly he came to enter Anlo, and at what juncture in its history, we may only speculate.[7] Ellis's accounts of Anlo in the 1870s indicate that the highest circles of Nyigbla worship were shrouded in secrecy: 'no one but the chief priest may enter the sanctuary and commune with the god' (Ellis 1965 [1890]: 75).[8] The chief priest, 'the mouthpiece of the deity, promulgator of his decrees' played a crucial role in the functioning of the cult. This chief Nyigbla *tronua* (priest) was an extremely important public figure, as both a political and spiritual leader, who had to be consulted on important state matters, especially decisions regarding war. He actually shared power with the *awoamefia*, the paramount chief of the Anlo. How exactly this institution of dual leadership evolved is unclear, although some historical sources indicate that it was well-established by the mid-nineteenth century.[9] Greene suggests that Nyigbla priests had secured and consolidated their political position as early as the 1770s, and that their rise to prominence was linked to the oracular powers they possessed.

What happened after Nyigbla's rise to prominence is well documented. Nyigbla priests instituted a series of social and political changes, which altered the nature of the religious terrain. After their rise in the 1770s, Nyigbla priests formed alliances with priests of other deities, in an attempt to bring them under their influence: Afu, Dzotsiafe, Awadatsi, and other clan and ancestral deities were organised into a hierarchical structure with Nyigbla at the apex (Greene 1996a: 87). Chief priests of

---

[7] Greene, who examined the various oral traditions that deal with Nyigbla's origins, suggests that the deity belonged to the stigmatised Dzevi clan, and assumed importance in Anlo during the eighteenth century (Greene 1996a: 27).

[8] A. B. Ellis was the fifth British District Commissioner of Keta, a position he held from 1878 to 1879. He wrote *The Ewe-Speaking Peoples of the Slave Coast of West Africa* (first published in 1890, reprinted in 1965), describing the customs and rituals associated with the parts of Ewe country that he knew best.

[9] Greene suggests that Nyigbla's ability to predict success and failure at war led to his growing popularity (Greene 1996a: 58–9).

other influential cults were forced to relocate shrines to Anloga, to facilitate regulation by Nyigbla priests. The search for influence in people-poor Anlo led shrines to strengthen their followings by taking *trokosiwo* (sing. *trokosi*) by the early nineteenth century. *Trokosiwo* were female initiates pledged to shrines by families, in return for spiritual services rendered by priests.[10] Priests usually retained control over their labour, exploiting it to their advantage. Apart from Nyigbla, several other Anlo deities, under the control of powerful patrilineages, engaged in the practice of recruiting *trokosiwo*. Cultic networks would have been organised around patron deities of Anlo clans, such as Sui and Adzima (of the Amlade clan) and Tomi (of the Adzovia clan) (Greene 1996a: 64). By the early 1800s, Nyigbla priests had initiated the *foasi* ceremony, by which they could induct two or more girls from every Anlo clan into the cult each year. Women in the service of Nyigbla had a special name, *zizidzelawo*.[11] Such *zizidzelawo* were initially voluntary affiliates (Akyeampong 2001b: 224). However, all such voluntary religious associations were gradually transformed into involuntary associations within a generation in the Anlo religious system: Greene tells us that *zizidzelawo* had to dedicate one of their children to Nyigbla's future service, and cultic recruitment came to be inherited through lineage ties (Greene 1996a: 88). The cult of Nyigbla was typical of all other Anlo cults of the period: by the 1860s, when the missionaries encountered Anlo religion, shrines dedicated to various deities had large followings attached to them.

A. B. Ellis, the fifth District Commissioner of Keta (1878–9), described several other religious networks that he encountered in Anlo, which resembled the workings of the cult of Nyigbla in terms of structure and recruitment patterns (Ellis 1965: 31–90). Ellis identified three categories of religious initiate: *vodu-sio*, *kosio/edro-kosio*, and *vodu-vio*. *Vodu* is the word used amongst the eastern Ewe for what the western Ewe refer to as *tro* (Ellis used the word *edro*). A *kosi* was pledged or dedicated to a god by his/her family in recognition for services rendered. *Vodu-sio* were shrine priestesses (though it is likely that Ellis is describing Dahomean initiates in this case).[12] *Vodu-vio* were not as closely affiliated to the shrine as the other two categories of initiate, worshipping only at festivals and ceremonial occasions. Ellis's accounts suggest that the priests of shrines had a great deal of control over *kosio/edro-kosio*, which corresponds with

---

[10] *Tro* = deity; *kosi* = servant. Male initiates, known as *trokluwo* (sing. *troklu*) were also recruited, although neither as frequently nor on the same scale as their female counterparts.

[11] The origins and etymology of this word are unclear. Greene suggests that it was a term used to refer exclusively to Nyigbla initiates (Greene 1996a: 87–8).

[12] Ellis's accounts of Anlo and the Slave Coast suggest that priests of most deities (whether they were common to all 'tribes' of the Slave Coast, or particular to certain locations), appear to have recruited members to enlarge their entourage.

the *trokosiwo* that Greene and Akyeampong describe.[13] Their labour was exploited, it is possible that their sexual services were controlled by priests to some extent, and children born out of such liaisons between priests and *kosio* belonged to the shrine. Ellis suggests that shrines in Anlo also recruited *kosio* through pledges made by families, implying that there may have also been replacement strategies in place. Interestingly, while men outnumbered women in the shrines of the Gold Coast, Ellis tells us that the ratio was more balanced amongst the 'Ewe-speaking people', including the Anlo (ibid.: 139).[14]

While the exact nature of the process of recruitment is unknown, what we can be sure of is that initiates were indeed replaced. This leads us to conclude that there was little individual choice with respect to religious affiliation and engagement with shrines in 1850s Anlo. So the majority of religious cults in pre-Christian Anlo all exhibited similar character-istics: they were replacement cults, with membership being transmit-ted through lineage ties; initiation into these cults demanded life-long commitment from their followers. In addition to Nyigbla, other deities recruited *trokosiwo*: Sui, Adzima, and Tomi were ancestral deities, and could be worshipped only by people with ties to particular clans and pat-rilineages. Ellis's study suggests that there was little competition between shrines for followers, which is congruent with Greene's analysis of pre-1850s Anlo (Greene 1996a: 89). Nyigbla's decline after 1850 was to have far-reaching consequences for the religious system. When the missionar-ies entered Anlo in the 1850s, the Anlo religious environment was on the cusp of a radical structural change. The popularity of the chief deity was on the decline, leaving Anlo open to alternative religious agents, namely the Yewe deities and in due course, Christianity.

Despite encountering it during its declining phase, the missionaries found the cult of Nyigbla rather daunting, and therefore decided that Anloga was not an appropriate base. Anloga's 'heathenism' served as an effective deterrent, and the Bremen missionaries chose Keta, a more cosmopolitan town, as the site for their first mission station in Anlo. In addition to its thriving port, Keta had numerous manufacturing firms and industries, and was home to several merchants from as far away as Sierra Leone and Cameroon, which made it more tolerant of outside influences, both ideological and material. Besides, the priests of the Nyigbla cult had little control in Keta.

---

[13] Such women are referred to as *fiasidiwo* (sing. *fiasidi*) in contemporary Anlo.

[14] Ellis refers to the entire region between Anlo and Dahomey as the Ewe-speaking belt. In addition to the Anlo, his book also includes descriptions of other non-Ewe societies of the Gbe cluster, such as the Fon of Dahomey. Therefore, Ellis's 'Ewe-speaking' peoples correspond to what contemporary ethnographers of West Africa would identify as the Gbe-speaking belt (Ellis 1965).

Tricks of the Trade: The Yewe Cult

Unfortunately for the missionaries, Keta was not exactly a 'heathen-free' zone either. While they had left the Nyigbla cult behind in Anloga, they were confronted by a similar challenge in Keta. Another new cultic network, which resembled Nyigbla in terms of structure and organisation, albeit superficially, was flourishing in and around Keta: Yewe, organised around a collection of Dahomean nature deities. Though a proliferating cult, Yewe was not as deeply rooted in Anlo society as was Nyigbla, a factor which proved encouraging for the missionaries.

Anlo oral traditions assert that Yewe worship was imported from the former Dahomey sometime during the late eighteenth century (Greene 1996a: 95–6; Akyeampong 2001b: 108). This is confirmed by missionary accounts, which record the westward diffusion of Yewe worship into Anlo from eastern Dahomey (Herskovits 1938, Vol. 2: 189–93; Debrunner 1965: 58–9). Most Yewe shrine owners in present-day Anlo have clear ideas of the regions from which their Yewe god-objects were originally imported to Anlo. For example, the Goku shrine in Anlo-Afiadenyigba identifies Ketakore in Togo as its spiritual base. Initiates of other shrines believe their original spiritual hubs were towns in the Republic of Benin and Nigeria, and make regular pilgrimages to these parent shrines to reinforce ties. Greene and Akyeampong suggest that while the three deities associated with the Yewe cult – Hevieso (thunder), Avleketi (sea), and Voduda (serpent) – may have been worshipped in Anlo for about a century and a half as *voduwo* owned by individuals, it was their organisation into Yewe shrine complexes that was novel in the early 1850s (Greene 1996a: 96; Akyeampong 2001b: 110). As Hevieso, Avleketi, and Voduda were standard nature deities present in the Gbe-speaking belt during the eighteenth century, it is possible that they were part of the pre-Yewe religious baseline in Anlo. Yewe shrines were owned by wealthy merchants (*hubonowo*; sing. *hubono*), and each *hubono* aimed to recruit several initiates into his shrine.

These shrines were complex organisations in themselves. Herskovits's monumental two-volume study of Dahomey helps us reconstruct exactly what sort of institutions Yewe shrines in mid-nineteenth-century Anlo may have been, although it is likely that there were some differences between Yewe in Dahomey and Anlo. Herskovits tells us that Yewe or 'Yehwe' was the generic term for *vodu* in Dahomey. Dahomean divinities were organised into three distinct recognisable groupings: (1) the Sky grouping, which revolved around the worship of Mawu and Lisa, the original cosmic couple; (2) the Earth deities organised around Sakpata; and (3) the Thunder divinities centred on Hevieso.[15] According to

---

[15] Hevieso is sometimes associated with the Yoruba thunder god Shango, and shares many characteristics with him.

Herskovits, Yewe had become so 'specialised in Togoland that it refers only to the Hevieso gods of Dahomey', implying that Yewe shrines in Anlo were focused only on the worship of Hevieso and related divinities (Herskovits 1938, Vol. 2: 192–4).

Admission into a shrine associated with either one of these cults groups was either inherited or relatively open in Dahomey, depending on the level at which one entered the cult. High priesthood was an inherited office, and high priests were known as *voduno*. Outsiders attracted by the power of the *vodu* joined the cult group as ordinary members. French colonial administrator, Auguste Le Herissé, who was based in Abomey during the 1890s, identified four degrees of initiation. The *voduno* was the owner or head priest of a shrine: he was responsible for the overall organisation of the shrine; he officiated over all ceremonies, and received tribute from ordinary initiates and potential members.[16] The *xunso* was the one who 'carried' the god-object at outdoorings, playing an important role during ritualistic performances of the shrine. A *vodusi* was vowed to its service and was an ordinary initiate. There were other categories of member known as *legbano*, who retained loose ties with the shrine (Le Herissé 1911; Herskovits 1938, Vol. 2: 175). Most of these positions were hereditary. The position of the *voduno* was for life, usually passed down matrilineally or patrilineally within the same lineage. Upon the death of an ordinary *vodusi*, an heir had to be appointed. The heir of a *vodusi* could be nominated by the *vodusi* or by the family. Recruitment into cult groupings in Dahomey took other courses too. Childless women often commissioned the services of the shrine and pledged children thought to be born out of divine intervention to its service. Every shrine had different taboos, rules, and regulations. During the initiation period, initiates were marked out with the scarifications that distinguished them as devotees of a particular cult, and were taught the ritual language, customs, and dances of the particular *vodu* they worshipped. They were generally supported by their families through this initiation process. Initiates were expected to remain loyal to their own shrines, and had to devote their activities only to the gods of their own cults (Herskovits 1938, Vol. 2: 185).[17] Unlike their Dahomean counterparts, where initiates were replaced, Yewe shrines were relatively open in 1850s Anlo, on account of the fact that they were new shrines in the religious system. Anybody could petition the Yewe deities, and the deities in turn could 'catch' devotees of their choice. *Vodusiwo* were not initially recruited through lineage ties: new cults usually had few restrictions on the recruitment of new members, as they aimed to attract as many initiates as possible.

---

[16] Le Herissé wrote extensively about Dahomean customs and history. *L'Ancien Royaume du Dahomey: moeurs, réligion, histoire* was first published in 1911.

[17] Yewe would come to resemble its Dahomean counterpart, by the 1870s, in that Yewe *vodusiwo* could not engage in the worship of any other deities or attain membership of other *cultic* networks.

By the 1850s, Yewe was growing in popularity all over Anlo, especially in the *dutowo* south of the Keta lagoon. 'Crowds stream to him,' wrote Schlegel, a disgruntled missionary, of Elias Quist, a pivotal 'mulatto' Yewe shrine owner in the Keta area (Schlegel, quoted in Greene 1996a: 98). Quist was one of the many *hubonowo* (shrine owners) who during that period transformed the individual worship of a number of nature deities, mainly Hevieso, Voduda, and Avleketi, by uniting them to form the characteristic Yewe triad, based on the structure of a Dahomean shrine. But Quist, like others who were behind the proliferating Yewe phenomenon, were members of the new class of wealthy merchants in Anlo. Many of these Yewe *hubonowo* lacked the credentials to participate in orthodox Anlo religious networks: Greene tells us that a large number of them, including Quist, were ethnic outsiders, who had amassed wealth and prestige through their trading activities. It appears that these Yewe *hubonowo* transformed their shrines into business cooperatives almost immediately (ibid.: 97). Yewe's rise in the 1850s corresponds with the golden age of the illicit slave trade in Anlo: Yewe shrines and the cult's occupational policy on secrecy were used to continue the trade.[18] A former Yewe initiate, Stephan Kwadzo Afelavo, who converted to Christianity *c.* 1890, describes the intimidation and threats involved during a Yewe *nukpekpe* (initiation) ceremony:

Say nothing of what you see in the Yewe compound to any man, unless he be a Yewe priest or one who frequents the Yewe compound. . . . If you betray Yewe, when you are coming from some place a thunderstorm will break and you will see a ram appear: it will butt you with its horns, so that you fall down and die.

(Afelevo, quoted in Greene 1996a: 97–8)

Other equally detailed descriptions of exactly how Yewe kills follow in Afelevo's rather grim account. Not coincidentally, the registered rise in the illegal slave trade in Anlo between 1850 and 1870, which was boosted by a brief period of British absence from Keta's Fort Prinsenstein, coincided with the proliferation of Yewe shrines around Keta.

Yewe's success in post-1850s Anlo was certainly facilitated by its economic and functional agility. Yewe members formed an easily available workforce for their *hubonowo*, who used their labour in the newly established industries that had developed in the openings created by the colonial economy. Yewe complexes continued to function as organised business enterprises: by the 1900s, Yewe initiates were involved in the production, marketing, and selling of copra in Dzelukope, in the environs of Keta (Greene 1996a: 99). In addition, palm oil, liquor, and other products that formed an integral part of the colonial economy were produced

---

[18] Debrunner (1965), Greene (1996a), and Akyeampong (2001b) all suggest that there was a link between Yewe's policy of secrecy and the slave trade.

in Yewe shrine complexes. The *hubonowo* also established themselves as moneylenders, and Yewe initiates worked as debt-collecting agents for them; these initiates generally appear to have served the interests of their shrine owners. A Yewe initiate's account bears testimony to the exploitative nature of work:

> Yewe is hard work,
> They have caught me for it
> I lacked the head to refuse,
> Now the misery has overtaken me
> I am totally worthless in the world
> And not able to refuse anymore
> That is the fruit of Yewe . . .
> Hard and heavy is Yewe.
>   (A Yewe initiate, quoted in
>   Spieth 1911: 183)

The Yewe cult has always been associated with the more clandestine aspects of the Anlo economy, and adapted well to the decline in the slave trade in 1870. Yewe shrine owners became engaged in smuggling prohibited commodities from German- to British-controlled areas. Smuggling European alcohol and firearms from German Togoland became a very lucrative business from the 1870s, and there was a sudden upsurge of Yewe shrines in Denu, a smuggling depot located west of Adafienu, which marked the eastern limit of British jurisdiction until 1879.[19]

Structurally, at this point in time, Yewe was unlike the dominant pre-1850s Anlo cults, like the Nyigbla and the *troxovi* networks. Yewe membership was open to all, and initiates were not recruited solely through lineage associations. Most new cults in Anlo functioned exactly like the Yewe cult during the first few decades of their inception: they had to attract as many devotees as possible, and therefore involved themselves in a range of activities that provided socio-economic support, in addition to spiritual services. Yewe's versatility as a social institution is evident from the fact that, by the twentieth century, the cult had become a channel for manifesting individual interests, which may explain its enormous appeal across diverse sections of society: not surprisingly, Yewe shrines drew their membership from petty criminals and social rejects (Greene 1996a: 99). Most narratives of why people came to join Yewe shrines were associated with perceived individual failure or insanity, and joining a shrine allowed people to pose as reformed members of society, as well as providing them with a shield against social stigma. In addition, it gave young men and women considerable freedom to make decisions about

---

[19] The border was extended eastward to incorporate Some and end at Aflao in 1879, primarily to combat illegal smuggling into the Gold Coast and Anlo (Akyeampong 2001b: 64).

their own lives in matters of marriage and divorce. There was also a general rise in relationships without parental approval during this period (ibid.: 105). Greene also argues that Yewe actually helped women in Anlo society take control of their own lives and conferred upon them extensive freedoms. The most effective of these measures allowed a Yewe initiate to declare herself or himself *alaga* when insulted and 'go wild', thereby inflicting damage on the offender; the latter would then have to pay a hefty fine to the shrine owner in order to compensate for the damage he had done the initiate.[20] Joining the Yewe cult was an attractive option for the Anlo precisely because it had turned into a platform for expressing individual interests (Debrunner 1965: 59).

As Yewe grew in popularity from the 1850s, the power of Nyigbla priests declined (Debrunner 1965: 62). Several Anlo oral traditions deal with the subject of Nyigbla's decline: in a bid to enrich themselves from the slave trade, Nyigbla priests are believed to have sold several initiates into slavery in the early nineteenth century. This act constituted the ultimate betrayal for the Anlo, and Nyigbla priests lost the trust of their devotees (Greene 1996a: 112–13). The decline of the cult may also be satisfactorily explained, however, by the profound social and economic changes that were unsettling Anlo. Nyigbla priests gradually lost their importance as they failed to perform their specific functions as war oracles: the Anlo were defeated a number of times between 1850 and 1870 by their immediate neighbours and the British, which led them to question the efficacy of the war god. Besides, Nyigbla priests simply could not compete with their Yewe counterparts, and involvement with the Yewe cult was a more lucrative option for the average Anlo person. Yewe was able to recruit followers who were formerly devotees of orthodox Anlo gods, like Nyigbla, Sui, Tomi, and other shrines under the control of Anlo patrilineages.

Most historical accounts of the 1850s and 1860s demonstrate another feature of interest: there was a degree of antagonism between Nyigbla priests and the newly established Yewe cult. The respective leaders of the two cults represented completely different sections of society. Nyigbla priests were the traditional ruling elites, who felt threatened by the rise of the new wealthy Yewe priests, and did their best to curtail the latter from spreading their influence. Therefore, ordinary membership of one cult excluded an initiate from associating with the other. This antagonism between Nyigbla and Yewe was apparent. As Debrunner observed, 'the man who belongs to the Yehwe community worships these and not the long established guardian spirits who are felt to be something different

---

[20] These fines were so large that the practice led to an increase in the incidence of loans, debts, and the pawning of family members (Greene 1996a: 101).

from the Yehwe spirits. . . . Yehwe is a world on its own' (Debrunner 1965: 58–9). While Nyigbla reigned supreme in Anloga, Yewe was more popular outside Anloga and along the coast. In fact, the Yewe cult had always been forbidden from operating in Anloga: it was only as recently as 1996 that they violated this age-old ban by performing an outdooring ceremony in the traditional Nyigbla headquarters, gaining rights to Anlo's capital (Greene 2002: 57).[21] Greene suggests that measures such as the ban on sewn clothing imposed by Nyigbla priests in Anloga were aimed partly at preventing African and Afro-European traders from extending their spheres of influence in Anloga, as most of the merchants who were initially associated with 'symbols of modernity' would have been Yewe shrine owners.

As Yewe initiates grew in numbers, another religious presence entered the system: by 1857, the Bremen mission had stations in two Anlo towns, Keta and Anyako. The establishment of the Yewe cult and the intro-duction of Christianity destabilised the religious system. They provided individuals with a degree of freedom to determine their religious affili-ations – whereas in Anlo before the 1870s an individual simply replaced a family member within the religious system. The Anlo seemed to be turning away from closed, replacement cults towards more open net-works that individuals could access without any prior familial connec-tions. The coexistence of deities organised under Nyigbla before the 1870s was gradually giving away to competition, as the two new reli-gious agencies sought to establish and gain followers. Association with both Yewe and Christianity also enabled the Anlo to participate in the changing economic conditions of the time, which explains why the two religious bodies became an integral part of religious and social life in Anlo.

Two Places of Refuge: Christianity in Anlo

'Our tribe is the wildest and gives most trouble to white men.'
(Missionary reaction to the Anlo, *c.* 1860s, quoted in Debrunner 1965: 78)

After about two decades of evangelical work in West Africa, F. M. Zahn, the head of missionary operations in Eweland, announced to the mis-sion headquarters in Bremen that the NMG had 'Four Places of Refuge on the Slave Coast' (Debrunner 1965: 77). Of these, two were in Anlo: Keta and Anyako. These early mission stations were self-sufficient units, run by one or two missionaries and their 'native' assistants, and were an

---

[21] Greene suggests that for about sixty years Yewe has faced an outright ban, instituted by Nyigbla priests, on operating in Anloga (Greene 2002: 57).

extraordinary mêlée of people, as the staff listings of a Bremen Mission station in Keta in the 1860s reveal. There were three Europeans at the outpost: missionary Plessing and his wife headed the station, while Lydia Schlegel taught at the girls' school.[22] As in some other parts of West Africa, Mission drew its first converts from people at the edge of Anlo society: stigmatised foreigners, former slaves, and indentured people became the first Christians.[23] Two 'baptised pagan recruits' were central to the functioning of the mission station at Keta: Samuel Kwist was an Anlo who served as an interpreter, while Mose Akuete, the laundryman, was a native of Accra 'in service of the brethren on account of a debt' (Debrunner 1965: 79–80). Though Akuete had been baptised, he was 'excluded from Church activities for obvious sins for which he has not done penance' (ibid.). In addition, there were a number of children that the missionaries had either freed from slavery or who had been pawned to the mission by their parents. Maurice Samuel, from the interior, was bought by the missionaries for twenty dollars; Henry, from Accra, cost them twenty-five dollars; Dina was purchased for thirty dollars.[24] Paul, Christian, and Joseph Reindorf were 'mulattos' from either Accra or Anlo. There were 'unbaptised pagans': Yofu, the stable man, Odoli the cook, and Onyame, who was also bought by the Mission for forty-five dollars. There were some other children: 'mulattos' Peter Kwist, Frederick, and Edward Lawson, in addition to Kwame, Kujeji, and Sisa, from areas within close proximity of Keta, who may have been given to the mission by indebted parents (ibid.: 81–2).[25] By 1860, according to Ustorf, 66 per cent of all adults who lived in the three stations of Keta, Anyako, and Waya were free, while the corresponding figure for children in the three stations was 50 per cent (Ustorf 2001: 247, fn. 19).

During its first decade in Anlo, the Mission vigorously pursued a policy of buying slaves from slave owners, as illustrated above: most of these children were initially sold by their parents to slave owners, during moments of extreme monetary crisis. In order to gain more influence in the community, the Bremen missionaries actually encouraged people to pawn their children to them, in exchange for loans provided to families. It was the hope of early missionaries that such children would form the backbone of the Christian community in Anlo. As stated by missionary Brutschin:

---

[22] Lydia Schlegel was the widow of Bernhard Schlegel, one of the first missionaries to arrive in Eweland. Bernhard Schlegel died at the mission station at Anyako, though Lydia stayed on in West Africa after his death.

[23] The first converts to Christianity in Yorubaland, for example, were also marginalised groups and the lowest strata of society (see Peel 2000: 233–45).

[24] The interior refers to the Ewe interior, or central and northern Eweland.

[25] For details of other mission outposts, see Debrunner (1965: 80–9).

It often happens that Anglo [Anlo] traders bring out slaves, including young boys and girls from the interior. If only we had money, we could free some of these boys and girls. Their price is usually 30 to 50 dollars. How good it would be for them and for us too; we should have people of our own whom we could educate on Christian lines.

(Brutschin, quoted in Debrunner 1965: 85).

Between 1857 and 1867 almost a hundred and fifty children, the majority the possessions of wealthy slave merchants, were either bought or accepted as pawns by the missionaries. Inspector Zahn eventually acknowledged the importance of their presence to the Christian congregation. According to him, five out of seven assistants were either ex-slaves or pawns (Debrunner 1965: 85). It was therefore inevitable that the Bremen missionaries eventually became involved in the politics of pawnship and slavery.

Anlo was at war, locked in conflict with its neighbours, for most of the period between *c.* 1850 and *c.* 1875. The British abandonment of the fort at Keta in 1856 had resulted in a sudden surge in the slave trade. In 1865, the Anlo went to war with the Ada, apparently because of an assault on the prestigious Keta-based trader Geraldo De Lima (Greene 1996a: 131; Akyeampong 2001b: 60). This war escalated into a full-blown regional conflict in 1866, when forces from Accra, Krobo, and Ada attacked Anlo, only to be defeated. In 1869, the Anlo formed an alliance with the Asante against their northern Ewe neighbours, the Peki-Ewe. Trade routes from Asante to the coast ran through Peki and Ho, and the issue of control over those routes caused the war. The Asante Wars were particularly destructive, and resulted in a surge in the numbers of enslaved prisoners-of-war in Anlo. The skirmishes between the Anlo and their neighbours meant that slave hunts were on the increase. The internal slave trade along the Salaga axis was regenerated during this period (Akurang-Parry 2002: 43). In 1862, a correspondent of the *African Times*, writing about the trade along the Salaga axis to the coastal Voltaic districts, noted that 'now and then we see slaves gagged, or put in log, passing to the Slave Coast' (Akurang-Parry 2002: 42, fn. 80). Within Anlo, there was a rise in random captures, kidnappings, pawnship, and abductions (Akyeampong 2001b: 70). A letter to the editor of the *African Times* in October 1863, submitted by somebody from Keta, bears testimony to just how endemic slavery was in the socio-economic landscape:

People who formerly traded in palm oil now buy slaves, and every petty trader invests his little money in this more profitable trade. The slaves coming from the interior by the River Volta are sent down to Popo and Ahguay; and the people of the latter places also send money here to the traders to buy slaves for them.

(*African Times*, 23 October 1863, quoted in Akurang-Parry 2002: 42)

One year before the proclamation, discussing the price of slaves, another correspondent told the *African Times* that

> At present it is thirty dollars and buyers complain. This is a great deal cheaper than what exists in the east... tribes on this side of the coast who are not British subjects... are privileged to buy what they call domestic slaves.
>
> (*African Times*, 23 February 1873, quoted in Akurang-Parry 2002: 42–3)

In 1874, the British finally abolished domestic slavery; they then established a force in Anlo to monitor the situation and ensure compliance (Akyeampong 2001b: 70). The slave trade out of Anlo did not decline instantly after 1874, however, and neither did slave holding within society. The British defeat of the Asante in 1874, which ended Asante control of the famous slave market of Salaga as well the slave routes that ran through Eweland, did not affect the supply of slaves into the Gold Coast (and Anlo). Procured from northern sources such as 'Bornu, Yoruba (mid-Niger region), Timbuktu, and the Sokoto Caliphate, Mahdi [the Sudan], Djeddah, Bornu, and Wadai' (Akurang-Parry 2002: 34–5), slaves – alongside wage labourers – continued to be exported through the Salaga trading axis[26] for longer than previously thought, and certainly well after the Proclamation.

Another direct consequence of the Proclamation of 1874, which outlawed domestic slave holding, was a rise in pawnship for debt security in Anlo (Greene 1996a: 102; Akyeampong 2001b: 70).[27] The practice of panyarring, which entailed capture of a member of a debtor's family upon non-payment of a loan, became rife in Anlo (Akyeampong 2001b: 70–1).[28] Anlo's proximity to German Togoland made it increasingly difficult for the British to curtail these practices. This was partly because panyarring was legal in German Togoland after 1896, while domestic slavery was tolerated by the authorities until 1902. Anlo and Ada slave merchants continued to bring slaves from Salaga, and smuggle them to Keta through German territory, where the authorities turned a blind eye to their activities (Dumett and Johnson 1988: 83). Kpando and Kete-Krachi (both in German Togoland) witnessed considerable slave traffic between 1880 and 90. Anlo slave masters simply relocated slaves to German Togoland, to avoid detection by the British (Akyeampong 2001b: 70). The British managed to bring the slave trade between Anlo and German Togoland under control only after 1900, convicting between

---

[26] The 'Salaga trading axis' in Akurang-Parry's study refers to trading centres north of Asante proper, such as Bonduku, Nkonranza, Kintampo, Atebubu, and Kete-Krachi (Akurang-Parry 2002: 33). Anlo traders would have accessed this trading axis for slaves.

[27] Most of the victims of panyarring were women. See for example: Pasoo v. Jiku, *Panyarring Three Persons*, District Commissioners Court, Quitta, 15–16 October 1888, (PRAAD/ADM 41/4/22).

[28] Also see cases in PRAAD/ADM 41/4/1.

ten and fifteen slave dealers each year in Keta District alone from 1903 to 1911 (Dumett and Johnson 1988: 84).

Regulating the activities of slave dealers in post-proclamation Anlo was particularly challenging for the British. On 28 January 1886, an officer of the Gold Coast Constabulary (GCC) received orders from Inspector Firminger (also of the GCC) to arrest Chief Amegashi of Afiadenyigba for slave dealing. Firminger had been notified that Amegashi was a slave holder and dealer and that it was 'well known in Adda [Ada] that he is able to get rid of slaves for anyone'.[29] Amegashi had been charged with enslaving and attempting to sell one Kwasi Moshi,[30] who hailed from Sanji in Mossi country. Amegashi owned a large plantation on the outskirts of Afiadenyigba, where he kept a number of bought people. Moshi's rather tragic life history is indicative of the experiences of slaves in post-proclamation Anlo. Moshi had been transported by a slave dealer from Mossiland to coastal Ada, from where he was bought by one of Amegashi's slave merchants. After years in Amegashi's service, Moshi had been entrusted with the task of selling 'two demijohns of rum'[31] for Amegashi. However, an incorrect account rendered by him to Amegashi meant that the latter had decided to sell Moshi to recover his losses. Amegashi put Moshi 'in log', and had him sent first to Port Segro, and then to Little Popo to be sold. As nobody purchased Moshi, Amegashi's men transported him back to Afiadenyigba and on to Dakpor (in central Eweland), where he was bought by a man named Akolu in exchange for 22 bags of cowries. Moshi worked on Akolu's farm for four months, after which he 'smuggled' himself with some market people back to Keta. Why Moshi chose to return to Keta, in close proximity of Afiadenyigba, we shall never know. Perhaps it was the only place where he felt comfortable; perhaps Moshiland was but a distant memory at this point in his life.

Amegashi was not the only person to sell/pawn Moshi. On 11 February 1886, another of Amegashi's slaves, Kwashi, was tried and convicted of slave dealing. Kwashi told a court at Keta that Moshi and his wife (also a slave) frequently disappeared to neighbouring villages, where they ran up debts in Amegashi's name. These villagers came to Afiadenyigba and demanded payment of Moshi's debts. Burdened by debt, Moshi and his wife sought refuge in a shrine in Klikor, a strategy frequently employed by slaves in need of protection. The 'fetish priest' of the shrine in Klikor had refused to help them. When Moshi's debts reached a staggering

[29] PRAAD/ADM/41/4/2; p. 142.
[30] Moshi hailed from Mossi (Moshi) country, and was probably given this name because of his ethnic origins. His first name, Kwasi (which is usually given to a person born on Sunday in Akanised cultures of southern Ghana) indicated that he was probably acquired on a Sunday.
[31] PRAAD/ADM/41/4/2; p. 139.

£12, Kwashi and another slave, Daku, took Moshi to a village in the Ewe interior – possibly in German Togoland – where they pawned him for £9. This deal was kept secret from Amegashi. Kwashi was found guilty of slave dealing and fined £5, even though he had intended to redeem Moshi after his debts had been settled.[32]

The history of the Bremen Mission in Anlo was rather tumultuous, as evangelical work was to be confronted by a number of challenges. The period between the 1860s and the 1880s was a turbulent one in Anlo history. The Anlo were involved in a number of wars: the regional conflict caused by Geraldo de Lima during the 1860s, and the Asante Wars of 1874–5. Mission stations in Anlo were plundered by advancing armies and mercenaries, though the Anlo eventually allowed the missionaries to resettle in those stations, and actively helped in their rebuilding (Debrunner 1965: 90). By 1874, skirmishes between the Anlo and the British became more and more frequent, given the increasing British influence on the coast. By 1874, the geo-political situation in southern Anlo had changed radically: the area had come under British control and been integrated into the Gold Coast colony, and the Proclamation which outlawed domestic slavery in the colony had come into effect.

Despite the obstacles encountered by the Mission, by the 1880s Christianity had become rather fashionable in one part of Anlo: Keta. Robin Horton's paradigmatic theory of religious change is only partially correct in explaining why Keta was the first nucleus of Christian conversion:[33] the residents of Keta were gradually brought out of the microcosm, which favoured engagement with localised deities, into the macrocosm, associated with the Supreme Being and the socio-economic changes of the early modern period in Africa (Horton 1971).[34] The economic situation

---

[32] Ibid: pp. 157–8. As Akyeampong points out, slavery, forms of unfree labour, and pan-yarring 'became fused in disconcerting ways' during this period in Anlo (Akyeampong 2001b: 70).

[33] I suggest that Horton's theory is only partially applicable on two scores: firstly, Keta's population consisted of a cosmopolitan mix of people from all over the Atlantic World, a factor which facilitated the Anlos' embrace of Christianity in that town; secondly, after the 1920s, against the backdrop of 'modernity', missionary activity, and integration into the colonial economy, certain sections of Anlo society began worshipping what could be described in Hortonian terms as 'lesser deities' from the geographical north with great gusto. As Baum suggests of Esulalu (Baum 1999: 128), insecurities associated with this era and the tumultuous changes associated with the Hortonian 'macrocosm' actually turned some people in some West African societies away from the Supreme Being; instead, as in Esulalu, some Anlo in the early twentieth century took solace in local deities, upon developing the belief that these deities had governed the progression of their micro-history, and had the potential to chart the course of their collective destiny as a people.

[34] It is difficult to ascertain retrospectively what exactly went on in the minds of newly converted people in Anlo. The missionaries promoted Mawu, one of the many deities in the pantheon, as the Supreme God. Mawu and Lisa, were, according to A. B. Ellis

in Keta was radically different from what was on offer in any other mission outpost in Anlo. Situated in a geographically privileged niche, Keta was the financial hub of Anlo, and had been a thriving seaport for about two centuries prior to 1850. It was a 'melting pot', accommodating influences from all its immigrant communities. After the abolition of the slave trade, it became the centre of the lucrative trade in palm oil. By the 1860s, it was inundated by German firms, as well as other European merchants and West African traders from as far away as Sierra Leone. Pioneering German firms, such as F. M. Vietor & Sons, later appointed as the commercial agents of the Bremen Mission, had a strong presence in Keta. F. Olloff & Company were also well established in Keta, and were joined by individual entrepreneurs from France and Germany.[35] The British firm F. & A. Swanzy and Sierra Leonean merchant G. B. Williams also had thriving businesses in the town. Keta was therefore, a macrocosm in Horton's terms, where the Anlo could – and were gradually forced to – engage with 'modernity'. Valentin Mudimbe's arguments successfully explain why the residents of the economic hub were the most eager to become Christian. Missionaries presented themselves as civilising agents, with Christianity portrayed as a superior cultural attribute, which supposedly aided economic advancement (Mudimbe 1997: 47–8)[36]. In Keta, not surprisingly, the Bremen mission and the German trading agencies, especially F. M. Vietor & Sons, were intimately connected. The Bremen Mission in Keta actually projected itself as the ideological arm of these companies, whom they had entrusted with the responsibility of 'showing the ignorant heathens that things go well with the devout' (Ustorf 2001: 217). This link made between piety and prosperity was constantly emphasised, and the image of the European and Christianised African businessman was manipulated by the Bremen Mission to this end. Indeed, Keta's large business community were catalysts in the process of adopting Christianity: the initial congregation consisted of

who was stationed in Anlo in 1874, the original cosmic couple credited with creating the universe (Ellis 1965: 32–3). As early as 1705, the Dutchman Bosman noted that the people of Ouidah revered something akin to a Creator God, called Mawu (Law 1991a: 65–7). Law argues (1991a: 69) that conversion in its early stages in the Slave Coast may have entailed an upgrading of the cult of Mawu and a downgrading of all other local *vodun* cults; similarly, in Anlo, Mawu and other Christian agents gradually came to overpower the various local *trowo*, *voduwo*, and other unseen forces (see Meyer 1999: 54–82). What would have occurred initially in most parts of Anlo, as in Ouidah, was a 'shift of emphasis within existing religion rather than the adoption of a totally new religion' (Law 1991a: 69).

35 German firms Luther and Seyffert, Funk and Risch, Alfred Kuhlenkampff; French firms Regis Ainé and C. Fabre were also present in Keta (Akyeampong 2001b: 84–5).

36 Similarly, Ifeka-Moller (1974) argued that in parts of Igboland, potential converts associated Christianity with a new kind of 'white power', which they believed would facilitate their access to the colonial economy and enhance their understanding of European 'technological superiority'.

traders and their relations, as many as 53 of them from the household of Williams, the Sierra Leonean merchant, alone (Debrunner 1967: 205; Ustorf 2001: 17).

People of slave origin also came to play a significant part in the spread of Christianity in Anlo. The year that Anlo came under British control, 1874, was also when the British attempted to outlaw slavery throughout the Gold Coast colony. The Proclamation of 1874 abolished the slave status of enslaved individuals. The manner in which anti-slavery policy was implemented in Anlo meant that conflict between the authorities and slave holders was largely avoided (Greene 2011: 142). The colonial authorities favoured a gradual phasing out of domestic slavery rather than a forcible, abrupt end to the practice. This law meant that there were a number of options available to enslaved people in Anlo during this period. First-generation slaves had the option of returning to their native places. Most first-generation slaves in Anlo during this period were women who hailed from inland Eweland, displaced by the recent Asante Wars of 1869–74. (What became of these slave women is discussed in detail in the following chapter.) But there were other categories of people of slave origin in Anlo. There would have been children of slave mothers and slave fathers, who would have been the least integrated into society. (Such children would have been sold on as slaves in the pre-proclamation environment.) The children of slave fathers and free Anlo women would have also been very vulnerable in patrilineal Anlo. The children of slave mothers and Anlo men were, in a sense, protected by the status of their Anlo fathers. The well-being of children of slave ancestry, especially those with slave paternal antecedents, greatly concerned some Anlo chiefs. Chiefs like Nyaxo Tamakloe of Whuti realised the value of Christianity and education in integrating such slave children into society and bettering their life chances in post-proclamation Anlo. He began sending intellectually gifted slave children to school. These children would form a large section of the English-language-educated advisers and clerks who would aid Anlo chiefs and elites in the transition to modernity. Their mastery of the English language in colonial Anlo meant that they were equipped to overcome the stigma attached to their slave status on account of their education.[37]

Thus Christianity came to be associated in the Anlo imagination with commodities like education, which facilitated participation in the colonial economy and ensured upward mobility in society. By 1890, the Roman

---

[37] This strategy, pursued by and through persons of slave descent, was enormously successful. It led to the enstoolment of a chief of slave descent in Keta in 1885 (Greene 2011: 151). This individual's maternal ancestor was brought to Anlo as a war captive. His Christianity and education actually qualified him, in the eyes of his contemporaries, for a political position in Keta, a town where 'virtually everyone' was a stranger (ibid.: 150).

Catholic Mission established itself in Keta and set up a school, while the African Methodist Episcopal (AME) Zion church followed suit in 1899. By 1903, Keta district had a boys' and a girls' primary school as well as a girls' middle school, and claimed to have '701 Christians and 394 scholars' that year, further strengthening the perception that Christianity and education were intertwined (Akyeampong 2001b: 82). The missionaries made baptism a condition for school attendance, presenting the two as mutually complementary. Christianity can also be understood within the context of increasing European political influence: Anlo had its first generation of Christian mission-educated chiefs on the eve of British colonisation.[38] Facing assimilation into Empire, these mission-educated chiefs perceived Christianity as the language of modernity, as well as an essential tool for engaging with the cultural and political developments of the era.

It was only after 1906 that Christianity acquired a firm foothold in Anlo and Anloga. Part of the reason was that, as modernity gradually changed the face of Anlo, Christianity suddenly gained the support of the most important individual in Anloga: the *awoamefia* himself. The single most significant event in Anlo's religious history was thus the death, in 1906, of *awoamefia* Amedo Kpegla, who had strongly opposed Anlo's flirtations with modernity and Christianity. Modern Anlo was largely the product of one man's imagination: Cornelius Kwawuhume, who was chosen to succeed Amedo Kpegla. Enstooled in 1906, and better known as Togbi Sri II, he is remembered to this day as the man who transformed Anlo: he reinvented the chiefdom's past and laid the foundations for its future. Sri was rather different from his predecessors, as he was a trader by profession who had lived and worked in Sierra Leone and Cameroon, and was educated in Bremen Mission Schools in Keta. He was as comfortable with the newly emergent Pan-West African middle class of professionals and intellectuals, as he was with the traditional ruling elites.[39] There

---

[38] While post-colonial scholarship retrospectively tends to represent mission and empire as part of the same structure (see, for example, Mudimbe 1997), there were numerous instances where missionaries and political administrators were in fact distrustful of each other (Isichei 1995: 92), as in Anlo. The Bremen missionaries were mainly German, and the most important European power in 1850s Anlo was Britain. Early British district commissioners, such as A. B. Ellis, disliked the Germans intensely: he claimed that 'the missionaries prayed daily against me in their chapel' (Ellis 1881: 256; also quoted in Debrunner 1967: 206). According to Ellis, the German missionaries had a low opinion of his governing methods, and in particular the policing tactics of his Hausa regiment. British administration, according to the missionaries, had been conducive to the growth of social evils, such as prostitution, drunkenness, and violence. Ellis's diaries, *West African Sketches*, were first published in 1881.

[39] Indeed, Sri's ascent may be attributed in part to the support of some powerful chiefs who identified with the traditionalist lobby, such as Nyaxo Tamakloe and Joachim Acolatse I (Mamattah 1976: 207; Greene 2002: 43).

was another feature that set him apart from previous rulers of Anlo: he was a Christian. The appointment of a Christian to the paramount chieftaincy divided the kingmakers: Sri's ascent to the stool created a stir amongst the non-Christians in Anloga, especially the Nyigbla priests. The modernising lobby however, recognised that it was only a man of Sri's calibre who could steer Anlo through this rather confusing period. This development was anticipated by others, as by the 1900s some other Anlo towns had Christian chiefs: C. T. Agbozo and James Ocloo I had been enstooled in Dzelukope and Keta respectively (Akyeampong 2001b: 112–13).

Sri's reformist agenda became clear during the very first decade of his reign. He implemented some rather dramatic political and social changes in Anloga. The *awoamefia* would henceforth be a constitutionally elected leader, devoid of the ritual cloak that hitherto had surrounded the figure.[40] The Traditional Council was created to replace the Council of Elders, though it would retain some key features and functions of the older body. The new Council was meant to serve as an elected organisation, run along the lines of any modern government, rather than on the principle of hereditary membership (Akyeampong 2001b: 113). But this move wrecked the dualistic structures of political authority in Anlo, and the Nyigbla priest no longer had any power. Sri revamped Anloga drastically, by measures such as lifting the ban on wearing European clothing imposed by the Nyigbla cult, ruling that corpses could no longer be buried in the houses of the deceased, and above all by extending a welcome to Christian missionaries and international traders (Akyeampong 2001b: 113; Greene 2002: 153). With its modernising rhetoric, at first glance Sri's project may be evaluated primarily as one of rebellion against the traditional Anlo ruling elites, from whom he tried to distinguish himself. However, it also resounded with revivalist undertones, striving to conserve what were in his opinion the more desirable aspects of 'traditional' culture and religion.

Several religious fault lines ran through Sri's Anlo. By 1906, Yewe shrine owners commanded large followings in most Anlo towns, the capital Anloga was under the dwindling influence of the Nyigbla cult, while Christian traders and their clientele were part of the urban religious landscape. With the introduction of Christianity, Anlo religion became a contested terrain between 'heathenism' and Christianity. After six decades of missionary activity, by the 1910s Anloga had a small class of western-educated Christian intellectuals, with whom Sri II identified. The greatest challenge during the first few decades of his rule was the negotiation between Christians and 'traditionalists', the intelligentsia and the chiefs, and indeed between modernity and tradition

---

[40] Ellis gives us a brief account of the *awoamefia*'s role and functions in Anlo of the 1850s (Ellis 1965: 75).

itself. Sri's sub-chiefs were an interesting mix: some were Christians in favour of his modernising agenda, while others were 'heathens'. British District Commissioner Harry Newlands's remarks capture the intermediary role that Sri often played between the colonial administration and the modernisers, on one hand, and the traditionalist lobby on the other:

The Fia [i.e. Sri] of Awuna [Anlo] who is a Christian, would certainly outrage public feeling if he acted on the opinion of the Government and most probably alienate the sympathies of many people including some of his most important sub-chiefs, e.g. those of the old regime like Chief Tamakloe of Huti [Whuti], the Fia of Avenor (who is a fetish priest in the position of Fia over the largest sub-division) and the Fia of Apipe [Afife] who is also a *tronshi* [*tro* priest].

(Newlands, quoted in Greene 2002: 47)

Sri had come to power at a crucial period in Anlo's history, during which the politico-religious structure of Anloga was gradually crumbling. Anlo had come under British control after 1874, the authority of the traditional Anloga elites was waning, and Anlo's experiments with modernity were, at that point, unalterable. In 1906, the year of Sri's enstoolment, Anloga witnessed a severe drought, earthquake, and fire in rapid succession. A series of misfortunes struck neighbouring Whuti, and priests there claimed that Nyigbla had sent the fire because the people of Anloga had invited missionaries in to construct a mission post. To them, this was a warning from Nyigbla to stop, or else Anloga, the capital, would soon be destroyed (Akyeampong 2001b: 115).

Soon after, Anloga residents apparently rushed to the farms to remove their valuables, and parents of school children forbade them from helping the missionaries in any way. To the missionaries, the fire was a conscious act of sabotage, for which the traditionalists were responsible (Akyeampong 2001b: 115). Part of the reason was that Sri had just prevailed over the traditionalist lobby and convinced them of the need for the Bremen Mission to build a church in Anloga. In the wake of these natural disasters, the traditionalists took their opportunity to attack Sri. The explanation was anticipated: Anlo was facing Nyigbla's wrath over its fascination with 'modernity' and alternative ritual networks, especially Christianity; the ancestors were registering their unhappiness at the appointment of a Christian chief. In 1906 priests of the Nyigbla and Mama Bate (associated with the sea) banned the use of sails on the Keta Lagoon (Greene 2002: 46). They blamed the declining productivity of the lagoon, and people's inability to make their livelihoods, on the political changes instituted by the new *awoamefia*. Sri eventually encouraged people to violate the ban in 1911. Indeed, the Nyigbla lobby constantly tried to undermine Sri during the first few years of his rule. Sri was in a rather tricky position: though a Christian, he could not afford to be too condemnatory of the religious preferences of his people.

The enstoolment of a Christian *awoamefia* in Anlo did not lead to mass conversion to Christianity as it had in neighbouring societies, where the spread of Christianity was intimately linked with chiefly conversions.[41] Anlo presented one of the greatest challenges in Eweland to the Mission, for apart from its business hub around Keta, the region was slow to accept Christianity. While Sri's conversion opened up Anloga and the *dutowo* south of the Keta lagoon to Christianity, the *dutowo* north of the lagoon showed little enthusiasm for Christianity until the mid-1930s. It was as late as 1936 that twenty of the first congregations were founded in northern Anlo, with Abor (located on the outskirts of Anlo) as the head station (Grau 1964: 172). According to Basel missionary Debrunner, the 'tenacious pagan beliefs' of the Anlo were the 'chief obstruction' to the spread of the Gospel (Debrunner 1965: 78). But Christianity was not identified as the solution to the social disruption that emerged out of the experiments with modernity in Anlo. Its slow uptake during the period 1910–40 can be explained partly by the arrival of several deities from the northern savanna, which made their way into Anlo via the Akan belt. It was these deities that captured the Anlo imagination, as their arrival was widely interpreted against the backdrop of locally construed perceptions of the tide of Anlo history. The popularity of these northern deities can be explained in part by the fact that their presence helped the Anlo interrogate their agency in slavery, a social practice that modernity and Christianity had come to frame as ethically problematic over the course of the nineteenth and twentieth centuries.

---

[41] This was unlike the scenario in other societies in the Gold Coast colony at the time. In Asante, the *Asantehene* Prempeh I had metamorphosed into the anglicised Mr Edward Prempeh, while in exile in the Seychelles. Prempeh was allowed to return to Kumasi in 1924. His conversion to Christianity gave the religion a degree of legitimacy in the eyes of his subjects. Prempeh's return paved the way for mass conversion to Christianity in Asante. This was because chiefs played an important role in regulation and the ideological management of the religious system in Asante (see Müller 2013). Anlo chieftaincy, by contrast, was significantly weaker as an institution, and lacked the symbolic value assigned to the institution in Asante (Venkatachalam 2007: 159–73).

6   Gods from the North, *c.* 1910–*c.* 1940

The Scourge of Witchcraft

Several new religious agencies swept into Anlo between the 1910s and the 1940s. The first such wave was associated with a cluster of deities that had their ritual hubs in an area simply known as 'the north' that referred to the savanna belt or the Northern Territories of the Gold Coast, which had historically formed the outer limits of the once-powerful Asante kingdom. Before they made their appearance in Anlo, the popularity of these gods from the savanna (Twi: *Sarem*) had reached epidemic proportions in Asante and the Akan-speaking regions of the Gold Coast in the early 1910s, where they were revered for their prowess in combating witchcraft, a proliferating social evil in early twentieth-century Akan society (Debrunner 1959; Field 1960). Ab(e)rewa, Kunde, Senyakupo, Sacrebode, and Tigare were some of these northern deities that enjoyed intense spells of fame in the Akan forest belt between *c.* 1890 and *c.* 1930 (Allman and Parker 2005). The worship of these northern gods eventually spread as far south as the Ewe and Ga coastal littoral, as the exchange of ritual commodities was a significant part of trans-regional trade in West Africa.[1]

By the mid-1920s, Kunde, one such deity whose widespread popularity had alarmed colonial authorities in Asante, was becoming a significant presence in the Anlo religious system. A police officer sent to observe the

---

[1] West African deities travelled widely, with several of them leaving the shores of the continent. For example, Hevieso, the thunder god, and chief of the Anlo-Ewe Yewe pantheon, has several manifestations in other Slave Coast societies – he is Sogbo amongst the Fon, and S(h)ango in Yorubaland, and has many incarnations as far as the New World, carried across as a result of the slave trade and subsequent waves of voluntary migrations to the modern nation states of the Americas. Sandra Barnes, in an edited volume, *Africa's Ogun* (1997), examines the numerous avatars of the deity Ogun, from his native Yorubaland to the Americas and the Caribbean islands, where he was taken by the slave diaspora. Ogun is the *orisa* most commonly associated with iron, metallurgy, and hunting in Yorubaland. As was the case with other *orisas*, Ogun was re-configured in the diasporan African cultures of the Atlantic World: for example, in Brazil, he merged with St George the warrior (Ortiz 1997: 90–104), while in Cuba he became conflated with St Peter (Ayorinde 2004: 22).

activities of Kunde worshippers in Anlo documented how these northern deities were being introduced into the chiefdom:

> A man named Adja Kwesi, a native of Ahamensu in the Buem District (near Kpando, British Togoland) claimed to have discovered the same fetish [i.e. Kunde]. Adja Kwesi consequently admitted one Tornyeviadzi and his brother Tetevi of Ablorgamey (a village near Lome, French Togoland) into the fetish, and later installed one for the village.
>
> In 1925, certain fishermen went to Togoland for fishing, and were admitted into the fetish and brought its worship to Anlo (Keta District) but did least towards its spread.
>
> The fetish recently became very wide-spread in the Anlo State when one Mensah Hiator, native of Adina, Keta, was personally initiated into the fetish by Adja Kwesi, the founder of the fetish at Ahamensu. Hiator is now the chief priest of the fetish at Adina.
>
> (Letter from Acting Police Commissioner of Keta District to Secretary of Native Affairs, 27 May 1939).[2]

Adja Kwesi, Tornyeviadzi, Tetevi, and Mensah Hiator were all small-scale 'ritual entrepreneurs',[3] typical of religious transmissions in West Africa: ritual knowledge was exchanged between societies by such individuals, eager to find novel practical solutions to the spiritual problems they faced.[4] Like their Akan neighbours, the Anlo also exhibited a keen interest in these savanna gods, and began worshipping them with enthusiasm. By the mid-1930s, colonial administrators noted that 'Kunde had several aliases' in Anlo, and was sometimes known as 'Brekete, Abrewa, Tigare, Goro, Atike, and Alafia', indicating that a number of northern gods were present in the chiefdom.[5] But later that decade the colonial

---

[2] PRAAD/A/ADM 11/1/637: Kune/Kunde Fetish.

[3] Ritual entrepreneurs played an important role in the exchange of religious ideas and practices between West African societies. This method of religious transmission contrasts sharply with the organised missionary activity characteristic of the world religions. Most scholars of religion in Africa suggest that religious transmissions between African societies did not assume a large-scale missionary-type approach associated with the world religions: new deities were introduced into societies by individuals such as traders, travellers, and ritual entrepreneurs; if these deities proved popular, they were transformed into cults with large followings. Like Adja Kwesi, Osei Kwaku, resident of Wirekye near Bonduku, travelled to Dagarti country in search of anti-witchcraft knowledge to address personal problems and returned with some ritual objects, which subsequently became known as Sacrabundi or Sacrebode, one of the most successful of the anti-witchcraft movements in the Akan-speaking belt (Allman and Parker 2005: 129). For a different view see Pashington Obeng (2006), who argues otherwise: African religions, according to him, were actively proselytising faiths.

[4] For the mechanics of exactly *how* these deities/shrines/ritual resources physically moved across cultural boundaries, see Parker (2011). Satellite shrines in the Akan belt retained relationships with Tongnaab, the 'mother' shrine in the Tong hills; this ritual relationship needed to be reinvigorated occasionally by acquiring physical substances (generally mounds of earth) from the mother shrine. The earth was transported in bags – which were considered portable shrines in themselves, known as *bo'artyii* – and used to empower satellite medicine shrines.

[5] PRAAD/A/ADM 11/1/1679: Native customs and Fetish.

Figure 6.1. Alafia shrine, established in *c.* 1900 in what was then the Keta District, Anlo-Afiadenyigba, December 2013

authorities became increasingly concerned by just how popular these gods had become in Anlo. In 1939, the same troubled police officer brought to the attention of the Secretary of Native affairs that '34 places in 31 villages where there are Kunde houses have been visited . . . each village has over 200 worshippers. It is estimated that at an annual festival of the fetish at Adina, more than 6000 worshippers attend . . . ' (Letter dated 27 May 1939).[6]

This large-scale movement of ritual commodities from the north to the central Akan forest belt at the turn of the twentieth century is well documented in the historical literature.[7] The burgeoning interest in anti-witchcraft techniques in the forest belt can be attributed to the sudden rise in witchcraft accusations. Several theories have been put forward to explain why witchcraft (Twi: *bayi*) became such a preoccupation amongst the Akan during that period. Margaret Field, the government sociologist, argued that the phenomenon was a direct result of integration into the

[6] Ibid.
[7] See McLeod (1975) on how witchcraft actually operated in small village-based communities; McCaskie (1981) on witchcraft and northern deities; Allman and Parker (2005), for a detailed study of the movement of thee northern deities from the northern savanna to Asante.

colonial economy, as the cocoa boom had broken up established social hierarchies, and altered patterns of wealth accumulation by providing opportunities to amass fortunes outside the traditional structures of Akan society (Field 1960: 105–33).[8] Power relations in Akan society changed considerably, as the traditional chiefly elites were eclipsed by the new class of 'youngmen' (Twi: *nkwankwaa*) and 'rich men' (Twi: *akonkofo*). These were people who hitherto had neither status nor inherited wealth; they had been propelled to prominent societal positions by their participation in the colonial economy. There was an established belief in Akan society that material prosperity was always obtained at the cost of somebody else's (re)productive capabilities. This belief meant that *bayi* had to be at work during this socio-economic transformation, and had to have been behind the successes of new social classes such as the *nkwankwaa*. *Bayi* facilitated wealth creation by attacking the productive and reproductive abilities of its victims. Witches (Twi: *obayifo*) could inhibit wealth acquisition by slowing economic productivity, by resorting to measures such as spoiling crops and destroying cocoa plantations. *Bayi* could also prevent an individual from accumulating human capital in the form of descendants, by rendering him or her barren. The epidemic of hitherto unknown sexually transmitted diseases in the Gold Coast colony, which significantly altered fertility rates across the forest belt, also reinforced the belief in the agency of *bayi* (Field 1960). Rural–urban migration in the Akan belt had given rise to a class of entrepreneurial women, who preferred to remain unmarried, freeing themselves from dependence on their husbands and lineages: their presence in urban areas fuelled a surge in prostitution, which partly explains the rise of viral and bacterial diseases (Allman 1996). Witchcraft was believed to attack and destroy the very channels by which wealth was generated and accumulated, as is illustrated by the emphasis on economic activity and fertility. Basel missionary Hans Debrunner concurred with Field, suggesting that what had ensued from the encounter with aspects of modernity, and especially economic mobility, was a kind of 'neurosis', which found expression in the belief in witchcraft (Debrunner 1959: 65).

That the Akan employed ritual resources from the *Sarem* to combat *bayi* is a curious phenomenon in itself. For the Akan, and Asante in particular, the peoples of the *Sarem* had been their closest 'other' for

---

[8] Field was also a psychiatrist, and she argued that the shrines of the new northern anti-witchcraft cults attracted people who suffered from types of mental illness, including depression, anxiety reactions, and more severe conditions such as paranoid schizophrenia. Most of her fieldwork was conducted in the Akan-speaking region. According to her, the incidence of mental illness could be understood against the backdrop of the rapidly altering ideology and value systems of society, a function of the sweeping economic and political changes that Gold Coast societies experienced in the early twentieth century (Field 1960).

centuries. Most of the peoples that the Asante enslaved in the past came from this area: they were generically known as *nnonkonfoo* (sing. *odonko*).[9] The Asante perceived the *nnonkonfoo* as primitive, and almost subhuman, lacking in civilisation and material development; their inability to forge large states, in the manner that the Asante had, further cemented the perception of their backwardness.[10] While the cocoa boom and integration into the colonial economy had fuelled social and economic change in the forest belt, the resource-poor societies of the *Sarem* had remained largely untouched by these developments. It has been argued that according to Akan cultural logic, therefore, the northerners, though not free from *bayi*, somehow did not suffer from the effects of the phenomenon as the Akan did. This led the Akan to conclude that the northerners must have powerful anti-witchcraft devices in their societies, which somehow neutralised the activities of witches (Allman and Parker 2005).

The reality was that the Akan had a long-established ritual trade with peoples of the north, which predated the early twentieth century: Islamic amulets and talismans obtained from Muslim traders from the *Sarem* were prized for their witchcraft-repellent properties, and integrated into Akan ritual culture as early as the seventeenth century (Owusu-Ansah 1983). During this particular outburst of *bayi*-related troubles in the early twentieth century, the previously established networks for the procurement of northern ritual resources were simply exploited more intensely. The Akan essentially facilitated the transfer of these deities, derived from the north, to their southern neighbours, the Ga and Ewe peoples, by setting in motion a general southward movement of ritual resources. Thus the Akan technique for dealing with *bayi*, which involved a number of practices, including the worship of anti-witchcraft deities, drinking protective medicines, and the use of specially treated charms, entered the Anlo religious system by the 1930s.

A letter addressed to the Secretary of Native Affairs, from a police officer based in Anlo, describes exactly how the priests of anti-witchcraft deities and their potential clients interacted with each other:

The entrance fee is 2/6 [2*s* 6*d*] with at least one kola-nut. The prospective member explains to the Priest his or her object, which is either a general protection from all evils (mainly witchcraft) from sickness, success in business etc. The ceremony of admission consists of dividing the kola-nut into two, half is given to the prospective member and half is taken by the priest. Both chew and shallow it. . . .

At the shrine of Suka of Achiave (Keta District) . . . the blood of a dog is also drunk by prospective members on admission. . . .

---

[9] *Odonko* (Twi: stranger), used most commonly to refer to a foreign-born northern slave.
[10] The term was used to refer to enslaved northern peoples of various ethnicities, such as Dagomba, Hausa, Tchamba, and Losso.

In the shrine of Tome of Agbosome [Agbozume], newly initiated members are vaccinated with black powder. They also use talismans and dress in Hausa gowns. They also practise fortune telling by killing fowls and throwing them on the ground in certain forms when in religious procession, they carry kola nuts on the point of spears.

...A member is forbidden to practice witchcraft, commit theft, murder and adultery. A member is forbidden to use any charm amulet or any form of juju....[11]

This cluster of deities eventually came to be known in Anlo as the Atike-vodu or Gorovodu deities.[12] As their northern origins were a significant part of their local appeal in Anlo, they derived their name from the *goro* – the prized kola nut, a gentle stimulant – which southern coastal peoples traded in from the north (Arhin 1979: 45–6).

Soon after the Gorovodu deities had appeared in Anlo, another distinct religious entity from Kete Krachi, located north of the Ewe-speaking region, was becoming established in the chiefdom. Kete Krachi was home to the famous Dente shrine and its oracle, the Dente Bosomfo, whose protective and clairvoyant powers were well-known throughout the sub-region. The Dente Bosomfo had established his credentials as a successful war oracle, and regional powers like the Asante turned to him for advice during every military campaign, including before the British invasion of 1873–4 (Maier 1983: 38). Krachi was a border province of the Asante kingdom in the eighteenth and nineteenth centuries, and was one of a cluster of north-eastern provinces that frequently challenged Asante supremacy. A rebellion against the Asante in 1874, orchestrated by the Krachi people, culminated in independence for Gwandjiowa, Kra-chi, Brunfo, and Buem. These states organised themselves into the Bron Confederation, over which the Dente Bosomfo exercised supreme polit-ical and spiritual authority. The Bosomfo's power rested on his control of the major trade routes that accessed large inland markets, such as Salaga. Aware of the threat posed by his presence, the Germans captured and executed him in 1894, whilst destroying his shrine and exiling most of his entourage (Maier 1983: 142–3).[13] Kete Krachi passed from German to British hands after the First World War. Although the British remained suspicious of cultic movements and monitored them closely, they were in favour of allowing the Krachi people to resurrect Dente worship, as they had developed the belief that suppressed cults surreptitiously worked to

---

[11] PRAAD/A/ADM 11/1/637: Kune/Kunde Fetish. Letter from Commissioner of Eastern Province to Secretary for Native Affairs, 27 May 1939.

[12] *Atike* = medicine; *Goro* = kola nut.

[13] In addition to the Bosomfo's wide influence, Dente's reputation and worship were spread by a number of individual ritual entrepreneurs during the 1880s. A Dente priest, Keteku Kwami, arrived in Peki in 1884. His arrival was celebrated in Peki, an indication that they displayed great enthusiasm for this god and its services (Meyer 1995: 68–9).

the detriment of colonial authority.[14] Dente's resurgence in Kete Krachi during the late 1920s was followed by the establishment of several satellite shrines in the central and southern Ewe-speaking region, as the southward movement of ritual commodities had become the general trend, set in motion by the Akan demand for northern ritual resources. By 1930, Dente worship began proliferating in the northern fringe of Anlo, in towns such as Agbozume and Klikor.[15]

In its original form, Dente was an oracular cult, consulted by states and individuals for guidance in moments of crisis. Like the Gorovodu deities, Dente was also associated with anti-witchcraft functions. In Anlo, however, Gorovodu and Dente did not retain their initial anti-witchcraft functions for long. The economic situation in Anlo was very different from the cash-crop-enriched forest belt. Anlo had suffered a severe blow after the abolition of the slave trade, and the sudden, prolific wealth creation associated with Asante was absent in this part of the western Slave Coast; there were no new social classes which corresponded to the Asante *nkwankwaa* and *akonkofo*. The incidence of witchcraft (Ewe: *adze*) in Anlo was therefore not as significant a concern as *bayi* had become in Asante. The Anlo had little use for these northern deities in their Akanised form, as anti-witchcraft ritual knowledge. Instead, they came to make sense of the arrival of these northern deities against the backdrop of their own perceptions of local history, and in particular, the rapid economic downturn and onset of poverty, caused largely by the demise of the internal and external slave trade.

The Wrath of the Slaves

The growing popularity of these unknown northern deities was a rather worrying development for the Anlo. In the Anlo religious imagination, spiritual entities and supernatural beings are invested with agency, and are believed to be capable of deliberate action. Further, the Anlo believe that religious entities attach themselves to potential devotees for a number of reasons. It is up to the devotee to discover why an entity is demanding his or her attention. The Anlo were initially at a loss to explain why so many people in their chiefdom were attracted to the worship of these northern gods. The *Sarem* was geographically further removed from Anlo than it was from Asante, and, unlike the Asante, the Anlo had not come into frequent contact with the peoples of this region.

[14] PRAAD/A/ADM 11/1/751: Dente Fetish. The Secretary of Native Affairs and the Acting Colonial Secretary exchanged a number of letters in 1921, debating whether the people of Krachi should be allowed to resurrect Dente worship.
[15] Much of this information has been procured from numerous informal conversations and formal interviews with Fofie/Krachi Dente initiates of Klikor-Agbozume and Anlo-Afiadenyigba, conducted between 2000 and 2014.

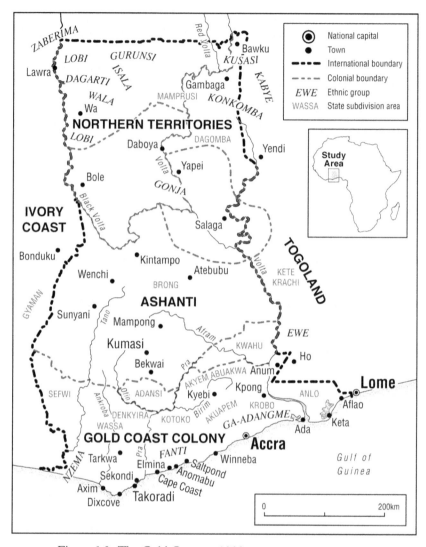

Figure 6.2. The Gold Coast, *c.* 1900

Many of my informants, including David Kwatsikor, a 78-year-old Gorovodu and Fofie devotee, echoed the views of several people in Anlo about the extensive ritual traffic from the North during this period:

The lineages of both my parents worship Gorovodu and Fofie or Krachi Dente. People in Anlo of my grandparents' generation were puzzled by the appearance of these deities, from so far away. Most of us had never been to the savanna or to

Kete Krachi. So we wondered why these deities had come here to demand our attention.[16]

Another individual from Anlo-Afiadenyigba, Komla Donkor, echoed David Kwatsikor's views:

My grandfather did not know why so many members of our patrilineage were attracted to these strange northern forms of worship. Instead of becoming Christians or worshipping our own Anlo gods, members of my patrilineage were, for some reason, being drawn to practise these northern rituals, such as drinking strange medicines and manufacturing magical objects. When they stopped doing these things, members of the family become sick and died. This was happening not just to members of our patrilineage, but to people all over the town. My grandfather and his contemporaries were mystified. Why were these rituals from these northern lands and Kete Krachi so important for our survival? It was like we were under some kind of spell. We, in Anlo, did not know much about those distant lands, as we had never been there.[17]

The Anlo began to interrogate the arrival of these deities against the meanings they attached to the savanna and Kete Krachi, the 'homes' of the Gorovodu spirits and Dente respectively. Kete Krachi occupied a special place in the Anlo imagination, as its position on the north–south trade routes made it very important for merchants from coastal societies throughout the eighteenth and nineteenth centuries. The salt–slave trade thrived along this north–south axis, and the Ada, Anlo, Ga, and other coastal peoples took salt to Salaga, which they exchanged for slaves from Dagomba, Gonja, and Mamprussi traders (Maier 1983: 28). Kete Krachi was located in close proximity to Salaga. Though it was just an intermediary location from where Anlo slave merchants bought their slaves, in the Anlo public consciousness Kete Krachi bore strong associations with the 'homes' of their 'bought people' or *amefeflewo*. Komla Donkor continued:

Most of us caught by these gods had another thing in common: we belonged to slave-owning lineages. So then we began to wonder if there was some connection between slave holding and this mysterious new religion. There were several slave women in Anlo around this time. Most were from Ewedome lands. They were slave wives to our forefathers at that time. We felt sure that the slave women must know something about this.[18]

Many of my informants, from contemporary Fofie worshipping lineages, do indeed suggest that the appearance of these northern deities caused a moral panic in Anlo. The inability of the Anlo to understand why these spiritual entities were demanding their attention became a matter of grave concern. The associations of the savanna and Kete Krachi with

---

[16] Interview with David Kwatsikor, Anlo-Afiadenyigba, 27 August 2006.
[17] Interview with Komla Donkor, Anlo-Afiadenyigba, 15 September 2007.
[18] Ibid.

slavery meant that, in a unique twist of events, the Anlo turned to their slave women – one of the most marginalised groups of people in their society – to help explain why these deities had descended upon them. There were a large number of enslaved people in Anlo during the 1930s, despite the British Proclamation of 1874, which abolished an individual's 'slave' status in the Gold Coast colony. In other Gold Coast societies, after the Proclamation, many ex-slaves sought to move back to their original homes to live among their own kin. Slaves acquired after 1874 were immediately granted their freedom, and the date of acquisition therefore came to be contested between masters and slaves in cases in colonial courts in Anlo, with slaves claiming that they had been bought after the Proclamation (Akyeampong 2001b: 70, especially fn. 125). The Proclamation was not well received in Anlo where slaves were reportedly killed when they attempted to return to their homes (Brydon 2008: 34, fn. 57). Moreover, many in Anlo believed that slaves who escaped would die soon afterwards as a result of severing ties with the deities of their adoptive patrilineages (see Nukunya 1983). Fearing this fate, the majority of inland Ewe slave women stayed in Anlo – where, in effect, they remained enslaved. David Nyamesi of Anlo-Afiadenyigba explained his slave great-grandmother's dilemma:

My great-grandmother Ama was brought to Anlo-Afiadenyigba after the Peki conflict when she was about six or seven years old along with her two sisters, who also became slave wives to my patrilineage. They hailed from a village near Ho. She had three sons for her husband (my great-grandfather), one of whom was my grandfather Kwaku Nyamesi. There is a very strong deity in our family called Mawuchoo. Ama was put under its control as soon as she came here and married her owner. This tied her to her husband and his ancestors and lineage. Her husband knew what she was thinking as a result of the magic of the deity. He knew when she was unhappy. He knew when she looked at or thought about other men. He knew when she contemplated escape. If she left her husband's household, Mawuchoo would have either brought her back to Anlo or killed her. So Ama was frightened. Ama never went back [to her natal home], but died here in Anlo.[19]

This family history reveals how, following the British Proclamation of emancipation, ritual strategies worked to detain slave women in Anlo. One such inland Ewe slave woman, the fourth wife of an Anlo slave owner, was Ablesi, who hailed from a village in the Peki area. Ablesi is credited with solving the mystery of the northern deities in Anlo-Afiadenyigba. A member of Ablesi's husband's patrilineage first brought Dente worship to Anlo-Afiadenyigba. Soon after, several members of his patrilineage followed his lead, believing too that they needed to appease Dente. Various members of this lineage also began turning to Gorovodu

[19] Interview with David Nyamesi, Anlo-Afiadenyigba, 9 December 2010.

worship, in addition to Dente. This did not please Ablesi's husband, who had converted to Christianity, and was encouraging members of his *afedo* to do the same. Seeking to understand why unfamiliar non-Anlo divinities had gained adherents in their household, members of the patrilineage were intrigued when Ablesi revealed that she had vague memories of Dente being worshipped in her ancestral village in northern Eweland. Encouraged by her Anlo owners, Ablesi travelled to her native village and then to Kete Krachi to collect more information about Dente worship.[20]

Upon returning to Anlo-Afiadenyigba, Ablesi explained that dissatisfied slaves and their gods were behind the appearance of both Gorovodu and Dente. Gorovodu was, according to Ablesi, a collection of deities from the northern savanna who were worshipped by slaves of Losso, Hausa, Kabye, and Dagomba extraction, while Dente, in her opinion, was a god from Kete Krachi that northern and inland Ewe peoples worshipped. She argued that all the slave ancestors of the Anlo, in conjunction with their gods, had attached themselves to potential devotees in Anlo to demand attention from their descendants. Slaves in Anlo, according to Ablesi, became dissatisfied spirits after their deaths. Upon marrying their Anlo masters, they were forced to accept Anlo cultural practices, speak the Anlo language, and worship Anlo gods. They became largely invisible members of society, and were erased from social memory. When they died, they were buried haphazardly without appropriate rituals being performed for them. Ablesi went on to insist that slave-owning lineages should establish shrines all over Anlo, dedicated to the memory of the slave ancestors and their gods. She proposed that a certain type of worship, which accorded slave ancestors the respect they deserved, be established in Anlo-Afiadenyigba. In response, a shrine – the first of its kind – was constructed in a settlement known as Ablesikope (Ablesi's village) in the Nyerwese division of Anlo-Afiadenyigba in the late 1930s. This shrine would serve as a focal point for slave-holding lineages to gather and worship their slave ancestors and the gods of these slaves.[21] The shrine at Nyerwese contains a stool carried away from a northern Ewe town by victorious warriors from Anlo-Afiadenyigba, and the remains of several northern spiritual objects, dedicated to the memory of slaves of the community and their gods. Ablesi's daughter, ritually renamed Nyomi, was initiated into the worship of Fofie in 1941: Nyomi's patrilineal ancestors had owned both northern Ewe and Hausa *amefeflewo* in the recent past, from whom she is descended.[22]

[20] Interview with Ajakoku, Anlo-Afiadenyigba, 15 April 2004.
[21] Ablesi's descendants continue to maintain this shrine in the Nyerwese division of Anlo-Afiadenyigba.
[22] Nyomi's initiation coincided with the burial of a prominent Anlo citizen. This date was assigned by identifying the grave that recorded the year of his demise.

Ablesi's argument was easily accepted as the Anlo had been slightly uncomfortable with the implications of slave holding for generations before the appearance of these northern deities. Historians of Anlo tell us that the Anlo were concerned about their moral responsibility as slave holders as early as the nineteenth century, as a set of practices called Fofie was dedicated to the well-being of slaves who died in Anlo (Greene 1996a: 67; Akyeampong 2001b: 69).[23] Fofie, in its original form, referred to small shrines maintained by slave holders, which contained relics or material remains associated with slaves, to keep alive the memory of enslaved people who had died in Anlo. We have little information about how popular or successful Fofie was in nineteenth-century Anlo, but the lack of records about these practices in missionary and colonial sources suggest that Fofie worship was a rather low-key phenomenon. The arrival of deities from the savanna and from Kete Krachi, the 'home' of so many of their slaves, was a deeply disturbing event in Anlo religious history, as it confirmed their dormant fears about slave holding. They were finally being punished by the gods of their slaves for their misdemeanours. Thus the newer arrival, Dente from Kete Krachi, and the older Fofie practices probably merged in 1930s Anlo into the set of practices we identify as the Fofie cult in Anlo today.

How exactly Fofie/Krachi Dente worship became established in each Anlo town probably differed slightly, depending on the individuals, circumstances, and agencies that found themselves engaged in the task of interpreting how the slave-holding past had shaped the present. What happened in Anlo-Afiadenyigba is therefore unique, though Fofie worship may have been configured in other Anlo towns through a similar sequence of events. Ablesi's role as interpreter demonstrates how inland Ewe slave women were critical to the institutionalisation of practices that aimed to address the aftermath of slave holding in Anlo. The power relationship between enslaved women and their Anlo masters had changed: no longer were the slave women frightened of Anlo deities that bound them to their adoptive Anlo patrilineages, but the Anlo hosts now lived in fear of their slave ancestors and their strange northern gods. Fofie worship, as advocated by the inland Ewe slave women, was essentially a practical and bold attempt to rewrite all non-Anlo slave women into the historical record, by exploiting the Anlo fear of these unknown deities.

---

[23] A deity called Fofie was worshipped not only in pre-1930s Anlo but also in the central and northern Ewe belt, though its functions and characteristics probably differed greatly from region to region. Spieth encountered a Fofie priestess in c. 1908, who converted to Christianity (Meyer 1999: 97). It is not clear if, in Peki of the 1900s, Fofie was a well-organised religious cult with a centralised priesthood (as in current-day Anlo) or whether it was merely a loose network of devotees, though the latter scenario is the more likely. Another possible scenario is that Fofie was brought to Anlo directly from the Akan-speaking region, and then made its way to the Ewe interior.

I collected a few detailed family histories of nineteen Fofie-worshipping lineages in Anlo-Afiadenyigba. These histories suggest that slave women of Ablesi's generation, following her example in the 1940s, went on to assist their respective lineages in the establishment of Fofie worship. Ablavi of the Nyamesi family and Akosua of the Agboado family were slave women carried away during the Asante Wars; during the 1930s, they helped these families construct Fofie shrines. These slave women suddenly found that the attitudes of their Anlo masters had softened towards them: they were no longer treated with indifference but became valued members of society whose help was needed to avert a spiritual crisis. This unexpected series of events began with the arrival of mysterious ritual techniques and ended with public recognition of the social value of all the slave ancestors.[24]

Fofie-worshipping lineages, with the help of the slave women of Ablesi's generation, sought to establish friendly ties with the households and villages from where they had obtained their slaves. These slave women began encouraging their Anlo owners and descendants to visit their natal villages in central and northern Eweland. This journey took Fofie-worshipping lineages in search of their non-Anlo kin, following the instructions of their slave women. Thirty of Anlo-Afiadenyigba's Fofie-worshipping lineages think they have been able to isolate the exact locations from which their Ewedome slave ancestors came. These Anlo lineages have continued to maintain cordial ties with their Ewedome kinsfolk. Anlo men are encouraged to marry women from the families of their Ewedome slave ancestors. As a mark of reciprocity, Anlo women also marry men from the households of their slave ancestors. To the best of my knowledge, as of 2010, there were about twelve Ewedome women living in Anlo-Afiadenyigba, related to the very women that their husbands' patrilineages once enslaved. Elias Agboado, a former magistrate I encountered, is married to Hope Agboado. Hope is one of Agboado's five wives, the great-granddaughter of Akosua, who was enslaved by the Agboado family during the 1870s; Akosua was Agboado's slave grandmother. Hope hails from Wumenu, a village near the Ho area, from where Akosua was abducted when she was in her teens; she left behind one young child in Wumenu, from whom Hope is descended.[25] Such moves are viewed by the Anlo as a means of reinforcing ties as well as making amends for the past. These gestures are essentially attempts to 'practise memory' (Tonkin 1992: 109), by making conscious attempts to keep the past alive in the present.

---

[24] Interview with Elias Agboado, Anlo-Afiadenyigba, 27 August 2005; Interview with Quasi Ajakoku, Anlo-Afiadenyigba, 29 August 2005; Interview with David Nyamesi, Anlo-Afiadenyigba, 8 December 2010.
[25] Interview with Hope Agboado, Anlo-Afiadenyigba, 27 August 2005.

As Fofie worship gradually developed into a corpus of ideas that rewrote slave women into social history, there were other mechanisms evolving in Anlo to obscure the slave origins of those with patrilineal slave ancestry. During this period, Anlo patrilineal antecedents were gradually becoming a prerequisite for full social membership in the community (Greene 1996a). Slave owners and chiefs were becoming deeply concerned about the plight of slave descendants, and especially those that lacked Anlo patriliny, in the post-proclamation landscape of 1874. These chiefs encouraged their subjects to view the descendants of male slaves as integral members of their masters' clans (*hlowo*); in time, over the course of the twentieth century, these slave descendants became virtually indistinguishable from other free members of slave-owning lineages. A range of other terminologies came into use for peoples of non-Anlo slave origin. Instead of *amefefle* (bought person), terms such as *ndokutsu* (someone you worked hard in the sun to get) and *alomevi* (person acquired through working with one's hands), became acceptable ways of referring to a slave, to 'blunt the assault on their slaves' self-esteem' and to encourage slaves to see themselves as integral parts of masters' families (Greene 2011: 144). It was becoming more acceptable for people of slave origins to participate in Anlo public life. In 1885, an individual of slave descent became a chief in Keta (ibid.: 151). This chief's maternal great-grandmother was brought to Anlo as a war captive from Ada; in terms of his patrilineal origins, he was classified as a 'mulatto' or someone of mixed European ancestry. His enstoolment was supported by the British, as well as by Chiefs Tamakloe and Acolatse, who were members of the Anlo traditional elite. This chief's maternal cousin was the trader whom Greene refers to by the pseudonym Paul Sands, whose diaries provide us with a wealth of information on the plight of persons of slave origin in late nineteenth-century Anlo. Sands reveals that members of his family continued to be insulted occasionally as '*da awa li fe ma-mayoviwo*', or grandchildren of a war captive (ibid.: 145). However, this detail did not prevent his cousin from becoming a chief. His cousin's mixed origins, paternal 'mulatto' ancestry, Christianity, and education actually made him ideal for a political position in a rapidly changing environment, in the eyes of his subjects and contemporaries. As male slaves and their descendants became more integrated into Anlo society, political authorities in Anloga gradually made evoking a person's slave patrilineal antecedents a punishable offence, to ensure and uphold social cohesion (ibid.: 144).

Slave owners with slave wives also worried about the life chances and well-being of the children of these non-Anlo women. It became common for such master-husbands to leave their property to the children of their slave wives. Children of free wives could inherit from their maternal Anlo kin, which was not an option for children of slave wives, who lacked matrilineal relations in Anlo. Bismarck Agboado (b. *c*. 1890) was the beneficiary of his status as the son of an Ewedome slave, for he inherited (along with his two brothers) all his father's property in the late 1920s, much to the indignation of his father's two Anlo wives and their children.[26] This would leave Bismarck and his brother's descendants in a better financial position than the children who were born to his father's free Anlo wives. Bismarck Agboado converted to Catholicism, and sent most of his children to mission schools; he became a prosperous textile merchant in the village. Several of his twelve sons obtained university degrees, and went on to work in a range of prestigious positions in the colonial administration and, later, in the Ghanaian civil service. The most famous of his sons is a successful lawyer. Some of Bismarck's descendants are also attached to Fofie in various capacities. Bismarck's half-brothers and half-sisters – descended from the 'free' Anlo wives of this patrilineage – have not been as fortunate or successful. There are many such instances of children of slave women, who benefited from the decisions of their Anlo fathers to bestow their wealth upon them. That these events took place during the period of soul-searching in Anlo, when Fofie worship was being configured, is significant. Ultimately, we will never know what led these slave owners to make such decisions: perhaps they were fearful of the wrath of the slave ancestors; perhaps, they were trying to demonstrate to their slave wives that they were deeply appreciative of their sacrifices and contributions to Anlo families and society; or perhaps these gestures were simply indicative of the strong affection these men had developed for their slave wives.

Chiefs, Christians, and the Northern Religion

The proliferation of Gorovodu, the strange northern religion, captured the imaginations of the colonial authorities and clergy. The campaign against these new northern deities was led by Church leaders in the Gold Coast and the neighbouring Togolands, who naturally despised these new religious cults. Church leaders were aware that cults and deities could be prohibited under the Native Customs Ordinance, if enough support was gathered against them (see Rosenthal 1998; Lawrance 2007). Gorovodu priests and worship were dismissed as 'charlatan enterprises' and 'money-making rackets'.[27] Kunde (used as shorthand for Gorovodu) practices were indeed represented as the very antithesis of modernity by Christians all over southern Eweland:

---

[26] Interview with Elias Agboado, Anlo-Afiadenyigba, 7 December 2010 (Elias is Bismarck's son).

[27] PRAAD/A/ADM 11/1/637: Kune/Kunde Fetish. Letter from Duncan-Johnstone, Commissioner of the Eastern Province to the Provincial District Commissioner, dated 10 August 1939.

It terrorises the population, prevents children from coming to school and the sick from going for attention to the hospitals and dispensaries and dupes the simple people that the fetish is the only cure for their maladies

(M. Cessou, Bishop of Lome, in a letter to Duncan-Johnstone, Commissioner of the Eastern Provinces, 1939).[28]

Kunde practitioners were blamed for several 'acts of lawlessness'. R. E. Walker, the Acting District Commissioner of Keta had, according to his successor Duncan-Johnstone, 'received complaints from Catholic priests of orgies and even wholesale slaughter of people in connection with the Kunde fetish, said to have taken place in towns at the northern edge of the Keta lagoon, such as Achiavi [Attiave] and Agbosome [Agbozume]'.[29] Another serious problem was that

'of thirty-two houses being burnt in the Agbosome division of the Keta District during the past two or three years . . . in nearly every case, the police have found it almost impossible to get any evidence. The incendiarism takes place always at night and last week, burnings which had stopped for some months began again, this time on the western side of Keta near Jitta' [Dzita].[30]

What alarmed colonial authorities most was the ease with which these religious movements crossed ethnic boundaries and colonial borders in West Africa. From their original home in the northern savanna grasslands, Kunde, Abrewa, and a series of northern gods had swept into the Akan forest belt, and, ten years later, were being worshipped in the Ewe littoral. The British colonial administration represented these cultic movements as a Pan-African scourge: as District Commissioner of the Eastern Province, Duncan-Johnstone warned his superiors in Accra that Kunde had been heard of as far as the French Congo and Gabon. Kunde was considered to be a 'politico-religious' movement, to be compared with Kimbanguism. Echoing the views of Father Dufenteny, a Catholic priest, Duncan-Johnstone wrote of Kunde:

The danger of these movements should not be under-rated. It is all the more dangerous that such movements exist in nearly every part of Africa. Should they come to understand one another and to fusion, it would be all-Africa against Europe.

Whatever the names of these movements, whether it be Kibangisu, Amieda, Amatsi or Kunde and the rest, they have several characteristics in common, and all have the same goal: leave Africa for the Africans. . . .

It is a religion essentially African, despite the things it has borrowed from the religions of Europe. It develops imperceptibility and only takes on a definite shape when it has assimilated all that can act upon the mind of the black man. Nationalistic ideas . . . need a system of mysticism capable of exciting the masses

[28] Ibid.
[29] Ibid. (Attiave and Agbozume are towns on the northern fringe of Anlo.)
[30] Ibid.

and a cement enough to unify their energies. And this they found in a paganism foreign to the European, and more particularly did they find it in the soul of paganism, the sorcerer, the born adversary of the European.[31]

Inspired by their Church leaders, the Christianised Anlo intelligentsia also encouraged the colonial government to suppress these cults. An outburst in a telegram to the District Commissioner from the Ewe League in 1940, concerning Anana Guasa, a series of practices associated with northern anti-witchcraft movements, bears testimony to the attitudes of members of such influential bodies:

Ewe League Keta and outstations comprising intelligentsia with prominent chiefs and elders strongly protest against petition to allow practice of fetishes prohibited by Anlo State Council. Practices dangerous to human life secretly and mysteriously also embodying superstition and generally demoralising and impeding civilisation.[32]

By 1939, colonial authorities had built up an admirable corpus of reports on the activities of the northern deities in several sub-regions of the Gold Coast colony. It was decided that Kunde and its different manifestations merited serious action: the worship of the deity was therefore banned by Sections Two and Three of Order in Council No. 43 of 1939, under the Native Customs Ordinance. Engaging in any aspect of Kunde worship became a punishable offence all over the Gold Coast. All outposts in the Keta District were instructed on how to deal with the prohibition order: Duncan-Johnstone advised local authorities in 1940 against a 'mass destruction' of shrines in Anlo, but advocated a 'steady and relentless drive'[33] in order to ensure that Kunde worship was gradually extinguished.

The case of one Gbedemah Dakpo of Afiadenyigba was typical of how the colonial authorities went about implementing their 'steady and relentless drive'. On 19 March 1940, the unfortunate Dakpo and an accomplice, Todokposhie, were arrested and taken into police custody at Keta. The police had obtained a search warrant for their houses. The search party was led by Ambrose Amewode, a native of Anlo, who had gathered evidence of an Alafia shrine operating from Dakpo's residence. Gbedemah Dakpo was convicted four days later in Keta, after having been found guilty of practising Kunde and not destroying his Alafia shrine. Besides, he 'had struggled with the police when handcuffed, and had allowed patients [clients/devotees] to escape by another door' as the police entered his house. Dakpo's punishment was a fine worth £25 or

[31] Ibid. These are the views of Catholic priest Father Dufenteny, echoed by Duncan-Johnstone.
[32] PRAAD/A/ADM 11/1/1679: Native Customs and Fetish.
[33] Ibid.

6 months' imprisonment, while his accomplice Todokposhie was released from custody. His 'fetish objects' were confiscated and destroyed.[34]

The role that senior Anlo chiefs, like the *awoamefia* Sri II, played in relation to managing these movements is also significant. Though a Christian, chiefs like Sri II were not condemning of all non-Christian practices. As *awoamefia*, Sri simply could not afford to alienate priests and followers of a cult that had gained such popularity in his chiefdom. Aware of the appeal of this new northern religion, Anlo chiefs actually devised methods of shielding the devotees of northern cults against the colonial prohibition order, and covertly encouraged the followers of these cults to resume their activities.

On 20 April 1940, the same man responsible for the conviction of Gbedemah Dakpo of Afiadenyigba, Constable Amewode, arrested a further six people for worshipping Kunde in two small Anlo villages, Tovieme and Zomayi. Much to his surprise, all six of them produced licences signed by Sri II that enabled them to continue worshipping Kunde, which was prohibited in the Gold Coast colony. According to Amewode's report, addressed to the Criminal Investigation Division, priests of various deities, among them Kunde, [A]lafia, Nana, Guaso, Afaga, and Apertorku, simply had to pay a fee of £30 per annum to the Anlo State Council to obtain such a licence. The money actually went directly into the Anlo Administration Treasury Fund, a step which only legitimised the presence of 'fetish' worship in Sri's 'modern' Anlo.[35] Amewode reported, in a letter meant to explain why it was so difficult to suppress Gorovodu worship in Anlo, that at least five hundred licences had been issued by the Anlo State Council.[36]

The documents about these northern deities, to be found in the National Archives at Accra, provide a rather skewed vision of the past. The alarm these movements caused and the close surveillance to which they were subjected by both the colonial authorities and some members of Anlo society may lead one to conclude that Anlo had a large modernised Christian community that saw its identity as at odds with 'fetish' worship. In practice, however, the dialogue between 'heathenism' and Christianity must have been far more complex, and the services of certain cults may have been used by precisely the people who overtly adopted a stance against it. The fact that these networks survive into the

---

[34] Ibid.
[35] In the southern Akan states, every herbalist or cult had to have a licence which was typically issued by local chiefs, and was renewable each year. These licences actually accorded practising herbalists and ritualists a degree of protection against the agents of the ever-suspicious and condescending colonial state (see Allman and Parker 2005: 143–81).
[36] PRAAD/A/ADM 11/1/1679: Native Customs and Fetish.

twenty-first century with large followings means that the moves to erad-
icate them, while being extensively documented, had little success. It is
also unlikely that the Anlo chiefs and colonial elites were aware, at that
point in time, that Gorovodu and Fofie – as well as being 'new religions' –
were also shaping broader social processes that were defining a sense of
self in the collective Anlo psyche.

Anlo-ness versus Ewe-ness (*c.* 1900–*c.* 1950)

While cultural logic was partly responsible for activating memories of the
slave-holding past, internal identity politics in Anlo and Eweland between
c. 1900 and *c.* 1950 also played an important role in coming to terms
with the ghosts of slavery. Two politico-cultural movements, which were
concerned with consolidating ideas of Anlo-ness and Ewe-ness (*Evegbe*)
as regional identities, were unfolding.[37] As a concept, Anlo-ness, which
sought to emphasise the uniqueness of the Anlo vis-à-vis other Ewe-
speaking peoples, was naturally at odds with Ewe-ness, which sought to
represent all Ewe-speaking societies as a single, unified, 'ethnic' bloc.
The reconciliation of Anlo-ness with Ewe-ness was particularly difficult
in Anlo, as the Anlo had largely come into contact with the inland Ewe
peoples through the institution of slavery: for the Anlo, the inland Ewe
were not their equals, but inferior, on account of being enslaved. The
negotiation of Anlo-ness and Ewe-ness in Anlo would therefore go hand
in hand with revisiting the Anlo agency in slave holding, and especially
their agency in enslaving inland Ewe peoples.

Anlo and 'Anlo-ness'

The Anlo *dutowo* were not unified for most of the pre-twentieth-century
past, though Anloga, the 'capital', maintained loose political and cultural
hegemony over the other towns. Anlo of the nineteenth century could be
divided into Anlo Proper, which consisted of *dutowo* from Dzita to Keta
and Anlo-Afiadenyigba; the *dutowo* north of the Keta lagoon had been
either semi-dependent or, at times, completely independent of Anloga.
While Anlo Proper had come under British control in 1874, the British
had actually signed separate treaties with other neighbouring states: Aflao
and Some in 1879 and Klikor in 1885, which suggested that they were
independent of Anlo Proper at the time of the British takeover.

Under the patronage of the colonial administration, the Anlo State
Council sought to expand the boundaries of the core Anlo state, or
Anlo Proper (Akyeampong 2001b: 113). The colonial government had

---

[37] *Evegbe* loosely corresponds to 'Ewe-ness' (Lawrance 2007: 26). *Evegbe* may also be used
to refer to the Ewe language, Ewe people, Ewe cultural attributes, and Ewe nationalism.

hitherto acknowledged that *dukowo* like Dzodze, Wheta, Afife, Avenor, Fenyi, and Some were bound with Anlo only for administrative purposes, although they were not part of Anlo Proper. In 1901, the Native Jurisdiction Ordinance, created to facilitate the British policy of indirect rule – which implied that the chiefs were administering their territories on behalf of the government – was applied to Anlo. The colonial government recognised most Anlo chiefs as independent rulers of their *dutowo* until 1910, when an amendment to the Native Juristiction Ordinance, implemented in the Keta District, made the *awoamefia* the head chief, and other chiefs in Anlo subordinate to him, rather than the District Commissioner. This sparked off protests in almost all neighbouring *dukowo*, as several of them had been independent of Anloga at the time of British colonisation, and had historically resented Anloga's political influence in the area.

F. K. Crowther, Secretary for Native Affairs, was responsible for assessing the sovereignty claims of several southern Ewe *dukowo* and assigning them to their administrative units. His investigations, enshrined in the Crowther Report of 1912, were implemented almost immediately by the Gold Coast administration. According to Crowther, the states of Aflao, Klikor, Dzodze, Fenyi, Kleve, Wheta, Afife, and Avenor 'serve Awuna [Anlo] without question', and hence did not need to have their independence recognised.[38] This declaration was unwelcome in most of the *dutowo* north of the Keta Lagoon; the state of Some put up the greatest resistance to this move, declaring independence and seeking to annex neighbouring Dzodze too, as an assertion of independence from Anloga (Amenumey 1997: 25).[39]

Anlo legitimisation of the Crowther report, which broadened the limits of the chiefdom considerably, rested on the fact that these areas had been part of the Anlo Confederation, or Greater Anlo, during the wars against Anexo and northern Ewe of the 1750s and the 1870s respectively. Traditions and myths in Anlo Proper were quickly realigned to accommodate this shift: one event that was alive in the public consciousness of the Anlo was the Asante Wars (1869–1874), when the Anlo *dukowo*

---

[38] Crowther subsequently published the 'The Epwe Speaking People' in *The Gold Coast Review* in 1927, which contained the gist of his report (see Crowther 1927).

[39] PRAAD/A/ADM 11/1/1091: Fia Adama of Agbosome vs Sri. The arguments in favour of Some's independence are examined by the Gold Coast government in this report. The traditions of the people of Some claim that their ancestors were refugees from Keta, driven out by the people of Anloga in collaboration with the Danes; they moved to land provided by Klikor and Aflao upon which they established their capital, Agbozume. But as Klikor and Aflao were under the control of Anloga, for Crowther, this rather clandestine oral tradition only justified Some's status as part of the chiefdom of Anlo. Another detail, however insignificant, needs attention: Sri II was supported fully in his endeavours to enlarge the geographical limits of Anlo Proper by Crowther, who was a personal friend (Akyeampong 2001b: 113).

had actually formed an alliance with the Asante to fight the central and northern Ewe *dukowo* (Mamattah 1976; Amenumey 1986: 51–2).[40] As the only historical experience that the majority of Anlo *dutowo* shared was their membership of this alliance, the memory of this event was exploited to shape a sense of unity: songs, myths, and folk tales based on the event came into existence to celebrate Anlo participation in these wars, which was represented as the legitimising reason for the unity of Anlo.[41] The Asante Wars, which disrupted Anlo life considerably, had resulted in a drastic increase of displaced people and an influx of slaves into the community, mostly prisoners-of-war (*ametsivawo*) and bought people (*amefeflewo*), who originated in central and northern Eweland. While it is difficult to estimate the exact foreign slave population of Anlo at any one time, it is widely accepted that the period between the 1870s and 1920s witnessed the peak of domestic slave holding: in addition to the slaves acquired during the Asante Wars, the collapse of the trans-Atlantic slave trade also contributed to a larger slave presence in Anlo as in most societies of the Slave Coast (Wendl 1999: 112).[42] As Dente made an appearance in Anlo while they were in the process of renegoti-ating Anlo-ness by othering the central and northern Ewe, the practices associated with the cult became a platform for articulating themes such as foreignness, slavery, and emphasis on an Anlo identity vis-à-vis the northern and central Ewe: the explanation of the slave women like Ablesi about the deity's raison d'être in Anlo was therefore widely accepted, as it made sense in the context of other public events.

As cultural projects which cemented a sense of Anlo-ness were play-ing out in the social and ritual spheres in the Anlo *dutowo*, other politico-cultural movements swept across Eweland. By the 1930s, vari-ous Ewe groupings, including some Anlo, participated in a movement to unite the Ewe-speaking peoples across the Gold Coast and the Togo-lands, arguing that colonialism had divided a people who historically had been one. The irony was that the evidence of the past provided little support for this political development: the Ewe-speaking societ-ies had entered the twentieth century through radically different histor-ical trajectories, sharing few similar experiences, and had been locked

---

[40] Amenumey depicts the Anlo Confederation as a willing alliance of states, rather than an imposition of Anlo Proper hegemony. According to Amenumey, the Anlo confederation came into being in the 1780s, and included *dukowo* east of Kedzi (Amenumey 1986: 51).

[41] Several literary works that legitimised an Anlo identity were produced during this dec-ade, the most noteworthy being Daniel Chapman's *Anlo Constitution*, published by Achimota Press in 1944.

[42] The proportion of slaves in societies of the Slave Coast did not, at any moment in time, exceed those in the neighbouring kingdoms of Dahomey and Asante, where a third of and half the total population respectively were enslaved during the nineteenth century (Wendl 1999: 112).

in several conflicts against each other throughout the nineteenth century. Why then, had they suddenly come to think of themselves as one people?

The Invention of Eweland

'I am as happy as a child on its birthday. I too see this day as a *birthday of our Ewe nation.*'

(Inspector Zahn, quoting one of his native assistant's reactions to the celebration of the jubilee (1847–97) of the Bremen Mission between the Mono and Volta, quoted in Debrunner 1965: 122).

The creation of the concept of an ethnic Ewe nation was, in a sense, an 'evangelical project' (Peel 1989: 198), the artifact of Protestant German missionaries who began their work in the area during the 1850s.[43] Even the very term 'Ewe' has its origins in missionary ethnography.[44] As Inspector Zahn's remarks above suggest, it was within the NMG that the idea of Ewe unity germinated: in tune with Protestant Germanic notions of nationhood, a common language was taken to be the obvious indicator of political and cultural unity, seen to be associated with all the linkages that made up a nation. Missionary discourse represented the Ewe not only as a cohesive linguistic entity, but also as formerly a single political unit, one which had degenerated into several 'tribes'. Missionaries envisioned their work in paternalistic terms: the warring Ewe sub-groups were to merge into one, 'like our German people' and 'to speak in a new tongue', the mission-standardised Ewe language, in a 'Christian manner' (Zahn, quoted in Ustorf 2001: 195). In accordance with this vision of a Christian Ewe nation, paramount importance was placed on standardising the dialectical variations of the Ewe language, and translating the Bible. In 1857, Bernhard Schlegel had produced *Key to the Ewe Language*, containing 2,400 Ewe terms and their German translations. The improvements made to this text by Westermann culminated in a Ewe-German dictionary of 20,000 terms. Another significant addition to the corpus of Ewe literature came in 1906, when Jacob Spieth translated the Bible in its entirety into Ewe.

---

[43] Similarly, Peel argues that the evolution of a Yoruba ethnicity was the 'cultural work' of missionaries of the Church Missionary Society (see Peel 1989: 198).

[44] Missionary Dauble, one of the first missionaries to visit the inland Ewe in 1853, wrote that people (i.e. the inland Ewe) described themselves as 'Weme', meaning people of the valleys, which Dauble transcribed as 'Eweme'. Missionary Schlegel called the language of the entire linguistic cluster 'Eiboe'; according to him, the coastal people, i.e. the Anlo, spoke a dialect of the language, which he called 'Aungla'. The word Ewe was probably a corruption of Eweme or Eiboe, and it originated out of the attempts of the early missionaries to name the language and the peoples amongst whom they were working (Kraamer 2005: 61–2).

The Ewe nation was born in the missionary imagination, invented through missionary ethnography, and became the shared burden of Christian converts across Eweland. As Meyer argues, the Bremen Mission applied romantic Herderian notions of nationhood to define and establish ideological control of the Ewe nation they had created (Meyer 2002). The main aim of the missionaries was to sponsor a reinvention of Ewe national characteristics, which, they believed, had been lost through centuries of warfare and division. It was only through Christianity that the Ewe nation could be realised, revived, and subsequently preserved (Ustorf 2001: 191–2). This conception of the Ewe nation existed in a discursive space only accessible to the Christian, mission-educated Ewe-speaking people, who naturally became the first exponents of the Ewe Unification movement. The Anlo engagement with the project of Ewe-ness was unusually difficult on two accounts. First, the inland Ewe peoples had been their closest other for centuries, their enemies in combat, and their slaves. Second, the concept of an Ewe nation appealed only to the Christianised Anlo, the mission-educated elites or 'ethnic intellectuals' in Peel's terms; it had little currency for the 'less concerned mass of the ethnic constituency' (Peel 1989: 200–1), the 'heathen' Anlo. How did the Anlo engage with the politics of Ewe-ness?

Anlo and Peki were the only two Ewe-speaking regions that had been integrated into the Gold Coast by the 1890s, while most other Ewe-speaking *dukowo* became part of German Togoland. Not surprisingly, ideas of Ewe-ness appealed to people such as the Anlo *awoamefia*, Togbi Sri II, who was educated in Evangelical Protestant schools, and was a Christian.[45] While, as a Christian, the idea of an Ewe nation probably had some ideological appeal to him, Sri was aware of the economic benefits of sponsoring the idea of 'Ewe-ness' as early as the 1910s (Greene 1996a: 142–3). German colonisation had put an end to Anlo traders frequenting Lome and other commercial centres in Togo, adversely affecting the Anlo economy. Movement across the border was severely curtailed, while taxation on either side was also a serious cause of agitation. In 1919, Sri visited Lome, in an attempt to convince the authorities to reverse the Simon–Milner agreement, which partitioned Ewe-speaking societies between the Gold Coast and the two Togolands (Akyeampong 2001b: 191–2). Thus many of the initial supporters of the Pan-Ewe movement

---

[45] Sri's position on the Pan-Ewe movement was fraught with contradictions. While he campaigned for free trade between British- and French-controlled spheres, he remained uncomfortable with the inland and northern Ewe. He did not want an independent Ewe nation, but wanted to unite all Ewe peoples under British colonial rule, which he believed was superior to German or French colonisation. His offer of 10,000 men to the British army to help defeat the Germans during the First World War is indicative of his pro-British position (Collier 2002; Greene 2002: 23).

were members of the Anlo political elite, who were in fact traders, suffering on account of the embargoes and restrictions at the border. In its earliest phase, Ewe unification was mainly advocated by coastal trading communities, whose support was motivated mainly by their own special interests. Other significant ideological players in the Pan-Ewe movement at this stage were the Ewe-Brazilian merchants (the 'returnees'), descendants of freed Brazilian slaves who made their way back to the areas around Anlo and Lome (Welch 1966: 68–9).[46]

Unlike the more potent ethnic nationalisms of the time, Ewe nationalism remained relatively ill-articulated, and never really transformed itself into a movement that enjoyed mass support amongst all the constituent Ewe groupings for whom it claimed to speak.[47] Ewe intellectuals, chiefs, and educated Christians produced two political movements after the 1910s, both of which metamorphosed into political parties that made use of Pan-Ewe sentiments to varying degrees. Ewe unification, a movement that aimed to unite the Ewe across the Gold Coast and the Togolands under British auspices, found its outlet in the All Ewe Conference (AEC), established in 1946. The Accra-based Anlo intellectual, Daniel Chapman, was one of the founding members of the AEC; this group enjoyed support from the Anlo elite.[48] The AEC occasionally evoked Ewe sentiments – belief in the unity of Ewe culture, common customs and a shared history – to justify its project. In addition to Anlo, the AEC was popular elsewhere along the coast, which further strengthened the perception that its politics were strongly controlled by an Anlo element, as promoting ties with coastal societies was a priority of the Anlo and their economy. The leaders of the AEC, nevertheless, did try to incorporate the northern and central Ewe in their conception of an Ewe nation, a move which was not appreciated by those groupings, alienated by historical rivalries (Nugent 2002: 147–98).[49]

[46] Sylvanus Olympio, (later head of independent Togo), though a 'Brazilian', was an Ewephile and did much to encourage support for the Pan-Ewe movement. Many other leading figures could trace their origins to such Brazilian families, whose diasporic origins made them active players in various West African cultural nationalisms.

[47] Ewe nationalism contrasted with Asante nationalism, which peaked during the 1950s, and posed a serious threat to the emergent Ghana (Allman 1993). Ewe-centric historians, such as Amenumey, tend to exaggerate the nature and intensity of the Ewe sentiments involved in this project (Amenumey 1989).

[48] Daniel Chapman was, like Olympio, of non-Anlo origin, with Afro-Brazilian patrilineal antecedents. How his non-Anlo patrilineal origins influenced his own sense of Anloness or Ewe-ness is unknown. It is significant that he was more comfortable with the politics of Ewe-ness: perhaps his non-Anlo patrilineal origins worked against him to some degree in Anlo society. Interview with Winston Churchill Van Lare, Accra, 20 April 2014 (Van Lare is an Anlo from Keta, of Dutch patrilineal antecedents).

[49] The Anlo were not the only Ewe-speaking grouping who had difficulty with Ewe identity politics. After the First World War, German colonies were divided between Britain and France. The administration of British Mandated Togoland was to be brought into line with procedures in the Gold Coast colony. It was decided to group the 68

The AEC was rivalled and superseded, however, by an organisation that championed the cause of Togoland unification rather than Ewe unification. After Germany's defeat in the First World War, German Togoland was divided into British and French Mandated Territories, and new colonial borders ran through Ewe-speaking areas. Togoland unification, championed by the Togoland Congress (TC), advocated the idea of reuniting the two Togolands. This project was backed by Ewe groupings within both Togolands, as well some of the non-Ewe communities in parts of Eweland, like the Central Togo minorities.[50] It was from the Ewedome belt that the TC drew its most committed supporters. Interestingly, the TC sought to exclude the Gold Coast Ewe – the Anlo and the Peki – mainly because they were fearful of creating an Anlo-dominated regional grouping. Skinner argues that Togoland unification was actually driven by a specific social group, with an identity based on professional activities rather than ethnic affinities: for the leaders of the *Ablode* (freedom) movement, their identity as educated intellectuals was more important than their membership of the same ethnic group (Collier 2002; Skinner 2007: 141–3).[51] Advocates of the *Ablode* movement felt that their recent integration into the Gold Coast colony and their location at its geographical fringes had resulted in the economic and political marginalisation of British Togoland as a region; their politics were acutely shaped by a sense of regional disadvantage, rather than a sense of shared Ewe or Togolander identity.

Although some Anlo had cultivated strong Pan-Ewe sentiments, they were opposed on two fronts, and excluded from participating in the

identifiable chiefdoms under larger kingdoms to aid in their administration. Authority to rule was to be vested in the hands of chiefs who would rule on behalf of Britain, in accordance with their policy of indirect rule. Historical patterns of organisation and ethnic similarities were taken into account during this enterprise (see Nugent 2000). Interestingly, ten major divisions resisted assimilation into the British-created provinces of Akpini, Avatime, Asogli, and Buem. Most of these units (namely Abutia, Adaklu, Anfoega, Gbe Ewe, Goviefe, Tsrukpe, and Ve) were ruled by Ewe chiefs and peopled by an Ewe majority. Many of these chiefs did not want to be subordinated to other chiefs whose status was the same as theirs. They insisted that they had always been historically separate entities and could not merge with other chiefdoms: elsewhere in Eweland, the idea of *Evegbe* simply did not unite people.

50 Avatime, Buem, Likpe, and Santrokofi were some of the states peopled by Central Togo minorities (see Nugent 1997).

51 Even the very word *Ablode* (freedom) is problematic, as it does not correspond to the actual aims of the TC, which were rather ill-articulated and confused. At times they appeared to be reunification of the two Togolands into an independent state, and, at other times, to resist integration of British Togoland into the Gold Coast. The CPP was the main enemy of the TC in the run-up to independence, as the former supported the decision to integrate British Togoland into Ghana, and leave French Togoland under the control of France. It would seem that *Ablode* was employed within this context – to mean not political independence, but rather a freedom from Gold Coast politics, CPP domination, and from the colonial border that divided the former German Togoland (see Collier 2002; Skinner 2007).

organisations that advocated the cause of regional unity. The TC further believed it could strengthen the position of Togolanders within the arena of Gold Coast politics only by excluding the Anlo and Peki, disliked for their domination of church and trading networks. The Peki and northern Ewe dabbled in the politics of both the AEC and TC. However, the Peki bitterly resented the Anlo, mainly because of the alliance the latter had made with the Asante during the Asante Wars, an event lodged firmly in the historical consciousness of the inland Ewe groups. Isolated by both the Peki-Ewe and the Togolanders, the Anlo were therefore prompted to look for links in their own hinterland, rather than wholeheartedly participate in Pan-Ewe politics. Not surprisingly, the AEC essentially became defunct by the late 1950s, as the representatives of the various Ewe communities within the Conference were driven apart by irreconcilable differences. By the 1950s, the TC, to which the Anlo paid little attention, was the only remaining organisation championing the cause of regional unity.

The Anlo position had been somewhat consistent throughout the previous decades: it was apparent that they valued their links with the coastal Ewe, rather than the inland (both central and northern) Ewe. In 1943, the Anlo State Council (ASC) petitioned the Secretary of State for the Colonies once more to eliminate controls at the frontier between Attiteti and Grand Popo (Akyeampong 2001b: 192), claiming that the peoples of the Keta District had much in common with all communities east of the Mono River. Keta drew a wide clientele from the coastal communities in French Mandated Togoland, and the Anlo State Council's demand was clearly motivated by a desire to maintain a dominant position in the economy east of the Volta. Nugent however, suggests that campaigns such as the one against the border controls were always half-hearted, and that the Anlo never sought unification with the coastal communities located east of Keta. Even though Pan-Ewe sentiments were developing on either side of the border in both colonial and post-colonial times, these communities actually favoured the existence of a border, as they constantly devised methods to exploit it for material and financial gain. Towns located at the border between the Gold Coast and French Togoland, and subsequently Ghana and Togo, became thriving centres of illicit trade, 'theatres of opportunity' for people who live in the borderlands (Nugent 2002: 272). Despite the occasional display of nationalistic and ethnic sentiments, sufficient groups of people actually preferred the maintenance of the status quo to ensure the survival of the borders that divided Eweland at various stages of its history (ibid.: 272–3).

Meyer offers us another explanation for why Pan-Ewe politics were unsuccessful (see Meyer 2002). The project of nation building, as undertaken by the Bremen Mission, was essentially contradictory: while the nation was to be realised within the Protestant Church, existing political structures that were put in place by the colonial powers, like chiefs and the colonial administration, could not be altered. Meyer argues that nationhood, or the process meant to bring about the organic growth of the nation, was encouraged, while nationalism, perceived as being anti-colonial and dangerous, was actively discouraged. The organic growth of the Ewe nation was therefore stunted, as the process lacked a viable nationalist project, one of the crucial elements of nation building. The Bremen Mission's experiment, which entailed creating an Ewe nation within colonial structures, therefore failed. In addition to the creation of a nation, the chief players within the Bremen Mission such as Inspector Zahn had made clear that the aim of the Mission was to have a self-sustaining, self-governing Ewe church, meant to serve as the moral backbone of the Ewe nation. Not surprisingly, in an Ewe nation without a political project, the Bremen Mission became the main arena of anti-paternalistic resistance: the pinnacle of Ewe nationalistic struggle was realised when they made the Church an Ewe one (Meyer 2002: 192). During the First World War, German missionaries were expelled from the British-administered areas, including Anlo. Although Scottish mission-aries were encouraged to fill the void, by 1922 the Bremen Mission had metamorphosed into the Ewe Presbyterian Church, run exclusively by Ewe clergy (Debrunner 1967: 292). Yet, even this display of 'Ewe-ness' was temporary, as by 1929 the Ewe Presbyterian Church had renamed itself the Evangelical Presbyterian Church.[52]

Perhaps Ewe political nationalism may have been a failure at the time, because it was devoid of a strong sense of Ewe-ness or *Evegbe*, which was needed to sustain it as a movement. Though the project of forging a sense of *Evegbe* amongst the culturally diverse and politically disparate Ewe-speaking communities was destined to take longer on account of its sheer complexity, it was, nevertheless, slowly but surely developing in the socio-cultural sphere. Several myths about the unity of the Ewe were being codified by Ewe-speaking societies in their oral traditions during the first half of the twentieth century: the idea of a common mass migration from Ife, followed by settlement and subsequent dispersal from Notsie, which was to become the unifying myth of all Ewe peoples, was probably first institutionalised in Anlo, initially by the Bremen missionaries. The 'Notsie paradigm' was firmly established only as late as the 1960s. Notsie had changed in status from being just a religious centre famed for the efficacy of its nature spirits to the mythic Ewe homeland from which all

---

52 The idea of an Ewe church could not be sustained for long. Eweland included several groups that claimed to be non-Ewe, like the Central Togo minorities. The change in the name was mainly to demonstrate to these minorities that the Church was not exclusively an Ewe one, and that they were not being excluded from church affairs or regional politics.

Ewe peoples had originated (Greene 2002: 19–37). The story of Togbi Agorkoli's oppression of his Ewe subjects, which resulted in their flight from the walled city, was common knowledge, as it had been taught in schools all over Anlo by the late 1950s.[53] The novelty of the concept of Ewe-ness is illustrated by the fact that the *Hogbetsotso* festival, supposedly commemorating the flight from Notsie, was instituted in Anlo only in 1962, by Togbi Adelaza II, successor to Sri II. *Hogbetsotsoza* – from the Ewe words *hogbe* (homeland, in this case Notsie) *tsotso* (exodus) and *za* (festival) – has become a celebration of Ewe-ness, reproducing the story of Togbi Agorkoli's oppression of his Ewe subjects. Chiefs from all the constituent subdivisions of Anlo are expected to send delegations to Anloga, to celebrate their flight from Notsie and arrival at Anlo. The problem of explaining relationships with the other Ewe peoples was overcome rather easily with the incorporation of the Notsie myth.[54] The differences between Ewe-speaking people were due to the three different migratory routes they took after the flight from Notsie: the northern Gbi Ewe eventually settled around Hohoe, Peki, and Kpando; the second grouping converged at Ho, Kpetoe, and Adaklu; while the final section comprising the Anlo and their neighbours settled along the coast.

From the vantage point of the early twenty-first century, Ewe ethnicity appears to be the result of the combined imaginaries and collective actions of many players: missionaries of the NMG who laid the conceptual foundations of the Ewe nation; early ethnographers, colonial officials, and travellers who painstakingly documented Ewe customs and traditions; Christianised Ewe who campaigned tirelessly for some form of self-rule; Ewe intellectuals who authored versions of their own history against the backdrop of their ill-fated ethno-nationalist project; and post-colonial politicians whose management of ethnicity within Ghana and Togo have led to a re-conceptualisation of the cultural parameters of Ewe-ness during the post-independence era. However, a paradigm has developed in relation to the study of the evolution of ethnicity in West Africa: the idea that the cultural processes, agencies, and actors associated with Mission Christianity were crucial in the creation of ethnic

---

[53] Christianised Ewe intellectuals also often draw parallels between the escape of the Israelites from Egypt and the Ewe exodus from Notsie, with the Ewe experience of oppression under Agorkoli's rule equated with the experience of the Israelites in Egypt (Greene 2002: 36).

[54] Christianised Anlo intellectuals inserted the story of the origins of the Ewe directly into biblical accounts and the mission-authored history of the Ewe: for instance, Anlo historians such as Charles Mamattah (1976) and Agbotadua Kumassah (2009) subscribe to the idea that the Ewe, along with all major African ethnic groups, were descended from Noah's son, Ham; their long migrations took them to areas which correspond to the modern nation states of Egypt, Sudan, Ethiopia, Mali, Nigeria, the Republic of Benin (Ketu), Togo (Notsie), and finally to their present abode in south-eastern Ghana.

identities in colonial Africa has become embedded in the academic literature (see Peel 1989, 2000; Ranger 1989; van den Besselaar 2000; Meyer
2002). Early missionaries and Christianised elites, or 'ethnic intellectuals' in Peel's terms (Peel 1989: 200), are accorded a pivotal position in
shaping the cultural and historical contours of ethnicities in some West
African societies.

An examination of the Anlo case reveals that the ideological project of
reconciling Anlo-ness with Ewe-ness was not undertaken solely by such
'ethnic intellectuals', and that the wider role of ethnic intellectuals in forging the actual linkages that sustained these ethnicities in West Africa may
been exaggerated. In Anlo, marginalised slave women like Ablesi, dissociated from the language, practices, and cultural capital associated with
Mission Christianity, were instrumental in erasing the difference between
the Anlo and the inland Ewe: practices associated with Fofie, instituted
upon the recommendation of these women, played a key role in acceptance of the idea of *Evegbe* in Anlo (see Venkatachalam 2012). Anlo-ness
was essentially negotiated by dual – and contradictory – processes of 'othering' the inland Ewe slave ancestors, as well as incorporating them into
Anlo society and lineage genealogies, as seen in the ritual sphere. Most of
the ancestors honoured through the Fofie cult, which became an important religious presence in the 1930s, were foreign Ewedome and northern
Ewe slaves, who were, prior to the 1930s, perceived to be very different
from the Anlo. Through Fofie worship, foreign Ewedome ancestors eventually came to be revered in Anlo shrines, and rewritten into the historical
record: these moves led to a broadening of the definition of kinship as
it was locally construed in Anlo, to include Ewedome peoples, a move
which enable the Anlo to regard the other Ewe-speaking peoples as similar and related to themselves. Fofie-related practices helped the Anlo
address their troubled historical relationship with their closest 'other' –
the inland Ewe – against the backdrop of growing Pan-Ewe consciousness. Anlo, where definitions of who merited the status of an 'insider'
were based on elaborate myths of origin, actually witnessed a redefini-
tion of the clan system to incorporate the supra-regional identity during
the 1940s (Greene 1996a: 148–52). While it may be argued that the
northern and central *dukowo* of Eweland had become Ewe through a
Christian trajectory (Meyer 2002), the Anlo had ironed out their differences with other Ewe groupings by engaging with a corpus of 'heathen'
practices (Venkatachalam 2012). It is this tension that differentiates the
Anlo from other Ewe groupings. In the popular Ewe and Ghanaian consciousness, it is the general 'idolatrousness' of the Anlo, that set them
apart then – and continues to distinguish them now – from other Ewe
peoples.

Ewe-ness as a concept and a supra-regional identity eventually came
to be further sharpened within the context of Ghanaian and Togolese

politics after each country achieved independence, respectively in 1957 and 1960. As an ethnic and political identity, *Evegbe* continues to have great currency in Anlo, as evidenced by ethnic politics within the parameters of the Ghanaian state. The Anlo also regard the northern and inland Ewe as part of the larger family of Ewe-speaking people, their closest political allies in contemporary Ghana (Nugent 2001: 411–12, 424–6; Venkatachalam 2012: 63–4).[55] The shift in the Anlo imagination, from seeing the inland Ewe as enemies and slaves to kinfolk, occurred in part due to the actions and interventions of slave women such as Ablesi. Thus, the arrival of mysterious northern gods in Anlo during the 1930s, from Kete Krachi and beyond, inadvertently set into motion a number of crucial socio-historical processes, which reworked definitions of ethnicity and identity by critically interrogating Anlo agency in the practice of slavery.

---

[55] One of the ways in which this sense of *Evegbe* has manifested itself has been through support for the same political party, the NDC, which has formerly been associated with Ewe interests.

7   *'Yesu Vide, Dzo Vide'*:[1] The Dynamics of Anlo Religion, *c.* 1940–*c.* 2010

Reconstructing a history of Anlo religious practices is extremely challenging on account of the ever-changing nature of the religious system. The Anlo have acquired the religious entities of their pantheon on a basis that is both whimsical and calculating. Trade, conquest, and warfare have introduced them to new gods and religious techniques, which they incorporated into their religious system if they found appropriate use for them. Individual ritual entrepreneurs have introduced new deities depending on their perceptions of existential concerns prevalent in the Anlo religious marketplace. The ancestors have been reinvented through each successive period in history to address changing spiritual needs of every generation, depending on how the relationship with the past has been re-evaluated. Large, structured cultic followings have developed around some spiritual entities, while other entities have quickly (and mysteriously) faded into oblivion. The more successful Anlo cults are malleable, changing structurally and functionally, capable of mutating to address the shifting existential concerns of their devotees. The less successful cults have lost their appeal over time, as their social and religious functions become obsolete. Fofie, I argue, is one such less successful cult, which has been steadily dwindling in importance from its institutionalisation in Anlo during the 1930s, as the plight of the slave ancestors has become less of a concern with every passing generation.

Anlo slave-owning lineages identified several specific measures needed to appease the slave ancestors and their foreign gods during the 1930s. During this period, the religious landscape in Anlo was also progressively becoming Christianised, with the establishment of many new churches. As in other parts of Eweland (Meyer 1992, 1999), the European missionary project and conversion to Christianity left some converted Anlo with negative impressions – varying in strength – about certain aspects of their culture and pre-Christian religious traditions. On conversion these Anlo Christians could not condemn all non-Christian practices in their

---

[1] *Yesu vide, dzo vide* (Ewe: A little bit of Jesus, a little bit of *dzo*), a phrase often used to describe the religious behaviour of less stringent Christians by more stringent ones (see Meyer 1999: 106).

entirety, since their multiple identities – as Anlo, Ewe, Gold Coasters, and later Ghanaians – meant that they had to honour, or at least tolerate, some 'heathen' practices that celebrated and upheld these identities. After the 1940s, Christian Anlo (including members of Fofie-worshipping lineages) found themselves locked into a debate on exactly which aspects of their non-Christian heritage were 'primitive' and undesirable, against the backdrop of colonial and post-colonial modernity. The form the Fofie cult assumed during the second half of the twentieth century was influenced by the broader negotiation between Christianity and non-Christian practices in the Anlo public sphere. The steady decline in the importance of the slave ancestors from the 1930s can be attributed not only to the uptake of Christianity, but also to gradual changes in the dynamics of the Anlo religious system, which has prevented replacement cults such as Fofie from thriving. I argue that two distinct phases in the development of the Fofie cult can be identified between the 1940s and the present, which synchronise with broader changes in the religious system: first, a phase of cooperation over followers with other cults and Christianities, between *c.* 1940 and *c.* 1990; and, second, a phase of competition with these other religious agents for followers, from *c.* 1990 to the present.

Chiefs and Religious Change (*c.* 1940–*c.* 1960)

By the 1900s, several Anlo towns had Christian chiefs, among them C. T. Agbozo of Dzelukope and James Ocloo I of Keta (Akyeampong 2001b: 115). Sri II, also a Christian, ascended the paramount chieftaincy in 1906. Christianised Anlo chiefs constantly made a conceptual divide between foreign gods and those native to Anlo, a thematic distinction first established in missionary ethnography. In *Die Religion der Ewe-Stämme*, Jakob Spieth argued that Ewe culture, language, and social institutions had been in a state of continuous decay: the Ewe had supposedly fallen from a prosperous, virtuous period in their history to a state of moral poverty by the 1850s (Spieth 1911). The explanation provided for this fall was their willingness to experiment with non-Ewe religious agents. So, according to Spieth, cults like Yewe, with its imported deities from Dahomey, had actually altered the balance of the Ewe religious system by negating the positive virtues and social functions of the 'authentic' Ewe gods. The two most important ideologists within the Bremen Mission, Spieth and F. M. Zahn, had always stated that one of the tasks of the Mission was to protect the Ewe identity (*Persönlichkeit*), by sponsoring a linguistic and cultural revival. Ironically, these two missionaries also went on to suggest that it was only through Christianity – and not the worship of the 'authentic' Ewe gods – that the real Ewe character could be elevated and purified (Ustorf 2001: 194–5).

Spieth's ideas gave rise to paradigmatic discourses of authenticity that were constantly reworked by Anlo intellectuals and chiefs throughout the twentieth century to legitimise their own positions. This strand of thought led many Anlo, Sri included, to believe that despite their Christianity, some 'authentic' Anlo gods were beneficial to their society, while foreign, non-Anlo deities were detrimental. Sri and his councillors repeatedly made attempts to destroy the Yewe cult, by evoking Spieth's argument about its foreign origins. This argument was used to disguise the fact that some Anlo chiefs felt threatened by the influence and prestige of Yewe priests: the Yewe cult was associated with the largest network of shrines in Anlo by the 1920s, and each shrine drew a large number of initiates; the services of the Yewe deities could be employed to deal with a wide range of spiritual and practical problems, from environmental disasters to personal issues. Yewe witnessed an upsurge in membership by 1929, especially in Anyako, which caused church attendance to fall drastically in and around the town (Grau 1964: 172). Akyeampong attributes this revival to the new role that the Yewe cult had assumed in relation to the natural environment. Sea erosion had become an urgent problem in Anlo, with Keta's coastline and inhabited structures under threat, and the Yewe cult had emerged as the preferred medium through which to appease the sea. By 1932, Yewe priests from Anlo had expanded their operations as far as Ho, in central Eweland. Later that year, Peki chiefs were complaining of 'the unlawful acts of one Awuku Bledjima, a native of Awuna [Anlo]', who had introduced a 'certain fetish known by himself and called Agbey or Yewhe'. Yewe shrines attracted 'children who refused training', and 'wives who rush into the compound to punish their husbands'.[2] In both cases, heavy fines had to be paid for the release of those who had submitted to Yewe. In 1935, the Anlo State Council (ASC) took definite steps to reduce the number of people attaching themselves to Yewe shrines:

It is ruled . . . that . . . a woman below the age of 21 years could not be admitted to the [Yewe] fetish. Any woman from the age 21 years upwards should not be admitted to the fetish without knowledge and consent of her parents and husband if any.

> (Anlo State Council of the Eastern Province of the Gold
> Coast and Protectorate held at Awunaga [Anloga] on
> 17 April 1935, Akyeampong 2001b: 73)

The ASC did not achieve much by passing this rather ambiguous law, as Yewe witnessed a dramatic upsurge in popularity during the 1930s, when the two biggest towns – Keta and Anloga – appeared to be threatened by sea erosion (Akyeampong 2001b: 122). Going *alaga* became such an extreme display of disorderly behaviour in Dzodze (a *duko* in northern Anlo) that in 1937 perplexed Yewe initiates were informed that it was mandatory to obtain written permission from the colonial government

---

[2] PRAAD/A/ADM 11/1/1679: Native Customs and Fetish.

before the deity came to possess them (Greene 2002: 57).[3] Not surprisingly, later that year, the colonial government sought to ban Yewe under the Native Jurisdiction Ordinance, following Sri's recommendations. However, influential Yewe priests and some Anlo chiefs in favour of the cult actually argued that it had become indispensable to the functioning of the Anlo state, and therefore, despite Sri's dislike of the cult, Yewe escaped prohibition (Akyeampong 2001b: 122). Thus the dividing line between 'native' and 'foreign' gods often shifted, depending on those making the arguments for their preservation or destruction.

As the popularity of Kunde and other northern deities grew in the Akan forest belt and coastal societies, they also came to be singled out for suppression. By 1940, the worship of Kunde (a deity of the Gorovodu cluster) was illegal under the Native Customs Ordinance not just in Anlo, but throughout the Gold Coast Colony. Rather than weakening the network of deities, these government-sponsored measures led Gorovodu priests to devise strategies to camouflage their activities, sometimes with the help of Yewe shrine owners and priests of other long-established deities in Anlo. These acts of collaboration were part of a series of moves that eventually forced Anlo cults to evolve into dispensers of specialised favours in order to complement each other functionally. A process which forced cults into cooperation – which involved sharing ritual resources, paraphernalia, and followers – probably began during the late 1930s. Soon after Kunde entered the Anlo religious system in 1925, the government sociologist Margaret Field interviewed a Kunde worshipper about the procedure for getting initiated into the order. When questioned about the priest's role in the process, the devotee revealed why he might not be accepted into the fraternity:

If there is a strong deity in your house already he [the priest] may tell Kundi not to accept you because it is protecting you already. A wise man goes to *his family god first* [my italics] and asks permission to serve another. Then this family god will help Kundi to protect him.[4]

This indicates that when Kunde first made an appearance in Anlo, there was some degree of antipathy between the different cults. Kunde was perceived to be spiritually incompatible with other protective agents on some level, or perhaps Kunde priests were more successful in diverting followers from other already-established cultic groups, hence inviting the anger and hostility of these other religious practitioners. When the worship of Kunde had been officially outlawed in 1940, colonial officers stationed

---

[3] This was a mechanism Yewe initiates used to protect or assert themselves in situations that did not work to their advantage. Greene suggests that *alaga* was developed by female initiates of the Yewe cult to deal with excessive patriarchal control (Greene 1996a: 100–1).

[4] PRAAD/AADM 11/751: Dente Fetish.

at outposts were entrusted with the task of scanning villages to ensure Kunde worship was indeed extinguished. Much to the dismay of these officers, Kunde 'fetish' objects had been rehoused in Yewe shrines and 'Yewe priests were either shielding Kunde priests or had actually become Kunde priests themselves'.[5] Such acts of cooperation between Kunde and Yewe priests are documented by the colonial administration. Commissioner Amewode complained in a letter to the Criminal Investigation Division in 1940 that:

The Fetish Priests of Yewe and Dah are also Priests of Kunde and its aliases. When these Licences were issued to them to practise Yewe or Dah, they secretly use it for the worshipping of Kunde. . . .
I noticed that on No. 212 and 214 dated at Keta 9th April 1940, signed by the State Clerk and Fia Sri II are bearing different names such as Yeweso, Yewe Amator respectively, whilst the actual fetish possessed by these people is Apetorku alias Kunde.[6]

This development, whereby Yewe priests 'became Kunde priests themselves', is crucial to my story of the dynamics of religious change in Anlo and the move from the phase of what I call religious or cultic 'competition' to 'cooperation'.[7] This suggests that, after the 1940s, supplicants or devotees could worship several clusters of deities simultaneously instead of committing to only one religious network or cult. At other junctures in Anlo's religious history, cults have actually competed against each other for followers – as Yewe and Nyigbla priests did in Anlo of the 1850s, for example (Greene 1996a; 2002). Barely forty years later, the better-established Yewe cult and the newer Gorovodu network were sharing followers. Two developments enabling cults to coexist were at work in Anlo by the 1940s. First, cultic networks were becoming increasingly specialised, so that each cult addressed particular problems, believed to be caused by a particular category of spiritual agent. Yewe came to be associated with suffering attributed to ancestral agency, Gorovodu with witchcraft and the worship of northern deities, and Fofie with slavery and non-Anlo ancestry. Problems from all these sources could affect

---

[5] PRAAD/A/ADM 11/1/637: Kune/Kunde Fetish.
[6] Ibid.
[7] Coordination between the newer anti-witchcraft cults and traditional deities became commonplace in other societies of the Gold Coast, especially after the former were banned by colonial authorities. State hostility towards anti-witchcraft movements led to villages uniting to disguise and preserve practices. For instance, long after Aberewa was outlawed in the southern Akan kingdom of Akyem Abuakwa, the inhabitants of the village of Fankyeneko continued to frequent priests of the deity for spiritual favours (Gray 2005). While shrines were monitored closely by the police and representatives of the colonial administration, these outsiders could not distinguish between anti-witchcraft movements and more traditional ones, the latter of which were considered an integral part of desirable local religious practices. Besides, in an attempt to camouflage their activities, newer anti-witchcraft cults either merged operations with older shrines, or began to imitate ritual practices of the latter (ibid.: 152).

one individual at the same time. Second, recruitment patterns of each cult facilitated this development: the degree of choice in the religious system lessened, as ancestral agency largely dictated which networks an individual could join. How did these two strategies interplay?

Anlo gods, like component elements of many West African religious systems, can be placed in one of two broad categories: ancestral spirits and nature spirits. Among the Anlo, this difference is registered in the word used for each category: *trowo* are usually ancestral gods or those associated with a particular clan, while *voduwo* are spirits associated with natural forces. This difference dictated who could join which cults: membership of the cults dedicated to the *trowo* was usually inherited and restricted to people that belonged to a particular clan or extended family, while the *voduwo* prescribed spiritual solutions to anyone's problems. The developmental trajectory of Yewe, the most successful Anlo cult, indicates how the dividing line between *trowo* and *voduwo* blurred with time, a feature which also changed recruitment patterns of this and most other Anlo cults. Yewe was a new cult in the 1850s and, in an attempt to attract as many followers as possible, Yewe shrine owners would have offered their services to anybody without restrictions. At the time of its configuration in Anlo, Yewe was an 'open' cult. By the 1940s, however, its recruitment pool was considerably reduced by social stigma and political regulation, as joining the cult appeared less appealing to the Anlo than it had in the past. But Yewe had become an integral part of the religious landscape by the 1940s, and its popularity meant that virtually every Anlo lineage had deceased Yewe initiates in their immediate past. This facilitated the idea that dead Yewe initiates had to be replaced within the cult by their family members. If a deceased Yewe *vodusi* was believed to be the *amedzoto* of one or more children in a lineage, those children immediately assumed membership of the cult. This indicates that a significant number of people did not join the cult solely on their own initiative, but were socialised and groomed specifically for it. When this shift occurred cannot be precisely identified, though Akyeampong dates it to the late 1930s (Akyeampong 2001b: 122). By 1965, Nukunya noted that reincarnation was the 'most effective' method of recruitment, suggesting that this strategy must have been in place for at least two generations (Nukunya 1969b: 2). Nukunya could therefore state that Yewe *vodusiwo* and the offices of the priesthood (*minawo* and *midawo*) were usually drawn from families previously associated with the cult. He also noted, in 1965, that there were no restrictions on Yewe *vodusiwo* and *ahewo* (casual members) worshipping other non-Yewe deities, and several Yewe *vodusiwo* were involved in the activities of other cultic networks (ibid.: 5), suggesting that cults were in cooperation with each other.

As a result of these changes, most people in Anlo towns today are able to identify a Yewe shrine with which they are associated, whether or not they are initiated into the cult. Yewe membership (into both inner and outer circles) is exclusively hereditary and not open to those whose ancestors were not cult initiates. In a town like Anlo-Afiadenyigba, for example, each Yewe shrine draws its *vodusiwo* and priests – the more-committed inner-circle initiates – from certain *afedowo*, whose members usually reside in specific geographical catchment areas in every town: members of the same *afedowo* claim affinity with a single shrine, even if they are not initiated inner-circle members, as less-committed, outer-circle members. In addition to the *voduwo*, each shrine houses a number of ancestral gods (*alegbawo*), ancestral stools (*togbui zikpi*) and 'symbols of interest' (Nukunya 1969a: 27), which relate to the common ancestors of the patrilineages that each shrine services. In fact, a closer analysis of why people join the Yewe cult suggests that the Yewe deities behave very much in the manner of troubled ancestors rather than whimsical *voduwo*, indicating that Yewe occupies an ambiguous space in the Anlo religious environment: a collection of nature spirits that function and crave attention both in the manner of dissatisfied ancestors and on behalf of them. A Yewe initiate is committed to the cult for life, and undergoes a change of identity and name, corresponding to the ancestor she or he is meant to replace; this initiate is then locked in a relationship with the Yewe deities, just as their ancestors were in the past.[8] Fofie also took the form of a replacement cult upon its institutionalisation in Anlo during the 1930s: there was little choice in becoming a *fofiesi*, as the slave ancestors choose which of their descendants they wanted to worship them. Only descendants of slave women may petition the Fofie slave spirits for protection; the number of less-committed followers is therefore also drawn from members of the same descent groups. Priests of Gorovodu and other anti-witchcraft cults, who own god-objects and are in command of specialist knowledge, also nominate successors – who will then assume the priesthood – within their families. Though Gorovodu is a more open

---

[8] Lovell, who conducted research on the Ouatchi (Watchi) Ewe in the early 1990s, argued that initiation into a *vodhun* shrine was determined by transmission of the *hunka*, which she translated as 'cord of blood' (see Lovell 2002: 41). *Vodhun* shrines amongst the eastern Ewe had metamorphosed into the Yewe cluster of the western Anlo Ewe during the 1800s–1850s (see Herskovits 1938, Vol. 2: 189–93). Yewe in Anlo was organised along similar lines as the *vodhun* shrines of eastern Togo, differing slightly in terms of initiation, ordinary membership, and priesthood. So upon the passing of a *vodhunsi*, the *hunka*, is passed on through matrilineal ties amongst the Ouatchi, typically matrilineal descent and other forms of matrifiliation (Lovell 2002: 41–4). Yewe shrines may have been relatively open associations in their early stages, and one can only speculate whether there was an intermediate stage where recruitment was chiefly matrilineal as amongst the Ouatchi Ewe, before it evolved into the pattern that favours ancestral recruitment leaning towards patrifiliation. Deceased Yewe ancestors appear to reincarnate randomly within both patrilineages and matrilineages, though from my fieldwork it appeared that various forms of patrifiliation (replacing paternal ancestors and patrilocality) constituted the preferred means of assuming Yewe membership in contemporary Anlo.

cult, a significant number of inner-circle devotees also accessed Gorovodu networks through prior family connections: these transmissions
follow both paternal and maternal descent lines, with more committed
inner-circle initiates such as priests and *trosiwo* replacing ancestors from
both branches of the family. It is possible for some individuals to seek
the services of Gorovodu priests, or become a *trosi*, without any prior
familial connections – although, in my experience, such cases are few
and far between, and most *trosiwo* are replaced in exactly the same manner as *vodusiwo* and *fofiesiwo* are: by family members, and through lineage
ties.[9]

The condition that enabled individuals to seek the favours of two or
more cults, and assume multiple spiritual identities vis-à-vis the cults in
question, appears to have been firmly in place by the 1950s. Accounts
of several Anlo people bear testimony to multiple initiations. Kwasi Aku
(b. *c.* 1950) of Havedji is a Yewe *midao* and a Gorovodu *sofo*. He explains
his association with both networks.

At my birth, we identified my *amedzoto*. An Afa *boko* told me that this was my
paternal grandfather. This man was a Yewe *midao*, and he had died about a year
before I was born. He was the *midao* of a small shrine in Havedji, which has ten
vodusiwo attached to it. So when I was about ten years old, I replaced him. We
performed ceremonies, and I lived inside that shrine for a few months to learn
about Yewe. For years, everything was alright, and the gods left me alone. Then I
started to have problems again. The causes of these problems were the Gorovodu
spirits. The same grandfather that I replaced in Yewe had Gorovodu, and those
spirits wanted me to worship them. I did not know where my grandfather had
kept his Gorovodu, so I bought Bangre Ketesi (one of the Gorovodu deities)

---

[9] Fofie membership is transmitted exclusively within certain slave-owning *afedowo* or patrilineages. (*Fofiesiwo* usually replace their paternal aunts rather than their paternal grandmothers.) The more committed inner-circle Yewe initiates such as *vodusiwo* and the
offices of the priesthood are reproduced in families, through both paternal and maternal
ties. I came into contact with about 100 inner-circle Yewe initiates over the last decade,
and 70 of them were replacements for Yewe members in their fathers' families, while the
other 30 were replacements for ancestors in their mothers' families. In the case of the
Gorovodu cult, out of the 70 *trosiwo* and *sofowo* (the inner circle) I encountered, 28 of
them (40 per cent) had accessed the network on account of deceased paternal ancestors;
28 (another 40 per cent) though maternal ties; while 14 initiates (20 per cent) had no
prior link with the Gorovodu deities, and were just 'found' by them. Verdon (1983) in
his description of the Abutia Ewe, suggests that all immigrant deities (corresponding to
Fofie, Yewe, and Gorovodu in Anlo, which in the classical scheme favour possession and
originate from outside), which he terms *mama trowo*, are usually transmitted matrilineally, which does not seem to happen in contemporary Anlo. Some of these immigrant
deities (such as Fofie) in Anlo appear to have acquired the characteristics of ancestral
deities, and have come to be transmitted chiefly through the *afedo*, the fundamental unit
of social organisation from one generation to another, through patrilineal descent groups;
others, such as Yewe and Gorovodu, are transmitted through loose paternal and maternal
associations, but nevertheless through ancestral associations. This is an area that could
benefit greatly from more research.

from another *sofo*, and learned how to make northern medicine. Now I have two types of gods.[10]

The story of Metumisi[11] of Anlo-Afiadenyigba is typical of the religious experiences of *fofiesiwo* during this period.

My mother, Metumisi, was born *c.* 1920. Her father had her baptised, and she grew up attending church occasionally. Her *amedzoto* was her great-grandmother, an Ewedome slave woman. Her family were aware of this at her birth. She became a *fofiesi* in the late 1950s, calling herself Metumisi. Then Yewe began demanding her attention. She realised that she was also meant to replace another grandmother from the maternal side, a Yewe *vodusi*. So she started calling herself Sowamare, a Yewe name, and was initiated into the cult around 1961. She served both the Fofie and Yewe deities and performed rituals for them throughout her life. Members of her family also worshipped Yewe and Fofie, because of the ancestors. Some of these people also used Gorovodu and Adzevodu when they needed it. Although mother was ritually married to Fofie and Yewe, she continued to attend church occasionally. She would describe herself as a *fofiesi*, *vodusi*, and even Christian, depending on whom she was interacting with. But she was much, much more involved with Fofie and Yewe than with church. Several of her contemporaries (my aunts for example) also behaved like this.[12]

That Metumisi could reconcile her identity as a *fofiesiwo* with church attendance is indicative that she could ascribe two religious identities to herself without conflict. The form that Anlo Christianity took between 1940 and 1990 actually facilitated this religious cooperation between cults in the religious system. Christianity developed from an antagonistic force in relation to non-Christian practices, to one which accommodated and complemented the networks dedicated to the *trowo* and *voduwo* in the imaginations of most Anlo.

Christianity in Anlo (*c.* 1940–*c.* 1990)

Between the 1940s and 1990s, two distinct strands of Christianity could be identified in Anlo: mainline Christianity and churches belonging to the first wave of African Independent Churches (AICs). Mainline Christian churches were products of the original Missions: the Evangelical Presbyterian (EP) Church that arose out of the Bremen Mission and the Roman Catholic Church, a product of the Steyl Mission,[13] were the most popular in Anlo. The Musama Disco Christo Church (MDCC) and the

---

[10] Interview with Kwasi Aku, Anlo-Afiadenyigba, 19 February 2004.
[11] No relation to the other individual by the same name encountered previously in this study.
[12] Interview with Babaa, Anlo-Afiadenyigba, 1 May 2004.
[13] The Steyl Mission was part of a German Catholic Society, the SVD (Society of the Divine Word), that established itself in German Togoland in the 1890s (Sundkler and Steed 2000: 221).

Apostles Revelation Society (ARS) were the only two African Independent Churches with significant congregations in Anlo. While they were founded in 1922 and 1945 respectively, both churches gained members in Anlo during the late 1940s. Of particular interest is how these two strands of Christianity – mainline Christianity and AICs – interacted with Anlo cultic networks and helped to fashion the religious system.

Mainline Christianity and Anlo Indigenous Religion

By the 1940s, it was impossible to talk of Christianity as a unified, undifferentiated phenomenon – rather, there were several different Christianities, differing in theology, culture, and their relationship to the issue of African tradition. Only Christianities that were able to coexist with non-Christian cultic practices were able to flourish in Anlo during this period. As religious cults and orders became functionally more specialised, the various strands of Christianities also carved out their own niches in the religious system, thereby allowing Christians to access the services of the different Anlo cults in addition to those provided by churches, allowing the two religious traditions to negotiate patterns of coexistence.

The initial Christian message was made intelligible by missionaries to potential converts by contextualising it against the backdrop of the local Anlo religious traditions. In the absence of shared cultural, historical, and linguistic cues, missionary understanding of the existing Ewe 'religion' became a key reference point in the translation process. As Meyer argues, central to this dialogue was the image of the Devil (Meyer 1999). In the ensuing encounter, the local religious tradition was diabolised and presented as the domain of the Devil, which made it the diametrical opposite of the Christian realm. The Ewe were told that they had been worshipping the Devil and his agents through their *trowo* and *voduwo* for centuries, and the expression *nku vu*, literally 'opened eyes', was used to describe missionary endeavours (Meyer 1999: 8). Christianity was thus equated with enlightenment, and the Ewe were encouraged to view their pre-Christian religion as part of a dark and shameful past, a strategy that left converted African Christians with a negative evaluation of their local religious traditions.[14]

By the turn of the twentieth century, colonialism, mission schools, and commerce had produced a class of elites, who began to reflect seriously on the very encounter that had created them. Against the backdrop of political independence in the 1960s, African theologians became preoccupied with assessing the significance of Christianity for Africans,

---

[14] Similar metaphors were used in other parts of West Africa: *olaju*, which also translates into 'to open one's eyes', was used to describe Christianity's role in Yorubaland (Peel 1987).

which gave rise to the movement to indigenise Christianity. They sought to isolate Christianity from its colonial heritage. To do this, they had to revisit and reconfigure the initial missionary dialogue between 'African tradition' and Christianity, which portrayed African traditions as not only primitive, but also sinful. This 'Africanisation' project had to attack the presuppositions upon which Christianity in Africa had come to be based: Satan versus God, African 'primitiveness' versus Western civilisation, African 'heathenism' versus European Christianity (see Mudimbe 1983). The Africanising lobby argued that in African traditional cultures there were already elements that were compatible with Christianity, which had provided a stepping stone for conversion. Christian conversion was represented as the next logical step in the progression from African 'traditional' religion. This idea was embraced by leading theologians in favour of indigenisation, the best-known among them in the sub-region being G. de Souza of the Ivory Coast, and J. Bahoken and E. Mveng of Cameroon (ibid.: 93–4). These changes could be understood against the backdrop of cultural and political nationalism, as these strands of thought borrowed heavily from other intellectual currents of that era, such as Negritude and Pan-Africanism.

The most important Anlo theologian of this period was the Keta-born Reverend Christain Goncalves Baëta, who was ordained into the ministry of the EP Church in 1936, and became the synod clerk (chief executive) of the church between 1945 and 1949. Baëta's high-profile career lasted over five decades, during which he held many influential positions: he was chair of the Christian Council of Ghana, and head of the Department of Theology at the University of Ghana.[15] Like other West African theologians of the period, Baëta also supported the movement to Africanise Christianity, arguing that the use of 'unmodified Western forms' in African Christianity was 'undignified' (Baëta 1971: 21). He constantly encouraged African Christians to engage in dialogue with practitioners of African traditional religion, which he saw as crucial if the two faiths were to coexist. Unlike the more radical exponents of the indigenisation programme, Baëta was not in favour of forcibly Africanising Christianity in either form or content. For him, the key to indigenisation lay in the translation of the Bible itself, as it would facilitate a deeper understanding of Christianity and its application to African life. In 1971, Baëta concluded that 'relaxed and natural' indigenisation was taking place at its own pace, and was visible in measures such as the increased use of African music at church services (ibid.: 20). Baëta also believed that Africanisation could not be imposed upon congregations, and that European forms should be replaced with local ones only if the former were a hindrance to the spread

---

[15] The Theology Department eventually became the Department for the Study of Religions. Baëta was partly responsible for this transformation.

of the Gospel. His views were representative of the leadership of the EP Church until the 1980s.

The other significant individual in the history of Ewe Christianity was the Rev. N. K. Dzobo, moderator of the EP Church between 1981 and 1993. Dzobo essentially took Baëta's position one step further, by suggesting that a truly African Christianity could develop only if the church leadership took an active role in the indigenisation programme. He advocated the reintegration of African tradition into Christianity through his *Mele agbe* (I am alive) theology (Meyer 1995; 1999: 123–5). He argued that African tradition and Christianity can coexist, as they have certain conceptual similarities. Dzobo tried to demonstrate that core Christian concepts such as God, priesthood, and sacrifice were already present in pre-Christian African traditions, and, although the African versions of these concepts were different, they could be reconciled with Christianity. Part of his project was to join the life-affirming aspects of both Christianity and African traditional religion: Dzobo argued that the Devil was not the all-powerful force behind African traditional religion, but only a product of the pietistic missionary imagination, the result of the missionary confrontation with the unfamiliar. Dzobo aimed to break away from the principles advocated by 'irrelevant and Western-oriented Christianity', which he believed were inappropriate for Africans (Gifford 1997: 75). Though controversial, Dzobo's theology found acceptance in the EP Church, and was embraced by some members of the Anlo intelligentsia.[16] This resulted in the EP Church becoming most liberal with respect to its attitude towards 'traditional' religion. Dzobo's theology still appeals to senior EP members. Many EP members, drawing upon his ideas, believe that local Anlo traditions can coexist with, and complement, Christianity. David Davor (b. 1948), a senior EP member in Anlo-Afiadenyigba, actually endorses 'traditional' religion by suggesting that cults such as Yewe and Fofie are to be equated with ancestor veneration, which is a legitimate part of African traditions, and necessary for a truly African Christianity:

Several 'heathens' often visit the EP church in this town, and have been doing so for as long as I can remember. Some of our members – people who consider themselves staunch Christians – also go to the Yewe and Fofie shrines in the town. We have no objection with that, as they are just honouring their ancestors, and that cannot be done in church. Going to those 'fetish' houses to pay respects

---

[16] The *Mele agbe* theology had its critics. The EP Church Moderator preceding Dzobo, Reverend Dovlo, strongly opposed *Mele agbe* theology. Dovlo played a central role in the split of the church, supporting the more Pentecostally inclined group. His son, Dr Elom Dovlo, formerly Head of the Department of Religious Studies at the University of Ghana, also adopted his father's position in relation to Dzobo and his supporters.

to the ancestors is a part of our Anlo tradition, and it does not make anyone a bad Christian.[17]

Christians from Fofie-worshipping families had little trouble reconciling their need to venerate the slave ancestors with their Christianity. Justice Agboado (b. 1938), is a member of one of Anlo-Afiadenyigba's oldest Christian families. He describes himself as a committed Christian, but he is also an enthusiastic Fofie worshipper. Agboado, who is in agreement with the arguments of both Baëta and Dzobo, actually justifies his engagement with Fofie in Biblical terms.

MV: Tell me about yourself.

JA: I was born in Lome in 1938, but I am an Anlo man with roots in Keta and Anlo-Afiadenyigba. I am a retired secondary school teacher. I have taught all over Ghana and also in Nigeria.

MV: Are you a Christian?

JA: Yes, I was baptised when I was young. My father wanted all his children to become Christians. I studied theology as a young man. I am involved in the affairs of the EP church in this town [Anlo-Afiadenyigba].

MV: But you are also always present whenever Fofie worshippers congregate together. I have seen you at Fofie shrines and ceremonies in Anlo-Afiadenyigba, Keta, Whuti, and Anloga. Can you still call yourself a Christian?

JA: My father was born to a Keta man and his third wife, who was a slave carried away from Ewedome. His half-brothers and half-sisters who were born to free wives inherited much more than him. He was keen to do well for himself. So he became a Christian and went to school. That is how I was encouraged to become a Christian. But two of my sisters were *fofiesiwo* until their deaths in the 1990s. My niece (brother's daughter) is a replacement for them. We have a household shrine dedicated to our slave ancestors. I often pour a libation for them.

MV: How can you still call yourself a Christian?

JA: Of course I am a Christian. I find nothing wrong with Fofie worship. Slavery was not a very enlightened practice. The Bible gives us many instructions on what to do with slaves. For example: 'Masters, treat your slaves justly and fairly, knowing that you also have a Master in heaven' (Colossians 4: 1); 'You shall not give up to his master a slave who has escaped from his master to you' (Deuteronomy 23: 15), and 'If your brother becomes poor beside you and sells himself to you, you shall not make him serve as a slave' (Leviticus 25: 39). But we, in Anlo, did not treat slaves well. We sold our own indebted relations and kinsmen into slavery. We forced people to stay here and work for

---

[17] Interview with David Davor, Anlo-Afiadenyigba, 8 April 2004.

us, sometimes in unpleasant conditions. All these things are most un-Biblical. Slavery is our collective Sin. Through Fofie, we are atoning for these sins now, begging forgiveness from those who we have wronged, and from God.

MV: What did other Christians in your family think of your stance?

JA: They agree with me. In my generation, even the initiated *fofiesiwo* went to church services. In church, everybody knew they were *fofiesiwo*, but this was not an issue. Virtually all members of my generation in my lineage are Christian, but they always came to perform rituals for our slave ancestors. Fofie worship is a very Christian thing. 'There is neither Jew nor Greek, there is neither slave nor free, there is no male and female, for you are all one in Christ Jesus' (Galatians 3: 28). Fofie worship is attempting to erase the differences between master and slave. It is about Repentance and Atonement, both great Christian themes. Every culture is unique, and there will be distinctive expressions such as the Fofie cult, to deal with things that have come to be regarded as morally unjustifiable. I am proud that my people, the Anlo, can confront the sins of our past in such a mature way. I believe this is an extraordinary way of thinking which has developed here in Anlo, in relation to slavery. If all societies made an attempt to identify the sins of their past, and rectify them, the world will become a more peaceful place.[18]

Justice Agboado's articulate endorsement of Fofie worship suggests that the veneration of the slave ancestors is a desirable part of Anlo traditional culture. Like Baëta, he suggests that there are African cultural expressions (such as Fofie), which are compatible with Christianity. Agboado's understanding of slavery and the raison d'être of the Fofie cult differs slightly from that of a typical *fofiesi*. While for the *fofiesiwo*, Fofie is concerned with the aftermath of forcibly incorporating slaves into society, Agboado uses slavery more loosely, to refer also to the practice of selling people into slavery.

The testimonial of Rose Aidam (b. 1960), an EP church member who hails from a Fofie-worshipping lineage, also suggests that ideas such as Agboado's are relatively mainstream in Anlo amongst a certain section of the church-going people.

I am an EP Christian, from Whuti. Although we have been church-goers for three generations, we have several *voduwo* and *trowo*. My father and his family are Fofie worshippers, and the Fofie deities can demand my attention, even though I am a Christian. I am not initiated into the cult, but I go to the shrine often to pay my respects. Fofie is all about honouring the ancestors, and this can be done alongside church activity. In addition to Fofie, we have Togbui Galazi, Nunge, and Nunke, which one of our patrilineal ancestors acquired from Benin. They

---

[18] Interview with Justice Agboado, Anlo-Afiadenyigba, 9 December 2010.

are *trowo* and the ancestors speak through them. Ignoring these three *trowo* had been the cause of my downfall: about fifteen years ago, they decided to punish me. I encountered a number of problems. In order to solve them, I took up the worship of these *trowo* and went back to my village in Anlo, until they decided to set me free. I still went to church throughout all this, because the ancestors and Church business is separate.[19]

What is noteworthy from the accounts of Agboado and Aidam above is that the older members of the Fofie cult – generally those that came of age between 1950 and 1980 – associate non-Christian ritual practices with the realm of the ancestral, making it a crucial part of their identities as Anlo people. The majority of such people managed to oscillate across the Christian–'heathen' divide with ease before the 1990s. *Fofiesiwo* (who were also *vodusiwo*), like Metumisi, occasionally came to church when they felt the need. Christians like Agboado and Aidam went to Fofie shrines to commune with their ancestors. A series of public events also bear testimony to this cooperation between 'pagan' Anlo cults and Christianity. Soon after he was enstooled, the new Christian *awoamefia* Togbi Adelaza sacrificed a cow to control sea erosion at Keta on behalf of all his Anlo subjects. In 1968, Adelaza sent a delegation to Notsie seeking spiritual assistance in alleviating severe drought conditions that had plagued Anlo (Greene 2002: 29). Anlo Christians and church leaders did not protest at these moves: they were a necessary method of appeasing the ancestors, and could not be done within the framework of Christianity.

African Independent Churches and Anlo Indigenous Religion

In contrast to the stance of mainline churches and their members stand the African Independent Churches (AICs). The AICs also operated in Anlo during the era of cultic cooperation between *c.* 1940 and *c.* 1990, though they were not as successful in attracting members as the mainline churches. AICs mostly started out as prayer groups within mainline churches, a prophetic figure was usually at the centre of the movement, the emphasis on healing and faith was significant, and African instruments were often used in prayer rituals (Turner 1978). Some of the earlier AICs, founded several decades before political independence, were the by-products of the Africanising programme, as illustrated by their rejection of European forms and their inclusion of indigenous rituals.[20]

The first AIC to emerge in southern Eweland was the Apostles Revelation Society (ARS), founded by a former EP member at Tadzewu, in

---

[19] Interview with Rose Aidam, Whuti, 3 April 2004.
[20] For example, the Musama Disco Christo (MDC) church, which was founded in the Winneba District in 1922, originated as a prayer group within the Methodist Church. Prophet Jehu-Appiah was at the helm of the movement, and the MDC church placed great emphasis on healing and prayer (Opoku 1978; Burnett 1997).

the northern hinterland of Anlo. Prophet Wovenu established the ARS in 1945, and by the late 1960s the church claimed to have 50,000 followers in Ghana (Debrunner 1967: 346). The position and personality of Wovenu was crucial to the success of the movement. As in other AICs, healing was a central theme in the ARS, though Wovenu placed greater emphasis on modern medicine than on the spiritual healing techniques favoured by most other AICs. He had several qualified nurses and medics working for him. The ARS was unique in some respects, as Wovenu often dismissed the preoccupation with witchcraft and evil spirits – central to healing sessions in other AICs – as fabrications of the human mind. Speaking in tongues, a prayer tactic in other AICs, was discouraged at Tadzewu. Church services often incorporated traditional dances and rhythmic performances. The ARS had branches in most Anlo towns – Keta, Anloga, and even the less-Christian villages like Anlo-Afiadenyigba and Afife – by the late 1950s.[21] Wovenu's activities and image as a prophet can be understood in the tradition of previous prophets and preachers like Harris and Oppong.[22]

The position of the AICs on tradition and modernity, and on how 'African' Christianity had to be, was far from well-defined. Ironically, members of most AICs did not understand their practices as an amalgamation between two mutually incompatible African and European traditions, as they thought of themselves as being 'modern', having discarded the undesirable elements of their African religious past.[23] Baëta argues that the AICs and 'traditional religion' were idiomatically similar: despite the former's strict stance against using indigenous resources for prayer, structurally and functionally, the AICs bore a greater resemblance to traditional religion (Baëta 1962). Though certain AICs adopted strong positions against 'traditional' religion, they were essentially the

[21] Personal communication with members of ARS branch in Afife, February 2004.
[22] William Wade Harris and Oppong had both been active in Ghana between the 1900s and 1960s. Harris preached in Côte d'Ivoire and southern Ghana at the turn of the twentieth century, baptising thousands of people during his 'crusade'. He fashioned his image into that of a Biblical preacher and healer with divine powers, teaching strict opposition to witchcraft and the aspects of African tradition that he identified as undesirable (see Haliburton 1973; Breidenbach 1974). Samson Oppong was active in Asante and Brong during the 1920s, converting several people to Christianity. Oppong was also a healer, much in the manner of Harris (see Hanson 2002).
[23] For instance, the Aladura movement, which began amongst the Yoruba in Nigeria, sought to incorporate the this-worldliness of African traditional religion into Christianity. Aladura Christianity was a pragmatic religion, which identified personal problems (fertility, financial troubles, and failing health) and attempted to treat them through diligent prayer, though it continued to maintain a focus on certain 'orthodox' Christian themes, such as Salvation and Judgement. While it appears that Aladura Christians' denunciation of 'pagan' worship constituted a conscious attack on aspects of African tradition, Aladura Christianity shared key structural characteristics with African religions (Peel 1968a; Ray 1993).

by-products of an experiment that sought to make Christianity more African in its focus, orientation, and theology.

Until 1985, the EP and Roman Catholic churches had the biggest congregations in Anlo-Afiadenyigba.[24] The ARS and the Musama Disco Christo church had small followings, precisely because of their rigidity with respect to their members accessing the non-Christian sphere. Dogbatse's study of neighbouring Afife confirms these trends (Dogbatse 1999): mainline churches were more popular in Anlo between 1940 and 1990. Part of the reason was that mainline Christians tended to be more open towards non-Christian practices. In spite of sharing structural similarities with 'traditional' African religion, the AICs were slightly more condemning of non-Christian practices and beliefs, and understood dabbling in African 'traditional' practices of any sort to be the cause of all spiritual problems. As most cults in Anlo had settled into specific niches and had begun to coexist with each other, mainline Christianity was the preferred option for the Anlo, as it enabled them to access services provided by all the cultic networks. Statistics from the report of the Ghana Evangelism Committee (GEC) also suggest that mainline Christians outnumbered members of AICs in Anlo during this period. In 1987, according to the GEC, 32 per cent of people in the Volta Region[25] attended the four main Protestant churches, while 27 per cent called themselves Catholic, bringing the figure of mainline Christians up to 59 per cent. Of the remainder, 25 per cent went to AICs, 13 per cent attended Pentecostal churches, and 1 per cent went to other very small churches (GEC report 1989: 64). The Catholic and EP Churches witnessed growth periods between 1940 and 1990, while the AICs maintained their numbers, registering only very small increases (ibid.: 66). However the 1990s were another turning point in Anlo religion: membership of the mainline churches declined sharply, when a new set of Pentecostal churches became part of the religious landscape. By the late 1980s, the sharpest increases were registered in this Pentecostal sector, while the mainline Protestant churches, the Catholic churches, and AICs appeared to have registered only very small increases in membership (ibid.: 66). A new phase of Anlo religious history began in the 1990s, during which the rise of Pentecostal churches changed both the structure and nature of the religious system once again, this time leading indigenous religious networks and strands of Christianities to compete with each other for followers.

---

[24] This information was obtained through personal correspondence with church ministers. The exact statistics for Church attendance over the second half of the twentieth century are unavailable.

[25] Although these figures reflect church attendance all over the Volta Region (of which Anlo is part), they are also representative of the situation in Anlo.

The New Christianity in Anlo (*c.* 1990–Present)

The late 1980s in West Africa were characterised by the growth of a new type of Christianity, mainly Pentecostal in its outlook and orientation. This wave of Pentecostal churches had little in common with the early Pentecostally oriented AICs of the immediate post-independence era (Larbi 2001: 89). Gifford suggests that the label 'charismatic' is more appropriate for this new wave of churches, given the emphasis they place on leadership, and the role that the leaders of these churches play in public life (Gifford 2004: vii). Leaders and executive bodies of these Pentecostal churches made extensive use of the mass media (radio, television, and Internet resources) and were involved in forceful advertising campaigns, especially in the post-PNDC era, to portray and display the popularity of their religious services through carefully choreographed images of the 'pastor star' and members of the ideal congregation, always well-groomed and extremely attentive (Meyer 2011: 162). These churches were characterised by a peculiar culture, previously unknown to Ghanaian Christianity: services often emphasised themes such as personal success, wealth creation, and the means to achieve these rewards. Crusades to gain new members are constantly launched, with existing members expected to recruit newer ones. All-night services and prayer camps are part of this new Christianity. Some of the better-known charismatic churches are Christian Action Faith Ministries, run by Nicholas Duncan-Williams, the International Central Gospel Church headed by Mensa Otabil, the Lighthouse International founded by Dag Heward-Mills (ibid.: 23–7), and the Synagogue, Church of All Nations (SCOAN), headed by the Nigerian-born T. B. Joshua. Unlike the Christianity of the 1960s in Africa, which was an integral part of the climate of optimism that characterised the early decades of independence, these Pentecostal churches have often been described as transnational and post-nationalistic in their approach (Marshall-Fratani 1998; Peel 2000: 315–17; Englund 2000, 2001, 2003, 2004; Daswani 2010, 2015; Piot 2010).[26] The popular appeal of this wave of Pentecostalism, with the emphasis on individual success, importance of community networks, and faith, has been theorised as a development in response to the harshness of life in African states under corrupt and ineffective political regimes. The transnational outlook and

---

[26] Meyer (1998b: 31) argues that Ghanaian Pentecostal church leaders, unlike their Nigerian and other African contemporaries, explicitly addressed national concerns during the PNDC era by trying to engage their congregations with issues of national political and social importance. However, contemporary Ghanaian Pentecostalism is overwhelmingly transnational and post-nationalistic in its orientation and outlook, attempting to move beyond the national sphere and concerns associated with it (as well as to transcend the internationalised space associated with diasporan Ghanaian and African networks) in its search for an ideal global Pentecostal Christian identity, community, and values (see Daswani 2015).

disillusionment with the state finds articulation in the denunciation of aspects of African culture, and the international, outward-looking character of these churches: many members aspire to forge overseas links and networks for work and business, and, often, hope to be able to travel abroad for personal betterment through the connections made through these settings (Daswani 2010: 457). Pentecostalism may therefore be read as a living socio-religious discourse that critiques national policy and political regimes that result in more severe economic conditions in African states (ibid.).

These Pentecostal churches are changing the face of Ghanaian Christianity, as many members of the more traditional mainline churches and older AICs have converted to Pentecostal Christianity in the last two and a half decades. According to the Ghana Evangelism Committee, the traditional AICs – the Musama Disco Christo Church and the ARS – have been losing members, and have witnessed declines between 17 per cent and 23 per cent, while the congregation of the Catholic Church, the single biggest Christian denomination in Ghana, declined by 2 per cent. Though the mainline Protestant churches, – the Anglican, Evangelical Presbyterian, Methodist, and Presbyterian churches – have registered a small 7 per cent increase, the biggest rise in numbers has occurred in this Pentecostal sector, with increases of 80 per cent in membership (GEC report, quoted in Gifford, 1997: 62–3). These trends are also visible in Anlo: according to Dogbatse's study of the northern Anlo town of Afife, Pentecostal churches like the Action Faith Ministries first came to Afife in 1985 and have been increasing their memberships steadily ever since (Dogbatse 1999). In Anlo-Afiadenyigba, the first Pentecostal churches were established in the late 1980s.[27]

As mainline churches and AICs were constantly losing members to the Pentecostal churches, there was pressure on the former to emulate the latter in terms of their theology, services, and ethos. The dialogue between African 'tradition' and Christianity continues in these Pentecostal churches. Though they remain opposed to 'nominal' Christians, they disapprove strongly of churches that seek to incorporate traditional African beliefs and rituals to any extent, like the older Pentecostally-oriented AICs and mainline churches (see Meyer 1998a). The key idea is that the progress of a Christian can be hampered by demons who wield power over him, notwithstanding his submission to Christ. A Christian may have no knowledge of this at all, and may be victimised by such demons.[28] It takes an agent of God to diagnose and attack the problem: the role of such an

---

[27] Personal communication with leaders and initial members of the Church of Pentecost, who established the Anlo-Afiadenyigba branch after 1987.

[28] Some of the most influential literature on demons and demonology has originated in Nigeria. See for example, *Delivered from the Powers of Darkness* by Emmanuel Eni (1987) of the Assemblies of God.

agent is crucial in this Christianity, and is a stage beyond the experience of being born-again and speaking in tongues. These demons could be brought upon an individual by a number of things, most importantly, 'attending an Aladura church, palmist, fetish priest, card reader, witch doctor' or using 'amulets or talismans for protection', having undergone 'puberty rites, maintaining a stool or shrine in the family' having an 'enema with any native medicine' from a fetish priest (Gifford 1997: 97). Spiritual advisers study the personal profile of every patient and determine if the problem was indeed a demon and suggest ways in which it could be cast out, often amid shouting and praying in a special enclosure.

Deliverance has come to dominate many of these churches, and the link between 'traditional religion' and demons is brought out perfectly through rituals such as these. While African tradition is vigorously denounced in these churches, the principles that lie beneath the deliverance phenomenon owe more to African traditional conceptions of evil than anything else, even though they are articulated in the language of international Pentecostalism. The dichotomy between the 'this-worldliness' of African traditional religion and the 'other-worldliness' of Christianity breaks down, as this new Christianity is not otherworldly, centred around success, wealth, and personal achievements in the present (Gifford 2004: 198).

Numerous theories have been put forward to explain the appeal of this strand of Pentecostalism on an individual level at this particular juncture in Ghanaian history. According to Birgit Meyer, it enables individuals to disconnect from selective aspects of their African past, represented in the image of the Devil, against which they could then position themselves and their own individual or collective trajectories of growth and progress. The image of the Devil became a convenient ritual space which could incorporate everything from undesirable modes of African religiosity, to outmoded cultural expressions, social obligations associated with unwanted aspects of culture, and the burden of an unprogressive past. Becoming born-again allowed people to be 'modern' in complex socio-cultural ways in Ghana: while on the surface, Pentecostal discourse appeared to be making a disconnection with 'tradition' and 'traditional religion' symbolised by the 'Devil', the constant denunciation of the same kept alive the debate about the relationship between modernity and tradition, and between the global to the local in the Ghanaian psyche (Meyer 1998a). Ruth Marshall-Fratani (1998) argues that being 'born-again' allows individuals to adopt local, national, and regional identities at the same time, as these other identities are always secondary to their Christianity. According to her, part of Pentecostalism's appeal is its transnational networks, resources, and goods, which remote local actors are suddenly able to incorporate into their actions, lives, and aspirations on a significant scale. Being born-again, and the complex plethora of internationalised images that accompanies the process enhances the lives of hitherto disconnected, disempowered individuals, immediately conferring upon them a new kind of agency on a global platform. Girish Daswani (2015) emphasises the transformative potential and capacity for personal growth and regeneration: becoming born-again implies a process of reordering individual subjectivities not just on a local level, but also on a national, regional, and worldwide scale. Participation in Pentecostal networks could improve an individual's life-chances significantly by breaking old burdensome social relationships associated with kinship ties and other hardships of life in small communities in Ghana, while presenting new opportunities for accumulating social and cultural capital in new national and global settings; membership of global Pentecostal churches also immediately ties an individual into a large international community of like-minded 'born-agains' who share the same hopes, dreams, and visions for humanity's future.

Interestingly, all the conflicts between the various strands of Ghanaian Christianity have been visible in the developmental trajectory of the EP church and its offshoots. Meyer's work shows how the EP Church has absorbed many of the prevailing theological currents in Ghanaian Christianity through the decades (Meyer 1999: 122–40).[29] The 1990s proved to be a watershed period, when the popularity of mainline Christianity gradually dwindled and Pentecostal churches became more and more appealing in Anlo. Matters came to a head for the EP church during Dzobo's term as moderator. For the more rigid Pentecostally oriented people in the EP church, Dzobo's controversial *Mele agbe* theology was perceived as a move back to 'heathenism'. Some senior members of the EP Church were also concerned that Dzobo's reforms would result in the declining popularity of the church. Seeing that the Pentecostal or charismatic outlook – which differed from the older wave of Pentecostal churches – was becoming more attractive by the late 1980s, these leaders feared that people interested in deliverance and healing would leave the EP Church for charismatic churches that catered to these rituals. Protests were organised against Dzobo's reforms. Meanwhile, a prayer group known as the Bible Society Prayer Fellowship (BSPF), founded in

---

[29] A prayer group formed at Tekirom (a village in the Peki area) during the late 1950s proved to be the first challenge for the EP church. The group differed in terms of worship methods: drumming, dancing, speaking in tongues, and tithing characterised the group's sessions. A number of conflicts between the EP church and the members of the prayer group – especially with reference to worship methods – ensued, polarising the two groups. This prayer group eventually metamorphosed into the Lord's Pentecostal Church (Agbelengor) in 1961. The use of the word Pentecostal in its name was significant, as it distanced their theological position not only from the mainline EP Church, but also from the AICs, characterised by their reliance on African artefacts during services. Despite its opposition to the AICs, Agbelengor had several features in common with this first wave of Pentecostal churches in Ghana, and is representative of that genre.

the Kumasi branch of the EP Church in the 1980s, had come to tolerate and integrate Pentecostal practices in its worship, making it unrecognisable as the original EP Church. Dzobo was re-elected moderator for a third term in 1992, a move which was met with great opposition from the leaders and members of the BSPF. The matter was taken to the courts, and resulted in the BSPF breaking away from the EP Church. This faction of the church called itself the new EP Church, the EP Church *of* Ghana, as opposed to the old EP Church, the EPC, [comma] Ghana. A branch of the new EPC appeared to have metamorphosed into yet another church, called the Global Alliance (GA) during the course of my first period of fieldwork in 2003–4. The membership of the GA consists of ex-members of the EPC, Ghana. The arrival of the GA has alleviated much of the confusion caused by the 'of' and 'comma', seeing that the EPC, Ghana has virtually disappeared from the scene in smaller Anlo towns, such as Anlo-Afiadenyigba.

In Anlo, the GA attracted younger people, many of whom resided in the bigger cities (Aflao, Accra, and Lome) and visited the village at the weekend. A sociological profile of these churchgoers is revealing: most of them were under thirty-five years of age, reasonably well-educated, literate, aspirational – and aiming to leave Anlo for better opportunities. These newer charismatic churches were attractive on account of their internationalised character and the networking opportunities they provide. In addition to the GA, there are churches such as Deeper Life, Church of Pentecost, and Armies of God: each church counted between twenty and fifty members in Anlo-Afiadenyigba in 2010, who ranged from extremely committed people to those who were not entirely convinced of the churches' suitability for themselves.

The services of the GA are like the other Pentecostal churches, and contrast sharply with those of the EP Church. Most members of the GA endorse a strict stance against incorporating aspects of traditional religion, as well as the attitudes of the more liberal churches. There is little interaction between the members of the GA and the non-Christian sphere, which is understood as the realm of the Devil. The following comments are typical of members of contemporary Pentecostal churches:

I go to the Global Alliance church, though a few people in my family go to 'fetish' priests. Church pastors and members do not approve of these shrines. I used to go to the shrines too: I was first a Gorovodu devotee. That did not work for me. Then members of my family told me that I was to replace my grandmother in the Yewe cult. So I went to the shrine. I became very unhappy there. My other family and financial problems did not stop. I could not even stay there until the ceremonies were done for me. I left my hometown (Afife), and came to Keta. Then I came to Global Alliance: I surrendered myself to Jesus, stopped dabbling with fetishes, and denounced all other family members who worship fetishes. I am covered in the blood of Jesus and protected by the Holy Spirit. In the EP and

Catholic churches, members openly associate with fetish houses and so there is a lot of witchcraft and evil in the church. The fetish houses – whatever deities they may be dedicated to – are the causes of most peoples' problems. Joining a church that does not tolerate such practices is the only refuge against this evil. Now, I am happy.[30]

Indeed, 'heathen' practices are understood as problems that can be alleviated by joining church, including the ancestral worship to which the mainline churches seem to have reconciled themselves. The vehemence with which Pentecostal churches denounce African tradition, however, gives rise to cases of classic 'backsliding' in missionary terms, given that members are not allowed to access both Christian and non-Christian spheres. Unhappy church members revert to traditional practices, intensifying the competition between the Christian and non-Christian religious agents. The rediscovery of 'traditional' religion in Anlo after the 1990s was also made possible in part by a religious body known as the Afrikania Renaissance Mission (ARM). The cultural and religious politics of the Mission has encouraged the polarisation of the non-Christian and Christian spheres in Anlo, leading to the formation of a clear-cut conceptual divide between the two traditions, and the re-emergence of debates about the foreignness and effectiveness of Christianity in Anlo.

The Afrikania Mission: The Reinvention of Tradition

During the early 1990s, the ARM, whose chief aim was to safeguard African 'traditional' religion, became an integral part of the religious landscape in Anlo. The Mission was highly critical of Pentecostal Christianity, and its stance on 'traditional' African religions, claiming that 'traditionalists' were persecuted when practising their religion.

The Afrikania Mission was founded in 1982 by a former Roman Catholic priest, Dr Kwabena Damuah (b. 1930), in western Ghana. He lived in the United States for twelve years, earning a PhD in theology from Howard University in the late 1970s. Damuah subsequently held lecturing posts in a number of institutions in the United States, as well as the University of the West Indies. He returned to Ghana in 1976, where he held many prestigious positions, including Head of the Agricultural Institute. In 1980, he was made President of the National Union of the Ghanaian Catholic Diocesan Priests Association. The deteriorating economic situation in Ghana led him to take up a lectureship at the University of Jos (Nigeria) in 1981. Damuah returned to Ghana from Nigeria just a year later, amid the tension of the 'Second Coming', the second military coup staged by Jerry Rawlings. He was in sympathy

[30] Adzo Amevedzi, Anlo-Afiadenyigba, 6 March 2004.

with the Rawlings revolution and actively encouraged people to participate in it. Damuah was made a member of the governing PNDC,[31] a move
strongly criticised by the Catholic Church. Though he left government
later that year, he continued to 'support the revolution wholeheartedly'
(Gyanfosu 2002: 290).

Damuah resigned from the Catholic Church in 1982, a move that
can be analysed against the backdrop of the Second Coming. Part of
the Rawlings project was to forge a populist movement, which would
restore in Ghanaians a sense of pride and control over their everyday
lives. Damuah's move away from the Catholic Church, a foreign body
with its roots outside Ghana, was highly symbolic. He had developed
the belief that Christianity had contributed to the problems that Ghana
battled with at the time: mass poverty, social inequality, corruption, and a
complete breakdown of state functions. Damuah claimed that the Pentecostal influx of the 1980s had worsened the situation, by creating a culture of passive acceptance and indifference, rather than critical political
engagement. He also argued that Christianity had worked to Africa's
detriment, leaving a legacy of moral and intellectual poverty. Missionary
demonisation of 'traditional' African religion and culture had resulted
in a serious confidence crisis (Gyanfosu 2002: 271–2). The message
of political engagement and patriotism spread by the Rawlings revolution provided the ideal backdrop for Damuah's religious experiments.
Subsequent Afrikania leaders would remain sympathetic to the ideals of
Rawlings, sharing his goals of nation building.

Like Nkrumah, who had spent his formative years in America, Damuah
was greatly influenced by African-American and anti-colonial thinkers:
Edward Blyden, Marcus Garvey, and Martin Luther King Jr. Damuah
advocated a curious religious revival, influenced by his understanding of
a shared African history and culture. While he was committed to protecting and actively propagating 'traditional' practices in Ghana, part of his
philosophy revolved around celebrating the psychic and cultural solidarity of all African peoples. Ironically, Damuah's preaching was rooted
in Biblical terminology and a Biblical understanding of Africa's place in
the world. Egypt occupies an important spiritual location in Afrikania
ideology: it was the cradle of the Kemetic race and of all black peoples;
Amen-Ra was the Creator, to whom every African subconsciously prayed
whatever African 'religion' he practised. 'African traditional religion'
was meant to take its rightful place amongst other world religions. It
was 'mankind's first recorded religion', with its origins in ancient Egypt,
'which had produced great spiritual leaders such as Imhotep, Black Egyptian born in 2700 BC, priest politician, adviser to Zoser of Egypt, archi-
tect, scientist, the world's first medical doctor and the great genius of the

[31] Provisional National Defence Council.

ancient world' (Damuah, quoted in Gyanfosu 2002: 272). The Afrikania faith was committed to 'religious and cultural emancipation of all African peoples' (ibid.). The best way to serve God, according to Damuah, was through one's own cultural perspective: for the African, this was through a religion that was born in Africa, rather than through Christianity which was the ideological arm of the colonial project.[32]

Soon after its inauguration, the Afrikania Mission embarked on a vigorous 'crusade' to open branches all over the country and win over followers. By 1984, it had offices in most regions of Ghana. Damuah wrote extensively about the ideology of the Afrikania Mission, and his vision for the movement.[33] In 1990, he formed a partnership with the Godian religion, a similar revivalist religious organisation based in Nigeria.[34] The Mission won sympathy from a very small section of society, mainly consisting of academics and intellectuals, while most rural non-Christian Ghanaians (the group that Damuah had hoped would form the heart of the movement) could neither understand nor engage with his ideas.

After Damuah's death in 1992, the movement suffered from a lack of direction, eventually splitting into two: the ARM (Afrikania Renaissance Mission or Sankofa Faith)[35] headed by Osofo Kofi Ameve and the 'original Afrikania Mission' headed by Kwasi Dankama Quarm, both among the first priests initiated by Damuah. While the ARM gained recognition as a vocal religious institution under Ameve's leadership, Quarm's Afrikania Mission remained in the background. Ameve, a successful building contractor, had lived in Egypt for several years, and he used his personal fortune to rejuvenate the ARM. Ameve believed that Ghana was on the verge of a complete Christian conversion, as a result of the aggressive evangelical strategy of the Pentecostal churches. He encouraged the practice of Sunday services (started by Damuah), as Afrikania's alternative to church attendance, holding most of his services in the Arts Centre, a well-known location in Accra. Ameve drew moral and financial support from African-American visitors to Ghana, who identified with Damuah's teachings.[36] He did much to popularise the cause of the ARM, including weekly radio programmes and training workshops for those interested in 'African traditional religion'. He rehoused the ARM in a new building

---

[32] For more on the Afrikania Mission see De Witte (2008).

[33] See the website of the Afrikania Mission, <http://members.tripod.com/afrikania/> (accessed 16 January 2013) for a detailed explanation of their religious beliefs and practices.

[34] Godianism originated in Nigeria during the 1950s, and aimed to unite practices of 'traditional' Igbo, Yoruba, Hausa, Efik, Ibibio, Urhobo, and Itshekiri religion. Early Godians were Nigerian nationalists, although the movement spread beyond its borders, gaining followers in several African countries and amongst Africans in the diaspora.

[35] Sankofa means 'to go back' or 'to return', and is associated with the Akan *Adinkra* symbol.

[36] Interview with Kofi Ameve, Accra, 3 August 2000.

in Odorkor (a north Accra suburb). Ameve attracted some high-profile recruits to his cause: Professor Kwakuvi Azasu, of the prestigious Teachers' Training College at Cape Coast, and Dr Atsu Kove, a prominent scholar and academic. Both men are highly respected public figures in Ghana.[37]

Ameve was himself from the southern Ewe belt and, not surprisingly, the ARM saw a rise in its popularity in Anlo. As most prominent leaders and spokespersons of this movement were southern Ewe, the ARM came to be recognised throughout Ghana as an Anlo movement. This erroneous perception only reconfirmed stereotypical perceptions of the Anlo within Ghana: they were a people enthralled by witchcraft, *juju*, and 'traditional' practices, which only led to their further demonisation within a progressively Pentecostalising environment. This greatly disappointed Ameve, who had hoped to give the movement a Ghana-wide presence. Many local Anlo intellectuals and chiefs joined the Mission, establishing Afrikania offices and centres in almost every Anlo village. That the Anlo found the message of the Afrikania Mission as appealing as Pentecostal Christianity, which was gaining an almost hegemonic acceptance in other parts of Ghana, is interesting. Over a century ago, missionary anthropologists had often noted that conversion to Christianity in Anlo was a notoriously difficult project, as the ancestors and *trowo* occupied an important role in peoples' perceptions of self, identity, and engagement with the world (Debrunner 1965: 78). Full-fledged initiates of the various Anlo religious networks, who see their identities as religious subjects first, vis-à-vis their *trowo* and *voduwo*, were sympathetic to the message of the Mission, despite not fully understanding the nuances of Ameve's arguments on race and religion.

Over the past two decades, the ARM has been encouraging 'traditional' shrines across Ghana to affiliate with them, in an attempt to bring together various cultic practitioners at their Sunday service, in order to rival church congregations in numbers. ARM's Sunday services are an interesting spectacle, precisely because they highlight all the contradictions and inconsistencies within the movement. During Ameve's leadership, they were conducted in the Arts Centre in Accra, and the vast majority of the congregation consisted of African-American tourists and expatriate residents of Accra. Afrikania elders, the chief linguist, and a few priests were usually positioned at a table in front of the congregation. A drumming group was usually seated beside the altar. Afrikania songs and hymns were recited in the manner of a church service. The congregation was invited to confess their sins. Passages from the 'Afrikania Bible' – authored by Damuah and Ameve – were read out. Ultimately,

---

[37] Kofi Ameve died in 2003, and Atsu Kove succeeded him as head of the Afrikania Mission in April 2004.

libation replaced the Catholic communion, with members invited to dip their fingers in a libation cup. The priest poured libation on the ground, an act that symbolised the unity of the living with the ancestors. In larger congregations, newcomers were introduced and requested to speak on why they chose to attend the services of the Afrikania Mission, a giving of personal testimony which resembles the practice of many Pentecostal churches.

Such Sunday services were held in all Anlo towns during the course of my fieldwork. In Anlo-Afiadenyigba, they were conducted by a secondary school teacher, Quasi Nyamesi, a trained Afa practitioner and a Fofie devotee. Nyamesi's profile is typical of an Afrikania leader: a well-educated intellectual, who has worked all over Ghana and Nigeria, and is involved in aspects of traditional religion and worship. He has detailed knowledge about the ARM, though he is slightly critical of its reliance on ancient Egyptian symbolism and other supposedly universal African ideas, which he believes have little relevance for the average rural Ghanaian. The factor that unites Nyamesi with other ARM enthusiasts is his distrust of Christianity, and a commitment to encouraging the youth to take an interest in 'traditional' religion rather than join Pentecostal churches. The Sunday services in Anlo-Afiadenyigba were organised very much in the manner of those in Accra described above. A few members of local religious cults – though members seldom congregated together – were united in worship of Amen Ra, while Afa, Fofie, Yewe, and Blekete (Gorovodu) drummers contributed to the service, accompanied by some dancing and possession. Passages from the 'Afrikania Bible', which usually revolved around the practical problems most frequently encountered in the village, were read out: the ills of womanising, drunkenness, borrowing money, and theft. The service ended in 'cultural lessons', which discussed the activities of local churches, as well as the conflicts between churches and 'traditional' religion, with the leader urging members not to join churches. ARM's services were not very well attended: while I was in Anlo-Afiadenyigba, the strength of the congregation usually ranged from ten to thirty-five.

The account below is just one of the many examples I encountered of former Christian, ARM sympathisers 'rediscovering' the cults they were formerly involved with, typical of the post-1990s.

My mother was a Yewe *vodusi* and a *fofiesi*, and I grew up worshipping them. I joined the army and left this village when I was young. I married a woman who was a devout Church of Pentecost member. She stopped me from worshipping these deities immediately. We lived in Accra, and I started attending that church. I did well in the army, but towards the end of my career, I experienced a series of problems with business and health. Three of my children died in different accidents. I was a broken man. I came back to the village to grieve: this was in 1999. My family was on hand with advice. They told me of a pact my mother had made with Fofie: she experienced difficulties at childbirth, and promised to pledge me to it if I survived. I had forgotten about this bond: it is on account of Fofie that I was brought forth into the world, and it had protected me when I was in the army. But throughout my married life, I had become a Christian because of my wife. Both Pentecostal Christianity [the older AICs] and the new churches [the Pentecostal churches] are so condemning of the ways of our ancestors, and had forced me into remaining indifferent towards them. So the ancestors, *trowo*, and *voduwo* were punishing me for ignoring them. I decided to revive my links with Fofie: I started pouring libation for my mother's household Fofie objects. I perform my responsibilities as an *agbota*, and usually dress in cloth and beads like other Fofie worshippers. My wife was horrified when I reverted to Fofie worship. She was advised by her congregation that my renewed affinity for Fofie would be the cause of her spiritual and economic downfall. So she left me. But I am better off now because Fofie spirits are looking after me. I attend ARM services whenever I can. I think the ARM can teach the youth not to blindly follow Christianity. It is not necessarily good for us. We must not forget our own ancestors and gods.[38]

The ARM also encourages priests of various cults in Anlo to make their services available to people irrespective of their families' spiritual histories, in an attempt to counter church attendance. This has led to acute competition between religious agents (both cultic networks and churches) for followers. Replacement cults, like Yewe, which are losing nominal and committed members to churches, are in the process of opening up, and recruiting people from lineages hitherto not associated with them. As a result, I came across several people during the course of my fieldwork who were accessing shrines, networks, and churches with which their families did not have a history of engagement. Most of these people had also sampled the services of a number of shrines and deities, before settling for one of them – as in the following two accounts.

I frequently visit the Yewe shrine in Gbanyaga, especially in times of need. Nobody in my immediate family is connected to the shrine, or the Yewe cult for that matter. I am not a fully-initiated *vodusi*, and I do not think I will ever become one. I was very sick once, and I tried a number of shrines and deities. I went to our family *trowo* (including Fofie and Gorovodu), and two charismatic churches, but was not cured. Then an ARM elder from this village suggested that I go to a number of shrines (he told me which ones). The deities and the priest-ess in the Gbanyaga shrine had a remedy for my problems. I have been a regular visitor to only this shrine since 2000. I usually go only there for everything. I do not go to church at all. I get what I need from here. I have formed a bond with the Gbanyaga deities.[39]

I have been to several shrines for advice. My father's family are involved in Fofie worship. I was put under the protection of Fofie when I was young. Most diviners told me that I should become a *fofiesi*. But worshipping those spirits and doing everything for them did not keep me happy and free of problems. So I went

---

[38] Interview with Babaa, Anlo-Afiadenyigba, 11 April 2004.
[39] Interview with Esi, Anlo-Afiadenyigba, 8 March 2004.

in search of a deity that could help me. I tried several shrines, Gorovodu, Yewe, Adzevodu, and eventually have become a devotee of Mamma, a new deity from Nigeria. Mamma can do just about anything for you, from healing sickness to pacifying dead ancestors in any form, and preventing witchcraft attacks. I have been a Mamma worshipper since 2002. I have broken my ties with Fofie. Those spirits cannot 'take me' now.[40]

The second account is indicative of competition between 'traditional' religious agents for followers. While, in theory, elders of the ARM believe that individuals may be able to worship more than one set of 'traditional' deities, the increasing number of new religious agents in the religious system – in the form of Pentecostal charismatic churches – means that all shrines, networks, and churches are competing against each other for followers. The competition is not just between Christian churches and the non-Christian sphere, but also between *trowo* and *voduwo* cults that have hitherto been complementary, and capable of sharing followers.

Historicising Religious Change

Accounting for religious change in African societies, based on the evolution of 'traditional' shrines and cults, is a notoriously difficult task. For example, Parrinder (1970) argued that it was almost impossible in view of the lack of conventional historical evidence. Horton (1971), in his attempts to explain the large-scale conversions to Christianity in Africa, approached the problem of the paucity in sources by developing a model of religious change that roughly explained general trends in most African societies. Religious cults and networks in West Africa, on account of their inherently unstable and dynamic nature, are ever-changing in form, character, and function, presenting the ethnographer-historian with a peculiar set of challenges. Tracing the historical evolution of such religious networks and practices is time-consuming when ethno-historical methods are employed. For example, it took Baum 23 years of fieldwork and seven fieldtrips to Esulalu in order to document the rise of certain categories of shrine that rose specifically in response to Diola society's integration into the Atlantic slave-holding and trading economy (Baum 1999: 21). Previous studies of religion along the Slave Coast (De Surgy 1981; Rosenthal 1998; Wendl 1999) have been notoriously ahistorical, a reflection of the unruly nature of Ewe-Mina religion, which lends itself neither to definition nor clear historical reconstruction.

During the course of my ethnographic fieldwork in Anlo, which has lasted over a decade, I sought to look for some patterns of order within the extremely disorderly and energetic religious field, which was populated by deities and ancestors that constantly changed form; supplicants who

---

[40] Interview with Faith Nyameshi, Anlo-Afiadenyigba, 29 August 2005.

associated and dissociated with several networks with ease; Christians who returned to the worship of the *trowo* and *voduwo*; traditionalists who surrendered to Christ; witches and witchcraft practitioners who operated superstitiously across all boundaries, and angry slave spirits. A pattern finally emerged: I realised that my informants could be divided into two groups, based on when they began accessing the services of the various entities in the religious system. Each group engaged with cultic networks in Anlo and the denominations of Christianity in different ways. These trends helped build up a picture of religious change at an inter-generational level, over a century.

The older informants I interviewed were born roughly between 1930 and 1970. They became active in the religious landscape between the 1940s and 1990s. The vast majority of these people inherited their asso-ciation with Anlo cults and religious networks through ancestral ties. Complete initiation into cults – becoming either a *vodusi* or *fofiesi*, for instance – appeared to be hereditary. Such people were considered to be following in the footsteps of their ancestral sponsors, or *amedzotowo*. Inner-circle memberships in these religious cultic networks were also inherited. Even the less-committed members of these cultic networks, located at the periphery, usually accessed the services provided by the cult in question only if their families had a history of association with it. Anti-witchcraft and protective cults, not usually associated with ances-tral agency, like Gorovodu (despite being new arrivals into the religious system) and Adzevodu also exhibited many characteristics of the replace-ment cults. Devotees of this age group appeared to be treating deities in the religious system like ancestral deities – worshipping only those with whom their families had prior connections. Also, older devotees (includ-ing the more committed inner-circle members) could be initiated into two or more cults at the same time, and access the different spiritual services provided by these. Although spiritual problems manifested themselves in the same way, through sickness and loss of wealth, the diagnosis behind each problem was specific, and warranted association with the particular cult that could rectify that particular problem. The Anlo deities appeared to have been quite specialised, occupying unique functional niches in the religious system: Yewe *vodusiwo* appear to have joined the cult on account of life crises attributed to ancestral neglect; Gorovodu (and worshippers of other anti-witchcraft cults) use the cult to gain access to priests' medi-cinal expertise and healing or protective powers; Fofie initiates believe their chances of progress were blocked by angry slave ancestors. All these problems could affect the same individual, making him or her associate with several cults, either in the inner or outer circles of worship, sim-ultaneously. So, for example, a person could be a full-fledged member of the Fofie cult (*fofiesi*) and a Yewe shrine member awaiting initiation (*kpokpo*), as well as an Adzevodu supplicant at the same time. Similarly, a person could be a Gorovodu *trosi* and a Yewe *vodusi* simultaneously. Being a Christian did not prevent a person associating with one or more of these cultic networks when the need arose at any point in their lives. In some cases, the association endured throughout their lives, as either casual supplicants to the *trowo* and *voduwo* or as fully initiated members of these cultic networks: indeed, mainline Anlo Christians born before 1970 practised dual worship with ease, accessing traditional cultic networks as well as Christian churches.

This scenario changed after the 1990s, especially after the influx of new religious agents – in the form of charismatic churches – into the religious system. The cultural politics of the Afrikania Mission has also led to competition between cultic networks, a move away from a state of functional coexistence. The generation, born after 1970, who associated with cultic networks and Christianities in Anlo now seemed to forge rather superficial relationships with a number of deities and churches, in their capacity as cult members located at the periphery or outer circle, or as potential church members. In the case of traditional cultic networks, they then proceeded to petition the various deities at the heart of these shrines for spiritual favours. Lineage connections were not a consideration when determining which shrines they accessed. This meant that priests of cultic networks were extending themselves beyond their traditional pool of followers, and recruiting people from outside their usual kinship- and lineage-based spheres of influence. Devotees in post-1990s Anlo are eventually coming to worship what they believe to be the most effective deity, shrine, or church for their personal needs, after sampling a number of religious agents. Therefore, choice plays a major part in which religious agent they finally come to adopt as their preferred one – unlike their predecessors, who could access most cultic networks mainly through ancestral ties. Unlike the supplicants in the first group, they did not engage with more than one cultic network, after they had settled on the network with which to engage.

These changes mean that Anlo cults are no longer believed to be dispensers of specialised favours. Most religious agents cater to an array of spiritual and practical needs. So Yewe, Gorovodu, and other protective cults appear to perform the same function in the religious system, and prescribe remedies for issues that range widely from witchcraft to non-specific illnesses. So the overwhelmingly lineage-based replacement cults, such as Yewe, are attempting to extend themselves beyond the descent groups to which they were limited, while priests of the more open networks like Gorovodu and Adzevodu are pursuing aggressive recruitment strategies, by marketing and advertising their religious services across diverse sections of Anlo society – by word of mouth and making contact with potential devotees – in a manner that resembles evangelical campaigns associated with pastors of the newer Pentecostal churches.

These cultic networks are moving to a greater degree of openness by aiming to recruit more outer-circle members, and competition between cultic agents for followers appears to be on the rise. How this may affect the Fofie cult in the near future, and the legacy of slavery as preserved within the framework of the cult, will be the focus of the conclusion.

8 Conclusion: Ritual Servitude, Trans-Atlantic Conversations, and Religious Change

The Problem of Ritual Servitude

During the 1990s and 2000s, a series of events would lead the Anlo to revisit their ideas about slavery in their past, and also reassess the efficacy of some of their religious traditions associated with what the media began terming 'ritual servitude'. Aspects of traditional religion in Ghana's southern Volta Region, especially in the regions of Anlo and Tongu, received unwanted publicity in the mid-1990s in the national and international media. This episode brought shrines dedicated to well-established Anlo deities into the national spotlight. Anlo is home to about seven or eight *troxovi* shrines. These shrines are characterised by the attachment to them of large numbers of female initiates. *Troxovi* shrines are centred around Nyigbla in Afife, Sui and Tomi in Anloga, and Adzima and Mama Vena in Klikor-Agbozume. *Troxovi* shrines[1] usually demand young women (called *trokosiwo*, sing. *trokosi*)[2] in return for spiritual services provided to families, or to address the consequences of ancestral (mis)conduct in the past. Traditionally, family members were responsible for the upkeep and maintenance of initiates in such shrine complexes. These women were free to leave the confines of the shrine after they had performed the religious rituals that cemented the relationship between themselves and the deities: they were not obliged to live in the shrine complexes. They were bound to the shrine to which they had been pledged for the rest of their lives, in the sense that they had to return to celebrate ceremonies to honour the appropriate *trowo* and *voduwo* at stipulated times. In the event of the death of a *trokosi*, a replacement would be sought out within the same patrilineage. The practice originated during the eighteenth century, to enable priests either to have access to labour or to enlarge their retinues. It is widely believed that there are a greater number of *troxovi* shrines in Tongu than there are in Anlo.

---

[1] These structures, which are peculiar to the ritual landscape of the southern Ewe-speaking belt, evolved in the eighteenth century to maintain control over the labour of female initiates (Greene 1996a: 64; Akyeampong 2001b: 224).

[2] *Tro* = deity; *kosi* = servant. *Trokosi* is usually translated in the Ghanaian media as 'shrine servant'. The term *fiasidiwo* (sing. *fiasidi*) has come to be widely used in Anlo since the 1990s (Jenkins 2012: 12).

The practice of pledging women, before or upon their births, to serve shrines and deities is very common in Anlo. The theme of replacing dead ancestors in religious cults is practised extensively: all Yewe *vodusiwo* and *fofiesiwo* inherit their positions and religious duties in fulfilment of ancestral ties. The very act of being pledged to a deity in this way implies attachment to the deities in question, but also a degree of subjugation within the context of the cultic hierarchy. Initiates of *troxovi* cults in Anlo are often referred to as *troklu* (m) or *trokosi* (f), which translates into slave or servant of deity. *Klu* is the term most commonly used to refer to a person who does not own his labour, while *kosi* bears connotations of servant or slave wife. Such individuals were presented to the *trowo* as offerings by their families in recognition of spiritual favours bestowed upon them. Women often made ritual pacts with deities, promising to dedicate their children to the *tro* that helped them conceive and give birth successfully; such children retained strong links with these *trowo* throughout their lives. Runaway slaves and condemned people historically sought refuge in such shrines, placing themselves under the protection of these deities, thus being able to keep their would-be captors at bay (Jenkins 2012: 112–14). As Anlo cults were hierarchical in their organisation, the services and labour of *trokluwo* and *trokosiwo* were controlled to a certain extent by senior initiates and priests. *Trokluwo* and *trokosiwo* were ethnic insiders, either born in Anlo or with strong kinship ties to people in the constituent *dutowo* of the chiefdom. Ritual servitude of this kind differed greatly from the other Anlo practices of slavery, even though some of these pledged people had no control over the decision to join a cult. They were regarded with a mixture of admiration and fear, their statuses elevated by the fact that they were familiar with some secrets of *trowo* worship, and were beneficiaries of large support networks in the form of fellow cult initiates.

Accounts of *troxovi* shrines first made their way into the Ghanaian media in 1977, when Mark Wisdom, a Tongu man, began writing about the life experiences of *trokosiwo*.[3] Wisdom, a Pentecostal Christian, claims that he received divine guidance in a dream that instructed him to free such women, supposedly held in ritual bondage. Discourses about *troxovi*, as he constructed them for the media, typically endorsed the stereotypes of African primitivism versus 'progressive' Christianity. These women were, according to Wisdom, helpless victims of their own superstitious beliefs; scheming priests kept them in a state of semi-slavery, from which there was no escape. Almost fifteen years later, in 1993, his efforts were backed by a Canadian woman, Sharon Titan, who was working for a Christian NGO called International Needs (IN). In collaboration

---

[3] See Jenkins (2012) for a detailed account of this controversy, and for the history of these shrines in the Klikor-Agbozume area.

with the national Commission for Human Rights and Administrative Justice (CHRAJ), IN led a high-profile campaign against *troxovi* shrines in Anlo and Tongu. These two organisations claimed that such *trokosiwo* were nothing but slaves of priests, and that their human rights were being infringed. They spearheaded a movement for the 'liberation' of these 'shrine servants', calling for the immediate release of all *trokosiwo*, believed to be victims of 'modern-day slavery': IN estimated the number of women in ritual servitude to be 4,042, of which Anlo and Tongu accounted for 92 per cent (Akyeampong 2001a: 12). By 1998 IN actually claimed that it had been successful in freeing hundreds of such 'enslaved' women, by creating awareness amongst priests, traditional rulers, and the initiates themselves about the pitfalls of the practice. Their anti-*troxovi* operations eventually attained national recognition when, in 1998, a bill passed in the Ghanaian Parliament made the practice of female ritual servitude a second-degree offence, punishable by imprisonment (ibid.).

Some Anlo intellectuals interpreted this anti-*troxovi* campaign as a direct attack on the moral backbone of their religious institutions. Under the auspices of the Afrikania Renaissance Mission (ARM), the revivalist religious organisation committed to safeguarding African 'traditions' from Christianity, these intellectuals mounted an equally ferocious campaign to counter the efforts of these NGOs. The ARM's activities received nationwide attention during this controversy. The leader of the ARM at the time was Kofi Ameve, who saw the campaign to abolish *troxovi* shrines as part of the larger evangelical project, aimed at destroying all 'traditional' African religions. The ARM started mobilising people in Anlo to resist this cultural onslaught.[4] The ARM maintains that *troxovi* as an institution is a fundamental aspect of Anlo religion that is extremely beneficial to society, as it performs the valuable task of educating women initiated into such shrines about the religion of their ancestors. A curious reinvention of tradition quickly took place, to endorse such *troxovi* shrines. Key members of the ARM argued in their sermons that the *troxovi* system first came into existence when the Anlo migrated from Egypt to Sudan centuries ago, and was thousands of years old.[5] Others insisted that the system was akin to a Catholic nunnery, and there was nothing fundamentally wrong with it. Shrines were, according to them, training centres for women who would eventually form the moral backbone of Anlo society. Some senior Anlo chiefs, notably Togbi Addo VIII and Togbi Honi III, both of Klikor, also keenly defended the efficacy of the system by insisting that a *trokosi*, (also called a *fiasidi* in Anlo) was not a

---

[4] The Afrikania Mission dismissed all liberation ceremonies as a set-up and accused International Needs of collaborating with 'fake' *trokosi* priests and staging such ceremonies in order to earn foreign exchange. The truth about the nature of these practices will probably never be attainable amidst the sound and fury of their politicisation.
[5] Interview with Kofi Ameve, Accra, 10 August 2000.

slave, but a woman fit to marry a chief, trained in a traditional institution, instilled with noble values. This was a play on the semantics of the word: *fia* = chief; *si* = wife/pledged; and *di* originates from the verb to marry.

IN claimed that its campaign was successful in Tongu, as they managed to 'free' hundreds of these 'shrine servants'. They also set up centres to provide employment for them after they left the confines of the shrine, and invested in rehabilitation programmes where these women could learn various vocational skills that would enable them to integrate back into the community and make an independent living. IN made very little progress in Anlo, mainly because of the influence of the ARM and its sympathisers. The ARM received much public recognition during this period, and became an important cultural institution in Anlo. Although these *troxovi* shrines are not related to the Fofie cult, the controversy became instrumental in reshaping perceptions of the slave-holding past. The Fofie cult mainly commemorates bought people and war captives from areas north of Anlo. Apart from *amefeflewo* and *ametsiavawo*, the Anlo had several categories of pawns, who were generally ethnic insiders: *awowawo*, *kluviwo*, and 'panyarred' individuals, all of whom could be redeemed upon repayment of debts. The *trokosiwo* or *fiasidiwo* occupied a curious position in Anlo society: while they were also ethnic insiders, they were neither pledged nor pawned; they were 'free' but yet under the control of the shrine (and deities) for life. The controversy conflated the different types of slavery in the popular imagination, as the traditionalist lobby compared the *troxovi* phenomenon with various episodes in Anlo's slave-holding past. Anlo 'slavery' (especially domestic slavery) was reinvented as a humane practice, one which respected the spiritual well-being of both slave and master. Anlo slavery in the past and shrines that practised 'ritual servitude' in contemporary Anlo were both upheld as the epitome of humanity and gentleness by these Anlo intellectuals, who were keen to portray their culture in a positive and progressive light.

The interest generated by the *troxovi* controversy brought several independent journalists, foreign and Ghanaian, to Anlo. In the 1990s, an Agbozume-based intellectual, Dale Maasiasta, had established an educational centre and museum, dedicated to the study of Anlo-Ewe traditions and religion, called the Blakhud Centre.[6] A number of people made their way to Agbozume, on account of the media frenzy generated by the 'discovery' of the *troxovi* system. This was the perfect opportunity to promote cultural tourism, and the members of the Blakhud Centre rose to the occasion. The *troxovi* controversy saw Anlo traditionalists

---

[6] Blakhud is an acronym for Black Humanity Development. The founder had hoped to set up similar cultural institutions throughout Ghana and the sub-region. See website: <http://www.hypertextile.net/BLAKHUD/> (accessed 1 March 2007).

reconfigure internal slave holding in the Anlo public consciousness, during the 2000s, as a humane practice that safeguarded the rights of slaves and masters, completely different from slavery as it was practised in the Americas. This reconfiguration of historical slave holding in Anlo was developing against the backdrop of a broader, ongoing conversation about slavery and the slave trade in the local, national, and international arenas.

Reshaping the Moral Contours of History: Trans-Atlantic Conversations

In 2001, Emmanuel Akyeampong observed that there 'has been a conspicuous absence of dialogue between Africans and African-Americans over slavery and the slave trade' (Akyeampong 2001a: 1). The past two decades have seen an increase in scholarship about the psychological effects of the legacy of slavery and the slave trade on the peoples associated with the institution in West Africa.[7] The ethical questions that arise in West African cultures from the commemoration of slavery at the local level appear to differ greatly from the moral emphases in Euro-American narratives of the same event. Scholars have noted the completely different attitudes towards the legacy of slavery: Klein rightly observes that African-Americans take pride in their ability to rise from humble origins – and thus break out of the legacy of slavery – but Africans generally prefer not to refer to their slave origins, which carry connotations of stigma, shame, and foreignness in their host society (Klein 1989). West Africans seem more concerned by their agency in slave holding and by issues arising from the presence of slave descendants in their societies, than by their participation in selling people into the trans-Atlantic trade (see essays in Rossi 2009). The presence of African-Americans in West Africa, in search of their roots, has added a new dimension to the politics of remembering slavery all over the sub-region, including in Anlo. It would seem that, in contemporary Anlo, divergent traditions with different moral and historical emphases on the slaving past inhabit the public sphere: rather than compete for prominence with each other, they coexist, and the details of the different traditions get layered, mixed, and superimposed upon each other as time goes by. As these historical discourses negotiate for space and legitimacy through various media – ranging from the ritual environment to the educational curriculum, the modern print media, and commemorative festivals – they have all come to inform and alter how slavery and the slave trade are conceptualised in the Anlo historical imagination in the early twenty-first century.

---

[7] For example, see Benson (2003), Bob-Milliar (2009), and Rossi (2009) on West Africa.

The idea of staging a dialogue about slavery between continental Africans and Africans in the diaspora began gaining ground in Ghana in the early 1990s, when the then President Jerry Rawlings lobbied for the country's slave forts (such as Cape Coast and Elmina) to be recognised as UNESCO World Heritage sites.[8] Rawlings also instituted the Pan-African Festival (PANAFEST) in 1994, a biannual event, meant to encourage members of the African diaspora to forge stronger links – in the form of financial investments, NGOs, and developmental projects – with the country.[9] Ghana also began to offer diasporan Africans the benefits of full citizenship. A number of African-Americans have also been made chiefs in various southern Ghanaian villages, in the belief that this may encourage them to strengthen their ties with Ghana (Benson 2003). Rawlings had complex motivations. At a conference in the Republic of Benin in 1999, he joined Beninois President Mathieu Kerekou in apologising for the slave trade, a gesture that was well received by Africans in the diaspora. Both West African leaders had hoped that this very public apology would attract tourists and investors alike, as well as seek out powerful allies in the form of African-American pressure groups in the Americas. Clearly, exploiting the economic potential of the diaspora by the commodificaion of the slave trade was uppermost on their agenda (Holsey 2008: 230).

The representations of the slave trade in the museums of the castles of Cape Coast and Elmina bear testimony to how the event has come to be lodged in the Ghanaian public consciousness. The museum exhibits range from the material culture of early Fante societies of the seventeenth century to the story of the European participation in the slave trade. The story of colonialism, the emancipation of Africans in the Americas, and Africa's political independence from European powers are also documented. In these museum displays, the slave trade had to be represented in a manner that would strike a chord with diasporic audiences without making them resentful of local African engagement in the practice. In order to do this, history had to be misrepresented to some extent, and the African agency in the slave trade had to be underplayed. This has been done by 'racialising' history, by looking at it through a set of uncritical binary oppositions of white versus black, oppressor versus oppressed, European versus African. The European involvement is identified as the factor which accentuated large-scale slave holding and slave trading on the west coast of Africa. By injecting narratives of race into West African history, and suggesting that Africans in general were unwilling

---

[8] Ghana's coastline is dotted with forts from which the slave trade was conducted. Cape Coast and Elmina are the best-known.

[9] See website, PANAFEST 2007, <http://www.africa-ata.org/gh_panafest.htm> (accessed 27 December 2012).

participants in the slave trade, this history is able to exonerate all African participation in the trade. Continental Africans and diasporan Africans are both represented as victims of European colonisation and expansion. The experience of being subjects of European colonial nations in Africa is equated with the experience of being enslaved in the Americas.

Interestingly, the position of former President Rawlings on the subject of the slave trade – reflected in the following excerpts from his speech at PANAFEST 2009 –highlights the gap in the trans-Atlantic dialogue with respect to responsibility and victimhood.

Emancipation Day is a painful reminder of the pain our ancestors had to go through when Africa was colonised by the Europeans and Americans. Our fore-bears were sent to the West in conditions not fit for any living being. . . .

Emancipation Day also serves as a reminder of the pain that we Africans can inflict on our fellow brothers and sisters.

Emancipation Day is not just a reminder of the day slavery was abolished. It is a call on all African people to champion the cause of true freedom and justice wherever they live.[10]

Rawlings puts the blame primarily on colonialism (as this is what a dia-sporan audience is likely to be comfortable with), and only secondarily on local African societies. By diplomatically acknowledging the suffering of 'our forebears', he situates sold African slaves firmly within a past which both continental and diasporan Africans share. But, more significantly, by 'calling African people to champion the cause of true freedom and justice wherever they live', Rawlings is using the slave trade as a meta-phor to highlight contemporary forms and processes that promote global inequality, and Africa's marginal position in the world. This statement, of course, is a poignant critique of 'capitalism, development, North–South flows, unequal access to opportunity, wealth, and realisation of dignity' (Holsey 2008: 234). Holsey further argues that most of Ghana's post-nationalist and 'post-optimistic' citizens see the slave trade as a metaphor for global inequality, and they are largely unable to see the benefit of apologising for their role in slavery to people across the Atlantic. This is partly because of how the slave trade has been constructed in the public consciousness and in their educational curricula: post-colonial textbook histories 'must make the slave trade a minor addendum to the emergence of the modern nation state', to restore and rebuild Africa's image, and to prevent it from being perpetuated as the Dark Continent that exported nothing but slavery to the rest of the Atlantic World (ibid.: 5). Indeed, the problems of 'owning up to the past' in West Africa vis-à-vis the slave trade are complex and multifaceted, especially within the context of the

---

[10] J. J. Rawlings, 'Give true meaning to Emancipation Day', *Wordpress*, 18 August 2009, <http://jjrawlings.wordpress.com/2009/08/18/give-true-to-meaning-to-emancipation-day-rawlings/> (accessed 6 July 2012).

trans-Atlantic dialogue: African-Americans in particular, with a substantial emotional investment in the idea of their African roots, find it difficult to come to terms with the fact that continental Africans participated in, and benefited from, the slave trade; continental Africans are somewhat offended when asked to take responsibility for the slave trade, as they believe it symbolises Africa's insertion into the modern world economy on unequal terms (Holsey 2011).

Keen to put Anlo on the tourist trail, the Keta District Assembly and the Anlo Traditional Council decided to build a monument to slavery and the slave trade. Among the sites they chose was the village of Atorkor, located west of Whuti. Atorkor had a curious legend associated with it. An Anlo slave merchant, Dokutsu, is said to have sold an entire drumming group into slavery, at Srogboe, to either a Brazilian or a Portuguese crew (Akyeampong 2001a: 8). According to the legend, Dokutsu collaborated with some Europeans and extended an invitation to Dogbe and his drumming group on behalf of some Europeans to entertain the latter on board their ship. Once on board, they were captured, and clandestinely sold into slavery. But Dogbe managed to escape from them, and swam ashore. Historians date this event to around the 1850s (Akyeampong 2001a; Bailey 2005; Greene 2011). While the details of the betrayal were not public knowledge in either Whuti or Atorkor, the descendants of Dokutsu and Dogbe were aware of the story, and nursed bitter grudges against each other. Dogbe is said to have composed songs and new drumming rhythms, which were passed on from generation to generation within his family, denouncing Dokutsu's treachery towards his own people. In Anlo, descendants of slave traders are more forthcoming in acknowledging their role in the trade, as their ancestors' positions as slave merchants symbolise wealth and prestige. Dogbe's descendants were rather embarrassed at the attention to which they were suddenly subjected, even though members of the drumming troupe were not originally slaves, but tricked into slavery. This was because selling people into slavery was regarded as a form of punishment. It was an effective method of expelling unwanted people from the community, and Dogbe's descendants did not, under any circumstances, want to have that stigma attached to them. While acknowledging female foreign slave ancestors (as is done by Fofie initiates) is unproblematic, being reminded of links with Anlo people who were sold into slavery – and therefore purged out of the community – was highly awkward. Not surprisingly, it was the descendants of Dokutsu who suggested that this story be used to attract tourists to Atorkor. Bailey is of the opinion that the vast majority of people in Atorkor would rather restrict the story to the personal domain, as it brings back many painful memories of the slaving era, and exposes deep fault lines within the village (Bailey 2005).

The presence of African-Americans in southern Ghanaian societies has met with a mixed response. There have been several moves to make African-Americans chiefs in Akan areas (see Bob-Milliar 2009). While some local Ghanaian chiefs identify these moves as an easy method of promoting investment and encouraging local tourism, African-Americans see it as part of an elaborate project that enables them to get in touch with their roots, 'to bridge the gap' between 'those who left' and 'those who stayed behind' (Benson 2003: 110). Some Akan chiefs, in particular, are deeply critical of enstooling African-Americans, arguing that their ancestors got rid of murderers and criminals by selling them into slavery: therefore inviting expatriates back in this manner results in a perversion of tradition and undermines the long chain of chiefs who are of royal birth (ibid.: 129). In Anlo, I have encountered two individuals from North America who believe they have traced their African ancestry to the chiefdom. Their presence had reminded the Anlo of their agency in the slave trade, a subject about which, unlike slave holding, they have not developed any deep-seated anxieties.

One evening in Keta in 2010, I came across Rexford Smith,[11] a secondary school teacher from New Jersey, in his late fifties. His presence in this corner of Ghana is far from coincidental: he believes he has been able to trace his African ancestry to this stretch of the Slave Coast, and that he is almost certainly descended from an Anlo man sold into slavery during the eighteenth century. Rexford's efforts to trace his ancestry, however, are methodical and systematic, involving DNA testing and the consultation of historical records on both sides of the Atlantic. He was made aware of a particular project associated with a comprehensive DNA database, containing up to about 25,000 samples from about forty-five African 'ethnicities'. This particular project sought to map the genetic origins of all African-Americans.[12] In the hope that his DNA might tell the story of where he came from, Rexford sent off his own DNA samples to one of these projects at the cost of about $350. In the case of men, it is the 'Y' chromosome that is tested and matched up against a database, providing information of a man's genetic ancestry inherited from the paternal line, from father to father to father. The result would ascertain to which *halpogroup*, or major genetic tree of humanity, Rexford's direct patrilineal ancestors belonged. He was delighted when he discovered that his *halpogroup* was E1b1a, to which most West Africans belonged, suggesting that there was a direct uninterrupted paternal link to somewhere in West Africa. This laboratory further matched his DNA with that of a

---

[11] Name changed at request.
[12] Source: African Ancestry, <http://www.africanancestry.com/> (accessed 15 June 2012).

sample of an Anlo man, with whom he eventually made contact. Further research on his part suggests that he and this Anlo man, whom he now refers to as 'Uncle Kofi', may have had a common ancestor about eight generations ago.

Rexford visited Anlo in 2009 for the first time, at Kofi's invitation. Kofi arranged for him to be introduced to members of his patrilineage in Anloga. Most members of Rexford's 'family' in Anlo were welcoming. The head of the family poured a libation as an offering to the ancestors to thank them for reuniting the lineage with a 'lost son'. There were prayers held at family shrines to thank the ancestors for returning him to Anlo. Maintaining connections with the ancestors is an extremely important principle in Anlo religious logic, the central idea that governs the philosophy of Fofie-related practices. Therefore, most Anlo see it as important, if not necessary, for them to help African-Americans like Rexford reconnect with their long-forgotten ancestors. Rexford is convinced that he will be able to find some record of his first African ancestor in the oral traditions of this patrilineage, which, he suspects, date from the eighteenth century. Rexford plans to learn Ewe, and keep coming back to Anlo for extended periods of research into stories, narratives, and oral tradition associated with this family in Anloga.

Kofi hails from a slave-owning lineage, and members of his extended family are Fofie worshippers. While Rexford is delighted at his 'discovery' of Anlo, he is equally perturbed by the fact that his Anlo kinsmen were slave owners and slave traders in the past. His subject position, as a twenty-first century American, inclines him to condemn all aspects of the slave-holding and slave-trading pasts; he is also deeply uncomfortable when the Anlo celebrate the slaving past as an economic golden age.

It is painful to think that these people were engaged in such barbaric practices. Internal slave holding here, which denotes prestige, could not have been a pleasant experience for the slaves. As for selling their own into the slave trade to be shipped away... words fail me.[13]

Even more disturbing for Rexford is the fact that people in his lineage, including several Fofie initiates, remain unperturbed by their ancestors' involvement in selling people into the slave trade. A number of *fofiesiwo* suggest to Rexford that being disconnected from Africa has worked to his advantage: the fact that he was born in North America has meant he has had a better life; though devoid of the spiritual link with the land of his origins, he is materially better off than they are. As Metumisi, a *fofiesi* from Rexford's patrilineage, proceeds to explain when I ask what she feels about his return to Anlo:

---

[13] Interview with Rexford Smith, Keta, 7 December 2010.

It is true that we sold some people into slavery, and they were taken across the water [Atlantic]. We did not know where they were going to be taken or what was going to happen to them. We just sold them. But now their descendants are better off in America than we are in Africa. They are rich while we are poor. So why should they regret what happened? Why should they blame us? History has been kinder to them.[14]

In this way, *fofiesiwo* are able to avoid a critical assessment of the ethical implications of Anlo agency in selling people into slavery; instead, they can argue that African-Americans are, on the whole, more prosperous than their African kinsmen by virtue of being positioned geographically in the global North, which makes them immune to the economic uncertainties of life in the global South. Gideon Nyamesi, a secondary school teacher and a member of a Fofie-worshipping lineage, sums up the Anlo position on the subject of African-Americans and the slave trade:

We, here in Anlo or in Ghana, are not solely responsible for the slave trade. It was the result of other things, and many other people are responsible for it. We have a lot of problems to deal with now: corruption, unemployment, low productivity, and economic decline in Anlo and Ghana. But most of the descendants of slaves we sold are much better off than us: they have job security, more prosperous lives, better education, and opportunities to travel the world. They are in a better place now. If anybody has suffered in Africa on account of slavery, it is us, bled of our human capital.

But we are paying for what we did to our own slaves here in Anlo. We captured people and forced them to stay here. Slave women bore us many children, worked for us, and made us rich. And we did nothing good for them. We are addressing spiritual problems which arose out of that now. We need to make amends to our slaves now, so that their souls will rest in peace. We do not really need to apologise to the descendants of the people we sold. If some of these people come from America and elsewhere and look for us now, by all means, we shall welcome them, and allow them to stay among us for as long as they want. They need to feel connected to their Anlo ancestors, and we will show them how.[15]

It is clear that Nyamesi, like most Anlo, is struggling to make sense of the slave trade in a complex setting: the 'geographies provided by theories of both post-colonialism and the Black Atlantic' (Holsey 2008: 14); the ethical implications introduced by the trans-Atlantic dialogue; and his unique subjectivity as an Anlo person with specific concerns about local slave holding. The slave trade is constructed as an injustice against African people, societies, and nations, and not against present-day African-Americans, who are, according to Nyamesi, wealthier and better off. In the present conversation, African-Americans who claim affinity with Anlo through ancestry have been drawn back into Anlo history through locally construed notions of destiny, kinship, and ancestral

---

[14] Interview with Metumisi, Havedji, 6 December 2010.
[15] Interview with Gideon Nyamesi, Keta, 9 December 2010.

agency; their Anlo interlocutors, on the whole, have not engaged with the psychological effects of the slave trade and slave descent on peoples in the diaspora.

The trans-Atlantic dialogue may make the Anlo confront another aspect of slavery, in which they are forced to acknowledge their role in selling not only their own people, but also other Ghanaians and Africans into slavery. As the Anlo are keen to develop tourism as an industry, it would be right to observe that the trans-Atlantic dialogue has only just begun, and debates about Anlo agency in the slave trade are only in their infancy. If cultural tourism does indeed flourish in this corner of Ghana, the Anlo may have to reconfigure their conceptions of their slave-trading past in both public consciousness and historical imagination, in order to present a version that sits comfortably with their guests' expectations. Their anxieties about slavery may shift from interrogating their agency in slave holding to confronting their role in the slave trade, especially within the context of forging their identities as, firstly, post-colonial citizens of an African nation and, secondly, global trans-Atlantic 'black' subjects. The history of slavery and the slave trade may come to be viewed through the prism of binary oppositions such as coloniser versus colonised and European versus African. Ideas of race and Africanness may play an important role in informing and shaping these discourses, especially if bodies which seek to promote a Pan-African outlook for political reasons (such as the ARM), succeed in influencing the reconfiguration of slavery and the slave trade in Anlo's public imagination. There are some slave-holding families in Anlo who have already come into contact with African-Americans in search of their roots. The presence of people like Rexford has led some Anlo lineages to reconsider their actions in relation to the slave-trading past. In an attempt to recognise their role in the slave trade and the suffering they may have caused the descendants of people they sold into slavery, these lineages have instituted ritual practices to honour people expelled from the community through enslavement.[16] At the moment, these ritual provisions take the form of pouring a libation: clan functions and local level meetings sometimes end with an offering to all the ancestors (*togbuiwo*, *mamawo*, and *ametsiavawo*), the peoples of the present, the future unborn, and, latterly, those sold into slavery and their descendants. What happens in future, and how these conversations will develop new moral subjectivities and histories about slavery in Anlo – attached to or detached from the philosophy of the Fofie cult – remains to be seen.

---

[16] There is evidence that some Anlo communities are begin to engage with their agency in the internal West African and external trans-Atlantic slave trades. Jenkins describes the *Gowu* enactment in Klikor-Agbozume, an annual performance which addresses the moral dilemmas and lessons of selling people into slavery in the past (Jenkins 2012: 123–30).

Laying the Ghosts of Slavery to Rest: Religious Change and the Future of Fofie

The Fofie cult is the platform through which the Anlo have engaged with the memory of problematic aspects of local slavery in accordance with their own conceptions of history. The practices of the cult and the memory of the slave ancestors are intertwined and in some ways dependent on each other. Any study of the evolution of the Fofie cult has to be contextualised within the development of modern Anlo religion. A sociological and historical study of Anlo religion has suggested that Anlo cultural institutions were characterised by an inherent extraversion: the religious system has absorbed deities that originated from outside with relative ease. Priests of such new deities had to draw followers by displaying the efficacy of their spiritual goods, in terms of Anlo perceptions of their existential needs. If there was a sudden injection of new agents into the religious system (as there was between the 1870s and 1920s, and then after the 1990s), competition between these agents for followers became rife. In order to secure a foothold in Anlo society, every deity (and the cultic network which gradually developed around it) had to adopt survival strategies and ward off competing agents. Initially, in a bid to interest as many followers as possible, there would have been no restrictions on who could worship a new deity. As a deity's prowess increased, it would be housed in a shrine or several shrines depending on the number of priests, full-fledged initiates, and casual supplicants that it had attracted; if it thrived in the system long enough, it may have turned into a full-fledged cult. Such new cults would have functioned as an open religious network, marketing its services to all potential devotees and clients. These cults were also typically non-specialised in terms of their functions, as priests constantly had to reinvent themselves to satisfy their clientele. But, in the long run, such open cults risked losing some or many of their followers, as little commitment was expected of them.

As soon as a cult had attracted a significant number of followers, priests and devotees devised survival strategies to establish it in Anlo society. (The Anlo believers, of course, would attribute the success of a cult to the potency of the deities around which they are organised rather than any form of human agency.) The most common of these strategies was to switch from an open cult to a replacement one, where members and initiates could be recruited through lineage and kinship connections. (In other words, the deities at the heart of these cults would metamorphose from a state of kinlessness to Anlo-ness, shedding their foreign attributes and forging ties with Anlo people, lineages, and deceased ancestors.) This also implied a practice whereby, when an initiate of a cult died, a replacement was sought from within their family. While open cults received a limited degree of attention from a larger pool of followers, ancestral or replacement cults received life-long attention from comparatively smaller bands of devotees. So the long-term viability of a cult depended on its ability to open (into cults that sought to attract followers from all sections of Anlo society) and close (into replacement cults) at appropriate times, depending on the level of competition in the religious system. Thus the recruitment dynamics of cults changed periodically, depending on factors such as whether there were new religious agents on the scene functioning as open cults; the degree of competition in the religious system; the issues addressed by the cults in the system; and the social, economic, and political conditions in Anlo. Therefore, Anlo cults were in constant flux: both structurally, in terms of whether they had to open or close, and thematically, in terms of their need to reinvent themselves according to the most pressing concerns of their devotees.

Examining Anlo religious history from the vantage point of the early twenty-first century, I suggest we can isolate three watershed periods, during which the nature and structure of the religious system changed. Our first records of Anlo religion date from 1850, and from this time to the present, three distinctive phases can be identified: c. 1870–c. 1940, c. 1940– c. 1990, and c. 1990 to the present. The interconnectedness of Christianity and 'non-Christian' traditions is apparent: religious change in Anlo cannot be understood without a history that seeks to include both sets of practices as part of the same developmental trajectory. During its 'long conversation' (Comaroff and Comaroff 1991: 17–18) in Anlo, Christianity has oscillated from an ideology antagonistic to Anlo religion (c. 1870 – c. 1940) to one that has evolved to being accommodative of the same (c. 1940 – c. 1990), to a religious discourse that has switched back to being hostile to aspects of Africanness (c. 1990 – onwards): throughout, it has selectively internalised Anlo traits in its structures, cultural forms, and ritual practices – irrespective of its official stance vis-à-vis African tradition.

Between the Devil and the Cross (c. 1870–c. 1940)

We have little information on how the Anlo religious system actually functioned before the arrival of the missionaries in the 1850s. The abolition of the slave trade in 1807 and the gradual decline of domestic slave holding from 1874 would have had far-reaching effects for features such as the composition of the labour force, migration patterns, and gender relations in Anlo, which in turn affected how religious networks, both new and old, mutated into instruments for the control of people.

After the 1850s, Anlo witnessed an influx of religious agents. The cult of Nyigbla, the most prominent deity before the 1850s, declined rapidly, as the Anlo suffered a series of defeats in war, which led them to question the war god's efficacy. By the 1870s, Yewe shrines had become an integral part of the religious landscape in Anlo. Yewe was successful precisely because it was an open cult – one of the reasons for the upsurge in Yewe worship was that Yewe shrine owners exhibited great versatility in organising their shrines into trading cooperatives. While Yewe shrine owners were patrons of the illicit slave trade after the 1860s, they also managed to focus their attentions on other lucrative industries of the colonial period, as and when they developed. The dominant religious preference of the Anlo changed from Nyigbla (and other ancestral deities) to Yewe against a backdrop of economic deterioration during the late nineteenth century. The cult of Nyigbla, by this time, had become the preserve of Anloga elites and chiefs, and was associated with the conservative anti-modernist lobby.

By the 1870s, Christian mission stations had become established in two Anlo towns. Christianity's success may be explained by a number of factors. Most broadly, the Anlo were pulled out of their microcosm, through a series of economic and political changes, and had to orient themselves ideologically in the macrocosm. Being Christian was synonymous with economic and social mobility in early twentieth-century Anlo, an essential prerequisite for participation in the colonial economy and for engaging with modernity. Christianity functioned as if it were an 'open' cult, with no restrictions on its membership, as missionaries sought to convert as many 'heathens' as possible. However, Christianity appeared in Anlo during a period when the older religious structures were crumbling, so conversion to Christianity may also be understood within the context of the chiefdom's religious history: Yewe and Christianity, the new arrivals on the scene, profited from Nyigbla's decline, and competed with each other for followers. In addition, both these new religious agents were able to empower their devotees – through very different measures – within the rapidly changing political economy, which contributed to their popularity.

Into the competitive cultic environment of the 1920s swept two new sets of deities. First, anti-witchcraft deities that were originally acquired by the Akan from the northern grasslands found a niche for themselves in Anlo, coming to be known as the Atikevodu or Gorovodu divinities. Second, satellite shrines of Dente, also an anti-witchcraft divinity from Kete Krachi, made their way southward to Anlo during the late 1930s. The initial success of these deities can be explained by the protection they provided against witchcraft, a rapidly proliferating phenomenon during this period, often rationalised as a consequence of the socio-economic changes precipitated by integration into the colonial economy. These anti-witchcraft deities became a presence in the Anlo religious system, after the first wave of Christian conversions.

This period also witnessed the spread of several other cults and deities, some of which are still present in Anlo today: in addition to Christianity,

Yewe, and the gods from the North, the Anlo were exposed to some other religious agents, most significant among them being Adzevodu, an anti-witchcraft deity from Dahomey, and Mami Wata, the mermaid associated with the sea. All of these came to be established in Anlo by the late 1930s. However, we have virtually no reliable sources that provide information on what their initial functions were, who their first devotees were, and how they entered the chiefdom.

The Middle Path (c. 1940–c. 1990)

After the 1940s, the successful religious agents devised survival strategies for themselves by either turning into replacement cults or identifying specific thematic niches in the religious system, though some religious agents employed both strategies simultaneously. Competition between cultic networks for members gradually ceased, as they came to share followers, by developing specialised remedies for different existential crises. The most striking thematic transformation occurred in the case of the Krachi Dente, originally an anti-witchcraft and oracular divinity, which entered Anlo in the 1930s, and gradually came to be associated with Anlo's slave-holding past. Slavery had been a dormant concern in the Anlo collective memory: there had developed, in Anlo cultural logic, a sense of discomfort about enslavement as early as the nineteenth century. The ghosts of slavery were, in a sense, revived during the 1920s, during the influx of northern deities into the chiefdom. The entrance of Dente into Anlo coincided with the appearance of other Gorovodu deities from the northern savanna. The ritual movement of deities fitted with Anlo perceptions of punishment by ancestral agency: they came to believe that their slave ancestors and their gods were demanding their attention after generations of neglect.

Other cultural and social processes, which were also set in motion by colonial modernity, were negotiated against the backdrop of dealing with the ghosts of slavery. The Anlo were in the process of redefining their chiefdom, as Sri II, the Christian *awoamefia* of Anlo, tried to expand its traditional boundaries by imposing the hegemony of Anloga over all neighbouring *dukowo*. In addition to the development of Anlo-ness, another broader ethnicity was coming into being, which contradicted notions of Anlo-ness – the Ewe identity. Protestant Germanic notions of nationhood based on linguistic unity were applied to the Ewe-speaking peoples by the Bremen Mission, and ideas of the oneness of the Ewe were taken up by Ewe Christians. While Ewe unity was brought about through the Christian sphere, Anlo identity was cemented through the 'heathen' sphere, with deities like Nyigbla and Yewe coming to be revered as symbols of Anlo-ness. The interesting contradiction between the movements for Anlo and Ewe unity was that while the Anlo tried to become Ewe, they also became Anlo through the process of othering and – eventually incorporating – their northern Ewe ancestors into the historical record through a set of ritual practices. Krachi Dente merged with the existing Fofie cult in Anlo, reviving memories of slavery, and allowing the Anlo to re-interrogate their agency in the practice against the backdrop of the events of the 1940s. Full-fledged Fofie initiates were always women, who represented slaves owned by their patrilineage in the past. It was this feature of Anlo-Ewe social organisation, the patrilineages or *afedowo*, that enabled people to claim descent from slave women rather unproblematically, without disadvantaging themselves in society. Not coincidentally, the Fofie cult became an established presence when patriliny was becoming a prerequisite for Anlo-ness; therefore the revelation of matrilineal slave antecedents did not strip a person of his or her Anlo identity.

While Fofie and the Gorovodu deities slotted into specific thematic niches, these ritual networks also changed structurally, following the trajectory of Yewe, the most successful Anlo cult at that time. Two factors were to change recruitment patterns of Yewe: the cult came under a degree of regulation under chiefs like Sri II by the 1920s, and Christianity had effectively reduced its recruitment pool. Reincarnation within families had become a strategy of recruiting initiates by the 1930s. But this strategy, which closed up the cult, was successful in the case of Yewe because it had a large pool of followers at that point in time. (Even in present-day Anlo, every single lineage has had some involvement with Yewe during this period. Each lineage will be associated with a different Yewe shrine. Shrines of the same cultic network are not usually in competition with each other.) Ancestral discomfort rather than personal choice drew members into the cult after the 1930s, and it remains the reason most often given for joining the cultic network in contemporary Anlo. Fofie also slotted into the religious system as a replacement cult, mirroring the trajectory of Yewe; it thus found a secure niche within a system that was tilting away from cultic openness towards membership based on heredity. Fofie came to resemble Yewe in terms of structure and recruitment patterns, as initiates came to be reproduced within lineages.

Other factors, such as regulation by chiefs and the colonial administration, also pushed religious agents towards cooperation with each other. The colonial authorities became more alarmed at the growth of northern deities in the Gold Coast colony, and subsequently, the worship of Kunde (and Gorovodu) was banned in 1940. In Anlo, this move forced Gorovodu priests into cooperation with Yewe shrines. Gorovodu objects came to be housed in Yewe shrines, forcing the two previously antagonistic cults into collaboration. Yewe and Gorovodu also came to occupy different structural niches in Anlo society, and adopted different membership regulations. Yewe initiates took on new identities that pledged them to Yewe for life, while Gorovodu priests dispensed their spiritual goods to anyone in need of them for remunerations. By the 1950s, all Anlo cults had developed specialised functions, which enabled people to participate in all of them simultaneously – involvement with Yewe rectified ancestral problems, Gorovodu worship was associated with northern medicinal knowledge, and Fofie with the slave-holding past. Adzevodu and Koku, both anti-witchcraft cults, came to be associated with protection against witchcraft within families, and protection against physical harm respectively. These strategies and developments meant that Anlo cults could share followers with relative ease during this phase.

The trajectories that developed within Anlo Christianity are also significant in our story of cultic coexistence. The Bremen Mission stations metamorphosed into the Ewe Presbyterian, and eventually the Evangelical Presbyterian, Church in 1929. The Anlo intelligentsia, and some African theologians in general, were deeply unhappy with Christianity's attitude towards traditional African beliefs by the 1950s and 1960s, and sought to create an African Christianity detached from its colonial heritage. Two developments took place during this phase. The tension between Christianity and Africanness resulted in the rise of African Independent Churches (AICs). The AICs that spread in the 1950s sought to marry African tradition with Christianity; they were deeply indigenised, used local languages, and incorporated African aspects of worship. While their efforts seemed to suggest that they sought to Africanise Christianity, they were critical of aspects of their 'pagan' tradition. Amid these ideas, mainline Christian churches were also forced to reevaluate their relationship with Anlo 'tradition'. Most mainline Churches in Anlo during this period turned a blind eye to their members visiting shrines and consulting with African diviners and priests. Practices associated with Fofie, Yewe, and related cults were seen as a means of communing with the ancestors: this was considered something that could not be done in church, and therefore did not conflict with Christianity and was deemed a necessary, desirable part of African 'tradition'.

While Africanisation has been explained in terms of cultural politics and undoing the missionary heritage, few have suggested that it could be understood as a strategy pursued by Christianity to survive in an immensely competitive religious environment. As we have seen in the Anlo case, during this phase, most cultic agents in the system devised methods of coexistence, and Christianity's inclusion of African rituals, methods, and general tolerance of pagan practices can be understood against a backdrop of trends reflected within the religious system as a whole. Religious agencies came to share followers in this period: a 'non-Christian' in Anlo could get initiated into more than one cult, while a Christian could visit 'heathen' shrines and rationalise it in terms of ancestral worship. AICs failed to attract large numbers of followers in Anlo because of their strict stance against involvement with the 'heathen' sphere. Mainline Christianity became the favoured option, as these churches adapted to the religious coexistence which was the norm in the chiefdom.

Pentecostalism versus Sankofa (c. 1990–Present)

The late 1980s saw the entry of new strands of charismatic or Pentecostal Christianity, highly critical of both African traditional religion and other strands of Christianity. The critique of some forms of Africanness within these churches can be viewed through the lens of the political and economic climate of the last three decades, punctuated by several military coups and economic crashes. This Christianity is visibly post-nationalistic in its approach, sharing none of the concerns of the early AICs and mainline churches of the 1960s that played important roles in the rise of political, anti-colonial nationalisms in Africa during that period. This post-nationalist focus finds an outlet in the international character of these churches, and the indiscriminate denunciation of African tradition. By the 1990s, some Anlo intellectuals' disillusionment with Christianity was manifested through their support for a neo-traditional organisation, the Afrikania Renaissance Mission (ARM). The ARM sees itself as the protector of 'traditional religion', and its biggest enemy is Pentecostal Christianity.

With the arrival of these two diametrically opposed religious movements in Anlo, the religious coexistence between 1940 and 1990 was set to give way once more to competition during the 1990s. Despite its larger goals, the ARM is uncritical in its conception of traditional religion, as it endorses the African Christian worldview that divides Anlo religion into the distinct spheres of Christianity and 'heathenism'. Essentially, the ARM is reinventing African tradition in a curious manner. In Anlo, the Mission draws its support from members of all religious cults, such as Yewe, Gorovodu, Fofie, Mamma, Adzevodu, Koku and older *troxovi* shrines, with the aim of discouraging people from joining the new charismatic churches. The reorganisation of cults by the ARM, and the implementation of rules by which all cultic initiates have to abide – frequently attending Sunday services, staying committed to the Mission and their cults, boycotting Church activities – suggests that cults are once more in competition not only with Christianity, but possibly amongst themselves as they search for devotees. It is interesting to note that most Anlo cults feel threatened – Yewe, Gorovodu, Adzevodu, and Koku – and appear to be in the process of relaxing membership restrictions to compete with various charismatic churches and other cults for followers.

In contemporary Anlo, Yewe and Fofie are still predominantly replacement cults. However, the membership structure and recruitment patterns of all Anlo cults appear to be changing once more. For the replacement cults, it is increasingly difficult to substitute dead initiates, who make up the bulk of such a cult's inner-circle membership, through the ancestral reincarnation mechanism. In the case of the Yewe cult, the number of *vodusiwo* per generation in every lineage has steadily declined over the last two decades. Even the 'more open than closed' cults in terms of their membership dynamics (such as Gorovodu and Adzevodu) have not been able to sustain numbers of their inner-circle initiates through the ancestral replacement method.

While Anlo cultic networks have seen their inner circles shrink over the last twenty years, they have witnessed a simultaneous increase in the numbers of people associating with their outer circles in less-committed capacities. Yewe priests and priestesses appear to be inviting people from outside their traditional spheres of lineage-based influence to frequent their shrines. These people have no familial links with the shrine they have begun to visit, which is a departure from Yewe's recruitment strategy between *c.* 1940 and *c.* 1990. Gorovodu and Adzevodu priests are also on the lookout for new methods to attract followers: like priests of the Yewe cult, they appear to be extending their services to address problems that were beyond their traditional specialised niche, a strategy that cults usually adopt when threatened. For the priests of Anlo cultic networks, the emphasis now appears to be on attracting more casual worshippers to the fringes of the cult from outside the traditional spheres of influence, in the hope that these new members will form committed relation-ships with the deities or cults in question, and eventually channel their resources towards the activities and worship of only one cultic network. A degree of antagonism appears to be developing between the different cults, a reflection of the emerging competition within the system.[17]

West African religious systems vary greatly in terms of the attitudes of devotees to their gods and religious agents. Karin Barber (1981) argues that the attitude of devotees in West African society towards their gods

---

[17] I followed the trajectories of 150 Yewe inner- and outer-circle members in Anlo towns over 12 years (2002–14). Thirty of the 100 inner-circle initiates died during the early years of my fieldwork (2003–6). Only seven of them have been replaced through rein-carnation as of 2015. Of the 50 outer-circle members who have joined the Yewe cult in the last three years (2012–15), 33 have no lineage ties with the particular Yewe shrines with which they have come to be associated.

In the case of the Gorovodu network, I interviewed 70 inner-circle members: 14 of these had no prior connection with the deities, and had come to adopt their worship between 2005 and 2008. I also came across at least 40 people by 2010 who had petitioned the Gorovodu deities for favours as casual supplicants over a five-year period, beginning in 2005: of these 40, about eight had decided to adopt the worship of Gorovodu in a more serious capacity, as *sofowo* or *trosiwo* without prior familial associations, after sampling a wide range of deities in Anlo; 12 remained loosely connected with the cult as outer-circle members, while the remaining 20 became disillusioned, and moved on to other shrines and churches.

is determined by the structure and organisational hierarchy of the society in question, and, by opportunities available for the accumulation of wealth (Barber 1981). Her argument centres on comparisons between the Talensi, Yoruba, and Kalabari peoples. Barber argues that the degree of choice available to devotees in each of these societies is different, which promotes different religiosities. Basing her descriptions of the Talensi of northern Ghana on Meyer Fortes's accounts produced in the 1940s, Barber argued that the Talensi were subsistence farmers who seldom produced an agricultural surplus, and that their socio-economic organisation coupled with their location in the inhospitable savanna belt meant that individuals in their society lacked channels for accumulating surplus wealth. Talensi society consisted of several lineage segments, and an individual's position within a segment was strictly regulated by his seniority. An individual's status in society was ascribed to him rather than earned by him, a situation that he was unable to alter through his efforts. Positions of authority were automatically conferred on the most senior members of every patrilineal lineage segment, while deference to these elders was expected, leaving no scope for the realisation of individual aspirations. The Talensi belief system reflected their social organisation. The most important positions in the Talensi spiritual world were occupied by the ancestors, who were very much like the earthly Talensi elders, commanding the unconditional respect and adoration of their living descendants.

This belief in the supremacy of the ancestors accounted for two unique features of Talensi religion. First, the element of choice in determining which religious agents were worshipped was virtually absent, as individuals could not choose their ancestors: rather, their ancestors chose them at birth. A devotee's attitude towards his ancestors was one of passive acceptance, as he could not approach new ancestors if his own were unable to satisfy his practical needs; he was attached to his ancestors for life, and had to bear the seemingly unfair treatment they sometimes inflicted upon him, rationalising it as punishment for wrongdoings. Second, an individual had virtually no personal choice in worshipping his ancestors: each ancestral shrine was placed under the custody of the head of a lineage segment. A Talensi individual was unable to approach or commune with the ancestors of his own accord, as these ritual acts were regulated by the lineage elders. Thus religious activity, strictly mediated through kinship structures and a hierarchical society, left Talensi individuals at the mercy of their ancestors with little little scope for altering their religious – and socio-economic – opportunities.

In stark contrast with Talensi society, social mobility and personal enhancement in Yorubaland was possible through a number of channels. The Yoruba held 'Big Men' in high esteem, celebrating their entrepreneurial qualities and admiring their wealth. Success was often contingent on personal enrichment at the expense of others, and a range of practical and spiritual measures were directed to achieving these ends, including the employment of witchcraft. This injected a degree of competitiveness into Yoruba society, with potential Big Men locked into relationships of rivalry, as they sought to outdo each other in their bid to control resources, wealth, and, above all, people. The prestige and authority of a Big Man depended primarily on his ability to attract and maintain a retinue of followers: he needed the active collaboration of his wives, children, junior kinsmen, helpers and, in the past, slaves, whom he in turn had to advise and support. The *orisa* were the Big Men of the Yoruba cosmological universe, locked into similar relationships with their devotees: their reputations and appeal depended on the willingness and ability of their devotees to praise and worship them. Devotees invested a considerable amount of time and effort into pleasing their *orisa* – for, if the deity's fame grew, it reflected beneficially on them. Once an appropriate *orisa* had been identified, the devotee would dedicate herself to the worship of this particular deity, remaining indifferent to others in the pantheon. Relationships between members of the various cults were competitive, as each tried to enhance the glories of its chosen *orisa* by acts of elaborate praise and sacrifice. This degree of competitiveness meant that there was an element of choice in the system: failure by the *orisa* to satisfy the devotee would lead to the devotee appraching another, more suitable, *orisa*.

More competitive than the Yoruba *orisa* were the Kalabari water spirits, mirroring the principles of that society. The Kalabari religious landscape, as described by Robin Horton in the 1970s, reflected the ruggedly individualistic and entrepreneurial temperament of the people of Calabar. The landscape of Calabar was dotted with trading houses, a feature of the aftermath of the region's integration into the slave-trading economy. Assimilating strangers into houses by forging fictitious kinship ties and attracting supporters was important for leaders of these trading houses, and there was a definite realisation that the powers of the leader of a house were conferred upon him solely by his entourage; his prestige was dependent on the size of his following and their continuing satisfaction and loyalty. Leaders of such houses in Calabar relied more heavily on the support of their followers than Yoruba Big Men did on their entourages. Attitudes towards spiritual agents mirrored the relationship Kalabari people had with their leaders: while the Yoruba had a relationship of reciprocity with the *orisa* and their Big Men, and while the Talensi were controlled by their ancestors, the Kalabari actually controlled their ancestors and spirits – as they did the heads of their houses – giving people in authority their power: in Calabar, men could strip gods of the powers they had assigned them.

My historical survey of Anlo religion, based on family and lineage histories and extensive fieldwork lasting over a decade, and drawing on secondary historical sources, suggests that Anlo cults have changed structurally and functionally three times in the last hundred and fifty years. I argue that the Anlo religious system at present resembles the Yoruba and Kalabari systems when there are a greater number of religious service providers in the field, a factor that directly influences choice. After there is an injection of religious agents into the system, recruitment dynamics gradually change, and the religious system comes to resemble the Talensi system as open cults mutate into ancestral ones. One such watershed period, when the recruitment patterns for cultic membership changed, was around the 1990s.[18]

In pre-1990s Anlo, people had less choice with respect to which cults they joined, as the ancestors were diagnosed as the cause of most of their problems. Like the Talensi who were tied to the worship of their ancestors, most Anlo were tied to cults with which their ancestors were involved. Initiation into the Fofie, Yewe, Gorovodu, and other cults was conceptualised as the answer to various problems, believed to be caused directly by a certain category of ancestor. All these ritual networks occupied different functional niches, and therefore did not need to compete with each other for followers. This degree of functional specialisation allowed Anlo cults to coexist with each other, often sharing devotees: for instance, it was not unusual to come across an individual who was a *fofiesi*, *yewesi*, and a *trosi*, as she could have had both slave and Yewe-worshipping ancestors in the past, and, in addition, could also have submitted to the Gorovodu spirits. There was little choice when joining the majority of cults: association with the Yewe, Fofie, *trokovi* cults, and, in a number of cases, Gorovodu deities, could only be inherited. Even supplicants who associated with these ritual networks in less-committed capacities, as outer-circle members, accessed them through familial or ancestral ties, and seldom approached cults with which they had no prior associations. While the nature of the problem determines which cult an individual joined, prior to the 1990s, an Anlo person seldom enlisted the services of a cult or shrine with which his family had no links in the past. Thus there was little competition between ritual networks in pre-1990s Anlo,

---

[18] I identify three watershed periods in Anlo religious history when recruitment dynamics changed: *c.* 1870, *c.* 1940, and *c.* 1990. In 1870 and 1990, the religious system turns from a less competitive one, where recruitment is motivated by ancestral considerations and realised through replacement, into a more competitive one that resembles a religious marketplace, while, in the 1940s, it reverts from a more competitive system to a less competitive, replacement-oriented one. It is difficult to draw correlations between wealth creation, accumulation, and religious activity in Anlo on a temporal scale, as the local economy has declined steadily from the era of the slave trade and never quite recovered. Colonial industries have never benefited the region significantly. Large-scale out-migration is the norm. Religious activity is better correlated to broader social and historical existential concerns, and religious agents have proliferated in certain eras to address these.

as the agents associated with them all occupied specialised niches, and were overwhelmingly associated with certain kinds of ancestral agency. What we have seen steadily developing over the last two decades is a move away from a relatively closed system with cultic membership determined by ancestral considerations, to an open, more competitive one, where individual choice plays a significant part in determining which deities maintain large followings.

The situation in post-1990s Anlo is different. The more committed members of the inner circle of cultic worship, who pledge themselves to the *trowo* and *voduwo* during the course of their initiation, are on the decline, while less-committed devotees that generally exhibit a lesser degree of involvement with the cult are on the increase. Unlike more-committed members, the less-committed ones do not actually participate wholeheartedly in any ritual network. They prefer informal associations with cults, tending to favour a more superficial mode of engagement which implies less commitment, and consequently commit lesser resources towards pleasing the *trowo* or *voduwo*. This level of engagement also confers upon them considerable freedom to experiment with other religious agents. In turn, 'religious service providers' such as cult leaders have to devise innovative new strategies to keep their retinue interested: these strategies range from new techniques and methods of worship; the use of new sacrificial animals and offerings, which are generally cost effective; and inventing new religious paraphernalia and practices to keep devotees interested. It could be said that the Anlo religious marketplace is rife with aggressive consumers constantly in search of customer satisfaction in relation to services provided by religious agents. This competitive atmosphere in the ritual sphere is accompanied by the notion that spiritual problems are caused by human agency, generated by competitiveness, greed, and competition for resources. *Trowo* and *voduwo* in post-1990s Anlo are functionally very much like the Yoruba *orisa*, in that devotees believe them to be capable of satisfying a variety of existential needs; they are consequently petitioned for a broad range of favours, such as demands for children, material well-being, health, and protection from evil. Even cultic networks that traditionally have been hereditary ones appear to be compromising – moving from total commitment on the part of a small number of followers towards lesser commitment from a greater number of followers. Some leaders of Yewe and Fofie, two replacement cults, appear to be encouraging people that have no history of association with them to access the spiritual services provided by the shrine. The situation between the 1870s and 1940s, an era that witnessed the entrance of Yewe, Christianity, and the gods from the north into Anlo, may have been very similar. Figure 8.1 showcases the major changes in the Anlo religious system from the 1870s.

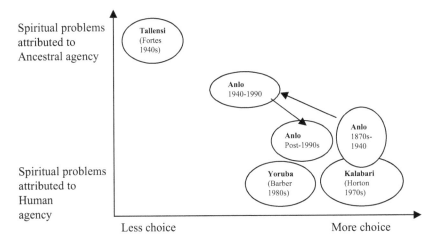

Figure 8.1. West African religious systems

What developments will the future hold for this incredibly complex historical trajectory? Pentecostal Christianity and neo-traditional movements are changing the landscape of twenty-first century Anlo, and the religious system may be moving towards more competition again, mirroring developments between the 1850s and 1940s.

Anticipating the Future

What will become of the Fofie cult, in a religious system leaning away from replacement as a recruitment strategy towards openness? A family history of a Fofie-worshipping lineage bears testimony to how the membership of the cult has dwindled rapidly since its inception.

Kofi Amegbor (b. *c.* 1840) was an Anlo slave merchant, who had one slave wife during the 1870s. She was a northern Ewe woman (simply referred to by her descendants as 'Mama Hohoe').[19] One of Mama's children (b. *c.* 1890), became the first *fofiesi* in this family, initiated by Ablesi into Fofie worship in the 1940s. She was known as Gbara ('leader'). Mama had eight daughters, and, in addition to Gbara, three others were also *fofiesiwo*. They were known as Tarosi, Blumesi, and Dzapkasi. In the next generation, there were only two *fofiesiwo* to replace these four women: Metumisi and Nanunsi, who joined the cult after the deaths of the first generation of *fofiesiwo* around the 1970s. The family members insist that they had the ability and resources to conduct the appropriate

---

[19] Whether this woman hailed from Hohoe exactly is doubtful, but what is certain is that that she is remembered as being of *Eweme* extraction.

ceremonies for potential *fofiesiwo*, and the decline in numbers in the successive generation is not a reflection on the lack of their resources. The
number of *fofiesiwo* had halved not because of financial constraints, but
because the slave ancestors had chosen only two people in the second
generation. The lineage had actually expected to have more than four
fofiesiwo in the second generation, as each of the deceased *fofiesiwo*, upon
becoming ancestors, is capable of guiding more than one descendant
into the world of the living. Nanunsi died in 1988 and Metumisi in 1990.
One woman in the next generation, known as Gbara, has replaced both
of them (her *amedzoto* is believed to be the first Gbara), in 2000. This
fofiesi died rather unexpectedly in 2006, and a single replacement has
been identified, but not initiated into the cult. The number of *fofiesiwo*
has decreased with every generation. Members of this lineage believe
that the slave ancestors are gradually retreating into oblivion after being
venerated adequately by their descendants.

In the last decade, some members of the Fofie cult in Anlo-
Afiadenyigba developed the belief that the slave gods and ancestors had
been effectively pacified. There were a number of people within the
cult who thought this way, including Babaa, my chief interlocutor. They
argued that slavery, an experience in the Anlo past, had been thoroughly
dealt with in the Anlo psyche; that people in Anlo had to turn their
attention to various other existential problems. Those in favour of abol-
ishing the cult argue that while the slave ancestors could not be forgotten,
Fofie worship was an expensive business. The cult consumed too many
of the resources of desperately poor people. Pleasing the slave gods has
often resulted – for the *fofiesiwo* and their families – in indebtedness for
months. This lobby suggested that the people of Anlo-Afiadenyigba were
better off turning their attention to other newer gods emerging in the
village, which were associated with the environment and development.
They constantly tried to convince members of the Fofie cult to take a
rather bold step: they recommended one big mass burning of all the
objects associated with the slave ancestors and their gods. This move,
they believed, would see the people of Anlo-Afiadenyigba resolve their
uneasy relationship with their slave ancestors: they could finally bid the
slave spirits farewell, and ask for their blessings one last time.

An opposing lobby within the cult believes that the slave ancestors are
angrier than ever. Fofie worshippers who subscribe to this view believe
that making decisions such as these are not up to cult members. Ajakoku,
the leader of the Fofie cult and a descendant of Ablesi, is associated
with this line of thought. He believes that the slave spirits will begin
attaching themselves not only to descendants of slave women, but also
to descendants of free Anlo women from slave-holding patrilineages. He
argues that descendants of free Anlo women prospered at the expense

of descendants of slave women. There were no indications of this actually happening as of 2010. But if the slave ancestors do indeed attach themselves to the descendants of free Anlo women, the recruitment pool of the Fofie cult will be much larger. If this happens, the Fofie cult will actually open up, and will be able to broaden its pool of devotees. If the cult is to survive, it will have to increase its pool of followers beyond its traditional constituency of a limited number of lineages with slave matrilineal antecedents.

The fate of the Fofie cult, ultimately, depends on whether the Anlo are prepared to put the ghosts of slavery to rest. Whether the trans-Atlantic conversations between the Anlo and diasporan Africans will change the moral emphases of slavery as dealt with within the framework of the cult remains to be seen. But if the Anlo have indeed come to terms with their slave-holding past, either one of two possibilities will occur in the near future. The cult may reinvent itself thematically or structurally in order to maintain a following, thereby disassociating itself from the aftermath of slavery, and linking itself to more contemporary existential crises in Anlo. Perhaps the slave spirits will begin attaching themselves to other members of society, and not just their direct descendants, which will ensure the survival of the cult. Ritual memories (in conjunction with oral traditions) would undergo a degree of realignment, to suggest that the slave ancestors are capable of affecting all members of society equally, and not only those with slave ancestry. The second possibility is that the cult remains unaltered. An unchanged Fofie cult may not hold much appeal, as there are other more urgent concerns in twenty-first century Anlo than the consequences of the slave-holding past. Besides, as a replacement cult associated with the aftermath of a distant historical practice, Fofie leaders would find it increasingly difficult to attract followers and maintain a competitive edge in a religious system full of antagonistic cults. Cultic networks in Anlo – and West Africa in general – survive only as long as the *voduwo* and *trowo* receive the affection of their devotees, and the inability of the slave ancestors and their gods to attract and sustain devotees may result in the Fofie cult fading into oblivion. In the event of either of these scenarios, we may be able to adopt a functionalist explanation, by arguing that the cult survived for as long as the Anlo needed to come to terms with the consequences of integrating slaves of non-Anlo origin into their society. Like all Anlo *trowo* and *voduwo*, the slave spirits are unpredictable: whether they disappear from Anlo religious history, remains to be seen. For the moment, however, the story of the Fofie cult is an unfinished one, as it is still a presence – although a dwindling one – in the Anlo religious system.

Bibliography

Adediran, B. 1994. *The Frontier States of Western Yorubaland, 1600–1889*. Ibadan: IFRA.

Adogame, A. 1999. *Celestial Church of Christ: The Politics of Cultural Identity in a West African Prophetic Charismatic Movement*. Frankfurt am Main: Peter Lang.

Akurang-Parry, K. 2002. 'Rethinking the "Slaves of Salaga": Post-Proclamation Slavery in the Gold Coast (Colonial Southern Ghana), 1874–1899', *Left History* 8 (1): 33–60.

———. 2004. '"We Shall Rejoice to See the Day When Slavery Shall Cease to Exist"': *The Gold Coast Times*, the African Intelligentsia, and Abolition in the Gold Coast, *History in Africa* 31: 19–42.

Akyeampong, E. K. 2001a. 'History, Memory, Slave-Trade and Slavery in Anlo (Ghana)', *Slavery and Abolition* 22 (3): 1–24.

———. 2001b. *Between the Sea and the Lagoon: An Eco-history of the Anlo of Southeastern Ghana*. Oxford: James Currey.

———. 2003. 'Environmental Folk Wisdom versus Scientific Knowledge: Producing and Contesting Knowledge in Anlo, Southeastern Ghana', in T. Falola (ed.), *Ghana in Africa and the World: Essays in Honour of Adu Boahen*. Trenton NJ: Africa World Press.

Allman, J. 1993. *The Quills of the Porcupine: Asante Nationalism in an Emergent Ghana*. Wisconsin WI: University of Wisconsin Press.

———. 1996. 'Rounding up Spinsters: Gender Chaos and Unmarried Women in Colonial Asante', *Journal of African History* 37 (2): 195–214.

Allman, J. and J. Parker. 2005. *Tongnaab: The History of a West African God*. Bloomington IN: Indiana University Press.

Amenumey, D. E. K. 1986.*The Ewe in Pre-Colonial Times*. Accra: Sedco.

———. 1989. *The Ewe Unification Movement*. Accra: Ghana Universities Press.

———. 1997. 'A Brief History', in F. Agbodeka (ed.), *The Ewes of Southeastern Ghana*. Accra: Woeli Publishing Services.

Argenti, N. 2006. 'Remembering the Future: Slavery, Youth and Masking in the Cameroon Grassfields', *Social Anthropology* 14 (1): 49–69.

Argenti, N. and U. Röschenthaler. 2006. 'Introduction: Between Cameroon and Cuba – Youth, Slave Trades and Trans-Local Memoryscapes', *Social Anthropology* 14 (1): 33–47.

Arhin, K. 1979. *West African Traders in Ghana in the Nineteenth and Twentieth Centuries*. London: Longman.

Ayorinde, C. 2004. 'Santeria in Cuba: Tradition and Transformation', in T. Falola and M. D. Childs (eds), *The Yoruba Diaspora in the Atlantic World*, Bloomington IN: Indiana University Press.

Baëta, C. G. 1962. *Prophetism in Ghana: A Study of Some 'Spiritual' Churches.* London: SCM Press.

_____. 1971. *The Relationships of Christians with Men of Other Faiths.* Accra: Ghana Universities Press.

Bailey, A. C. 2005. *African Voices of the Atlantic Slave Trade: Beyond the Silence and the Shame.* Boston MA: Beacon Press.

Barber, K. 1981. 'How Man Makes God in West Africa: Yoruba Attitudes towards the Orisa', *Africa* 51 (3): 724–45.

_____. 1991. *'I Could Speak until Tomorrow': Oriki, Women and the Past in a Yoruba Town.* Edinburgh: Edinburgh University Press and the International African Institute.

Barnes, S. (ed.) 1997. *Africa's Ogun: Old World and New.* Bloomington IN: Indiana University Press.

Bartlett, F. 1995. *Remembering.* Cambridge: Cambridge University Press.

Bascom, W. R. 1969. *Ifa Divination: Communication between Gods and Men in West Africa.* Bloomington IN: Indiana University Press.

Baum, R. 1999. *Shrines of the Slave Trade: Diola Religion and Society in Precolonial Senegambia.* Oxford: Oxford University Press.

Behrend, H. 2000. 'Spirit Possession and War in Northern Uganda (1986– 1994)', in H. Behrend and U. Luig (eds), *Spirit Possession: Modernity and Power in Africa.* Madison WI: University of Wisconsin Press.

Bellagamba, A. 2009. 'After Abolition: Metaphors of Slavery in the Political History of the Gambia', in B. Rossi (ed.), *Reconfiguring Slavery: West African Trajectories.* Liverpool: University of Liverpool Press.

Benson, S. 2003. 'Connecting with the Past, Building the Future: African-Americans and Chieftaincy in Southern Ghana', *Ghana Studies* 6: 109– 33.

Blier, S. P. 1995. *African Vodun: Art, Psychology, Power.* Berkeley CA: University of California Press.

Bloch, M. 1998. *How We Think They Think: Anthropological Approaches to Cognition, Memory and Literacy.* Oxford: Westview Press.

Bob-Milliar, G. 2009. 'Chieftaincy, Diaspora and Development: The Institution of Nkosuohene in Ghana', *African Affairs* 108 (433): 541–58.

Boddy, J. 1989. *Wombs and Alien Spirits: Women, Men and the Zar cult in Northern Sudan.* Madison WI: University of Wisconsin Press.

Bourdieu, P. 1990. *The Logic of Practice.* Stanford CA: Stanford University Press.

Breidenbach, P. S. 1974. 'The Wandering Preacher', *African Studies Review* 17 (1): 306–8.

Burnett, D. 1997. 'Charisma and Community in a Ghanaian Independent Church: a Study of the Musama Disco Christo Church', PhD thesis, School of Oriental and African Studies, University of London.

Brydon, L. 2008. 'Constructing Avatime: Questions of History and Identity in a West African Polity, *c.* 1690s to the Twentieth Century', *Journal of African History* 49 (1): 23–42.

Capo, H. B. C. 1991. *A Comparative Phonology of Gbe.* Berlin: Foris.

Chatwin, B. 1980. *The Viceroy of Ouidah.* London: Jonathan Cape.

Chapman, D. A. 1944. *The Anlo Constitution.* Accra: Achimota Press.

Cole, J. 1998a. 'The Uses of Defeat: Memory and Political Memory in East Madagsacar', in R. Werbner (ed.), *Memory and the Postcolony: African Anthropology and the Critique of Power.* London: Zed Books.

_____. 1998b. 'The Work of Memory in Madagascar', *American Ethnologist* 25 (4): 610–33.

_____. 2001. *Forget Colonialism? Sacrifice and the Art of Memory in Madagascar.* Berkeley CA: University of California Press.

Collier, K. A. 2002. 'Ablode: Networks, Ideas and Performance in Togoland Politics, 1951–2001', PhD thesis, University of Birmingham.

Comaroff, J. and J. L. Comaroff. 1991. *Of Revelation and Revolution: Christianity, Colonialism and Consciousness in South Africa.* Chicago IL: University of Chicago Press.

_____. 1992. *Ethnography and the Historical Imagination,* Boulder CO: Westview Press.

Connerton, P. 1989. *How Societies Remember.* Cambridge: Cambridge University Press.

Crowther, F. G. 1927. 'The Epwe Speaking People', *Gold Coast Review* 3 (1): 11–55.

Daswani, G. 2010. 'Transformation and Migration among Members of a Pentecostal Church in Ghana and London', *Journal of Religion in Africa* 40 (4): 424–74.

_____. 2015. Looking Back, Moving Forward: Transformation and Ethical Practice in the Ghanaian Church of Pentecost. Toronto: University of Toronto Press.

De Boeck, F. 1998. 'Beyond the Grave: History, Memory and Death in Postcolonial Congo/Zaire', in R. Werbner (ed.), *Memory and the Postcolony: African Anthropology and the Critique of Power.* London: Zed Books.

De Surgy, Albert. 1981. *La Géomancie et le culte d'afa chez les évhe du littoral.* Paris: Publications Orientalistes de France.

_____. 1988. *Le Systeme Religieux des Evhe.* Paris: Harmattan.

De Witte, M. 2008. 'Spirit Media: Charismatics, Traditionalists, and Mediation Practices in Ghana', PhD thesis, University of Amsterdam.

Debrunner, H. W. 1959. *Witchcraft in Ghana.* Kumasi: Presbyterian Book Depot.

_____. 1965. *A Church between Colonial Powers.* London: Lutterworth Press.

_____. 1967. *A History of Christianity in Ghana.* Accra: Waterville Publishing House.

Dogbatse, S. A. 1999. 'The Influence of Modernisation on Traditional Shrines and Its Religious Implications to the Anlo-Ewe of Ghana', BA dissertation, Department of Religion, University of Ghana.

Drewal, H. J. 1988a. 'Performing the Other: Mami Wata Worship in Africa', *The Drama Review* 32 (2): 160–85.

_____. 1988b. 'Interpretation, Invention, and Representation in the Worship of Mami Wata', *Journal of Folklore Research* 25 (1/2): 101–39.

_____. 2008. 'Mami Wata: Arts for Water Spirits in Africa and Its Diasporas', *African Arts* 41 (2): 60–83.

Dumett, R and M. Johnson. 1988. 'A Historiographical Debate: Britain and the Suppression of Slavery in the Gold Coast, Ashanti, and the Northern Territories', in S. Miers and R. Roberts, *The End of Slavery in Africa.* Madison WI: University of Wisconsin Press.

Dzobo, N. 1975. *African Proverbs: A Guide to Conduct.* Accra: Waterville Publishing House.

Ellis, A. B. 1881. *West African Sketches.* London: Samuel Tinsley and Co.

———. 1893. *A History of the Gold Coast of West Africa*. London: Chapman and Hall.

———. 1965. *The Ewe-Speaking Peoples of the Slave Coast of West Africa*. London: Chapman and Hall.

Englund, H. 2000. 'Ethnography after Globalism: Migration and Emplacement in Malawi', *American Ethnologist* 29 (2): 261–86.

———. 2001. 'The Quest for Missionaries: Transnationalism and Township Pentecostalism in Malawi', in A. Corten and R. Marshall-Fratani (eds), *Between Babel and Pentecost: Transnational Pentecostalism in Africa and Latin America*. London: Hurst and Co.

———. 2003. 'Christian Independency and Global Membership: Pentecostal Extraversion in Malawi', *Journal of Religion in Africa* 33 (1): 83–111.

———. 2004. 'Cosmopolitanism and the Devil in Malawi', *Ethnos* 69 (3): 293–316.

Eni, E. 1987. *Delivered from the Powers of Darkness*. Ibadan: Scriptures Union.

Evans-Pritchard, E. E. 1937. *Witchcraft, Magic, and Oracles among the Azande*, Oxford: OUP.

Falola, T. 1999. *Yoruba Gurus: Indigenous Production of Knowledge in Africa*. Trenton NJ: Africa World Press.

Fardon, R. O. 1990. *Between God, the Dead and the Wild: Chamba Interpretations of Religion and Ritual*. Edinburgh: Edinburgh University Press and the International African Institute.

Fiawoo, D. K. 1976. 'Characteristic Features of Ewe Anscestor Worship', in W. H. Newell (ed), *Ancestors*. The Hague: Mouton.

Field, M. J. 1960. *Search for Security: An Ethno-Psychiatric Study of Rural Ghana*. London: Faber and Faber.

Fisher, H. J. 1973. 'Conversion Reconsidered: Some Historical Aspects of Religious Conversion in Black Africa', *Africa* 43 (2): 27–40.

Fontein, J. 2014. 'Anthropology and the Question of Unknowability in a Criminal Trial', *Journal of Ethnographic Theory* 4 (1): 75–103.

Friedson, S. 2009. *Remains of Ritual: Northern Gods in a Southern Land*. Chicago IL: University of Chicago Press.

Gaba, C. 1969. 'The Idea of a Supreme Being among the Anlo People of Ghana', *Journal of Religion in Africa* 2 (1): 64–79.

Geschiere, P. 1997. *The Modernity of Witchcraft: Politics and the Occult in Postcolonial Africa*. Charlottesville VA: University Press of Virginia.

Geurts, K. 2002. *Culture and the Senses: Bodily Ways of Knowing in an African Community*. Berkeley CA: University of California Press.

Ghana Evangelism Committee. 1989. *National Church Survey: Facing the Unfinished Task of the Church in Ghana*. Accra: Ghana Evangelism Committee.

Giddens, A. 1984. *The Constitution of Society*. Berkeley CA: University of California Press.

Gifford, P. 1997. *African Christianity: Its Public Role*. London: Hurst and Company.

———. 2004. *Ghana's New Christianity: Pentecostalism in a Globalizing African Economy*. London: Hurst and Co.

Gilbert, M. V. 1982. 'Mystical Protection among the Anlo Ewe', *African Arts* 4: 60–6.

Giles, L. 2000. 'Spirit Possession and the Symbolic Construction of Swahili Society', in H. Behrend and U. Luig (eds), *Spirit Possession: Modernity and Power in Africa*. Madison WI: University of Wisconsin Press.

Gocking, R. 1999. *Facing Two Ways: Ghana's Coastal Communities under Colonial Rule*. Lanham MD: University Press of America.

Grau, E. E. 1964. 'The Evangelical Presbyterian Church (Ghana and Togo) 1914–1946: A Study in European Mission Relations Affecting the Beginnings of an Indigenous Church', PhD thesis, Hartford Seminary Foundation.

Gray, N. 2005. 'Independent Spirits: The Politics of Policing Anti-Witchcraft Movements in Colonial Ghana 1908–1927', *Journal of Religion in Africa* 35 (2): 139–58.

Greene, S. E. 1996a. *Gender, Ethnicity and Social Change on the Upper Slave Coast*. London: James Currey.

_____. 1996b. 'The Individual as Stranger in Nineteenth-Century Anlo: The Politics of Identity and Social Advancement in Pre-Colonial West Africa', in N. Lawler and J. Hunwick (eds), *The Cloth of Many Coloured Silks*. Evanston IL: Northwestern University Press.

_____. 1996c. 'Religion, History and the Supreme Gods of Africa: A Contribution to the Debate', *Journal of Religion in Africa* 26 (2): 122–38.

_____. 1997. 'Sacred Terrain: Religion, Politics and Place in the History of Anloga (Ghana)', *International Journal of African Historical Studies* 30 (1): 1–22.

_____. 2002. *Sacred Sites and the Colonial Encounter: A History of Meaning and Memory in Ghana*. Bloomington IN: Indiana University Press.

_____. 2003. 'Whispers and Silences: Explorations in African Oral History', *Africa Today* 50 (2): 41–53.

_____. 2011. *West African Narratives of Slavery: Texts from Late-Nineteenth and Early-Twentieth Century Ghana*. Bloomington IN: Indiana University Press.

Gyanfosu, S. 2002. 'A Traditional Religion Reformed: Vincent Kwabena Damuah and the Afrikania Mission, 1982–2000', in D. Maxwell and I. Lawrie (eds), *Christianity and the African Imagination (Essays in Honour of Adrian Hastings)*. Leiden: E. J. Brill.

Hahanou, E. K. 2009. 'Slavery and Politics: Stigma, Decentralisation and Political Representation in Niger and Benin', in B. Rossi (ed.), *Reconfiguring Slavery: West African Trajectories*. Liverpool: University of Liverpool Press.

Halbwachs, M. 1992 [1950]. *On Collective Memory*. Chicago IL: University of Chicago Press.

Haliburton, G. M. 1973. *The Prophet Harris: A Study of an African Prophet and His Mass Movement in the Ivory Coast and the Gold Coast, 1913–1915*. New York NY: Oxford University Press.

Hanson, S. 2002. *A History of Pentecostalism in Ghana, 1900–2002*. Accra: Heritage Graphix.

Hardung, C. 2002. 'Everyday Life of Slaves in Northern Dahomey: The Process of Remembering', *Journal of African Cultural Studies* 15 (1): 35–44.

Herskovits, M. J. 1938. *Dahomey: An Ancient African Kingdom* (2 vols). New York NY: J. J. Augustine.

Hill, P. 1986. *Talking with Ewe Seine Fishermen and Shallot Farmers*. Cambridge: African Studies Centre.

Hobsbawm, E. and T. Ranger. (eds) 1992. *The Invention of Tradition*. Cambridge: Cambridge University Press.

Holsey, B. 2008. *Routes of Remembrance: Refashioning the Slave Trade in Ghana*. Chicago IL: University of Chicago Press.

―――. 2011. 'Owning up to the Past: African Slave Traders and the Hazards of Discourse', *Transition* 105: 74–87.

Horton, R. 1971. 'African Conversion', *Africa* 41 (2): 86–108.

Ifeka-Moller, C. 1974. 'White Power: Social Structural Factors in Conversion to Christianity in Eastern Nigeria', *Canadian Journal of African Studies* 8: 55–72.

Isichei, E. 1995. *A History of Christianity in Africa: From Antiquity to the Present*. Grand Rapids MI: Eerdmans Publishing Co. Ltd.

Jenkins, J. 2012. '"Wives of the Gods": Debating *Fiasidi* and the Politics of Meaning'. PhD thesis, University of Sussex.

Klein, A. Norman. 1981. 'The Two Asantes: Competing Interpretations of Slavery in Akan-Asante Culture and Society', in P. Lovejoy (ed.), *The Ideology of Slavery in Africa*. London: Sage Publications.

―――. 1994. 'Slavery and Akan Origins?', *Ethnohistory* 41 (3): 627–56.

Klein, A. 1998. 'Fishing without Formality: An Economic Anthropology of the Ewe on the Lagos-Badagry Seabeach, Nigeria'. PhD thesis, School of Oriental and African Studies, University of London.

Klein, M. 1989. 'Studying the History of Those Who Would Rather Forget: Oral History and the Experience of Slavery', *History in Africa* 16: 209–17.

Kleinman, A. and J. Kleinman. 1994. 'How Bodies Remember: Social Memory and Bodily Experience of Criticism, Resistance, and Delegitimation Following China's Cultural Revolution', *New Literary History* 25: 707–23.

Kopytoff, I. and S. Miers. 1977. 'African Slavery as an Institution of Marginality', in S. Miers and I. Kopytoff (eds), *Slavery in Africa: Historical and Anthropological Perspectives*. Madison WI: University of Wisconsin Press.

Kraamer, M. 2005. 'Colourful Changes: Two Hundred Years of Social and Design History in the Hand-Woven Textiles of the Ewe-speaking Regions of Ghana and Togo (1800–2000)', PhD thesis, School of Oriental and African Studies, University of London.

Kramer, F. 1993. *The Red Fez: Art and Spirit Possession in Africa*. London: Verso.

Kleinman, A. and J. Kleinman. 1994. 'How Bodies Remember: Social Memory and Bodily Experience of Criticism, Resistance, and Delegitimation Following China's Cultural Revolution', *New Literary History*: 707–23.

Kumassah, A. 2009. *The Migration Saga of the Anlo-Ewes of Ghana*. Keta: Photo City Press.

Laidlaw, J. 2004. 'Introduction', in H. Whitehouse and J. Laidlaw (eds), *Ritual and Memory: Toward a Comparative Anthropology of Religion*. Walnut Creek CA: AltaMira.

Lambek, M. 1996. 'The Past Imperfect: Remembering as Moral Practice', in M. Lambek and P. Antze (eds), *Tense Past: Cultural Essays in Trauma and Memory*. London: Routledge.

―――. 2002. *The Weight of the Past: Living with History in Mahajanga, Madagascar*. Basingstoke: Palgrave Macmillan.

Larbi, E. K. 2001. *Pentecostalism: The Eddies of Ghanaian Christianity*. Accra: Centre for Pentecostal and Charismatic Christianity.

Law, R. 1991a. 'Religion, Trade, and Politics on the "Slave Coast": Roman Catholic Missions in Allada and Whydah in the Seventeenth Century', *Journal of Religion in Africa* 21 (1): 42–77.

―――. 1991b. *The Slave Coast of West Arica, 1550–1750: The Impact of the Atlantic Slave Trade on an African Society*. Oxford: Oxford University Press.

_____. 2001. 'The Evolution of the Brazilian Community in Ouidah', *Slavery and Abolition* 22 (1): 22–41.

_____. 2003. 'On Pawning and Enslavement for Debt in the Precolonial Slave Coast', in P. Lovejoy and T. Falola (eds), *Pawnship, Slavery and Colonialism in Africa*. Trenton NJ: Africa World Press.

_____. 2004. *Ouidah: The Social History of a West African 'Slaving Port', 1727–1892*. Oxford: James Currey.

Lawrance, B. 2007. *Locality, Mobility and 'Nation': Periurban Colonialism in Togo's Eweland, 1900–1960*. Rochester NY: Rochester University Press.

Le Herissé, A. 1911. *L'Ancien Royaume du Dahomey: moeurs, réligion, histoire*. Paris: Emile Larose.

Lewis, I. M. 1989. *Ecstatic religion: a study of shamanism and spirit possession*. London: Routledge.

Lorand Matory, J. 1994. *Sex and the Empire That Is No More: Gender and the Politics of Metaphor in Oyo-Yoruba Religion*. Minneapolis MN and London: University of Minnesota Press.

Lovejoy, P. E. 1994. 'Background to the Rebellion: The Origins of Muslim Slaves in Bahia', *Slavery and Abolition* 15 (2): 151–80.

Lovell, N. 1993. 'Cord of Blood: Initiation, Gender and Social Dynamics among the Ouatchi-Ewe of Southern Togo', PhD thesis, School of Oriental and African Studies, University of London.

_____. 2002. *Cord of Blood: Possession and the Making of Voodoo*. London: Pluto Press.

Maier, D. J. E. 1983. *Priests and Power: The Case of the Dente Shrine in Nineteenth-Century Ghana*. Bloomington IN: Indiana University Press.

Mamattah, C. M. K. 1976. *The Ewes of West Africa*. Accra: Woeli Research Publications.

Manoukian, M. 1952. *The Ewe-Speaking People of Togoland and the Gold Coast*. London: International African Institute.

Marshall-Fratani, R. 1998. 'Mediating the Global and Local in Nigerian Pentecostalism', *Journal of Religion in Africa* 28 (3): 278–315.

Maupoil, B. 1943. *La Géomancie à l'ancienne Côte des Esclaves*. Paris: Institut d'Ethnologie.

McCaskie, T.C. 1981. 'Anti-Witchcraft Cults in Asante: An Essay in the Social History of an African People', *History in Africa* 8: 125–54.

_____. 1986. 'Komfo Anokye of Asante: Meaning, History and Philosophy in an African Society', *Journal of African History* 27 (2): 315–39.

_____. 1995. *State and Society in Pre-Colonial Asante*. Cambridge: Cambridge University Press.

McLeod, M. 1975. 'On the Spread of Anti-Witchcraft Cults in Modern Asante', in J. Goody (ed.), *Changing Social Structure in Ghana: Essays in the Comparative Sociology of a New State and an Old Tradition*. London: International African Institute.

Meyer, B. 1992. '"If You Are a Witch You Are a Devil and If You Are a Devil You Are a Witch": The Integration of "Pagan" Ideas into the Conceptual Universe of Ewe Christians in Southeastern Ghana', *The Journal of Religion in Africa* 22 (2): 98–132.

_____. 1995. '"Translating the Devil"': An African Appropriation of Pietist Protestantism, the Case of the Peki Ewe in Southeastern Ghana, 1847–1992', PhD thesis, University of Amsterdam.

_____. 1998a. '"Make a Complete Break with the Past": Memory and Post-colonial Modernity in Ghanaian Pentecostal Discourse', in R. Werbner (ed.), *Memory and the Postcolony: African Anthropology and the Critique of Power*. London: Zed Books.

_____. 'The Power of Money: Politics, Occult Forces, and Pentecostalism in Ghana', *African Studies Review* 41 (3): 15–37.

_____. 1999. *Translating the Devil: Religion and Modernity among the Ewe in Ghana*. Edinburgh: Edinburgh University Press and the International African Institute.

_____. 2002. 'Christianity and the Ewe Nation: German Pietist Missionaries, Ewe Converts and the Politics of Culture', *Journal of Religion in Africa* 32 (2): 167–200.

Mittermaier, A. 2011. *Dreams That Matter: Egyptian Landscapes of the Imagination*. Berkeley and Los Angeles CA: University of California Press.

Mudimbe, V. Y. 1983. 'An African Criticism of Christianity', *Genève Afrique* 21 (2): 91–100.

_____. 1997. *Tales of Faith: Religion as Political Performance in Central Africa*. London and Atlantic Highlands NJ: Athlone Press.

Müller, L. F. 2013. *Religion and Chieftaincy in Ghana: An Explanation of the Persistence of a Traditional Political Institution in West Africa*. Münster: Lit Verlag.

Norregard, G. 1966. *Danish Settlements in West Africa, 1658–1850*. Boston MA: Boston University Press.

Nugent, P. 1995. *Big Men, Small Boys and Politics in Ghana: Power, Ideology and the Burden of History*. London: Francis Pinter.

_____. 1997. 'Myths of Origin and the Origin of Myth: Local Politics and the Uses of History in Ghana's Volta Region', *Working Papers on African Societies*, No. 22. Berlin: Das Arabische Buch.

_____. 2000. '"A Few Lesser Peoples": the Central Togo Minorities and Their Ewe Neighbours', in P. Nugent and C. Lentz (eds), *Ethnicity in Ghana*. London: Macmillan, 162–82.

_____. 2001. 'Winners, Losers and Also Rans: Money, Moral Authority and Voting Patterns in the Ghana 2000 Elections', *African Affairs* 100 (400): 405–28.

_____. 2002. *Smugglers, Secessionists and Loyal Citizens on the Ghana-Togo Frontier*. Oxford: James Currey.

Nukunya, G. K. 1969a. *Kinship and Marriage among the Anlo Ewe*. London: Athlone Press.

_____. 1969b. 'The Yewe Cult among Southern Ewe-Speaking People of Ghana', *Ghana Journal of Sociology* 5 (1):1–7.

_____. 1983. 'A Note on Anlo (Ewe) Slavery and the History of a Slave', appendix to C. C. Robertson, 'Post Proclamation Slavery in Accra: A Female Affair?' in C. C. Robertson and M. A. Klein (eds), *Women and Slavery in Africa*. Madison WI: Heinemann.

_____. 1997. 'Social and Political Organisation', in F. Agbodeka (ed.), *The Ewes of Southeastern Ghana*. Accra: Woeli Publishing Services.

Obeng, P. 2006. 'Religious Interactions in Pre-Twentieth-Century West Africa', in E. K. Akyeampong (ed.), *Themes in West Africa's History*. Oxford: James Currey.

Opoku, K. 1978. 'Changes within Christianity: The Case of the Musama Disco Christo Church', in E. Fashole-Luke, R. Gay, A. Hastings, and G. Tasie (eds), *Christianity in Independent Africa*. London: Rex Collings Ltd.

Ortiz, R. 1997. 'Ogum and the Umbandista Religion', in S. Barnes (ed.), *Africa's Ogun: Old World and New*. Bloomington IN: Indiana University Press.

Owusu-Ansah, D. 1983. 'Islamic Influence in a Forest Kingdom: The Role of Protective Amulets in Early Nineteenth Century Asante', *Transafrican Journal of History* 12: 100–33.

Palmié, S. 2003. 'Africanizing and Cubanizing discourses in North American *Orisa* Worship', in R. Fardon (ed.), *Counterworks: Managing the Diversity of Knowledge*. Routledge: London.

Parker, J. 2000. *Making the Town: Ga State and Society in Early Colonial Accra*. Portsmouth NH: Heinemann.

———. 2004. 'Witchcraft, Anti-Witchcraft and Trans-Regional Ritual Innovation in Early Colonial Ghana: Sakrabundi and Abrewa, 1889–1910', *Journal of African History* 45 (3): 393–420.

———. 2006. 'Northern Gothic: Witches, Ghosts and Werewolves in the Savanna Hinterland of the Gold Coast, 1900–1950s', *Africa* 76 (3): 352–80.

———. 2011. 'Earth and Shadow: Substance, Medicine and Mobility in the History of Ghana's Tongnaab Shrines', *Anthropology and Medicine* 18 (2): 257–70.

Parrinder, G. 1970. *West African Religion*. New York NY: Barnes and Noble.

Parsons, R. T. 1963. *The Churches and Ghana Society, 1918–1955: A Survey of the Work of Three Protestant Mission Societies and the African Churches Which They Established in Their Assistance to Society Development*. Leiden: E. J. Brill.

Peel, J. D. Y. 1968a. 'Syncretism and Religious Change', *Comparative Studies of Society and History* 10: 121–41.

———. 1968b. *Aladura: A Religious Movement among the Yoruba*. Oxford: Oxford University Press.

———. 1983. *Ijeshas and Nigerians: The Incorporation of a Yoruba Kingdom, 1890s–1970s*. Cambridge: Cambridge University Press.

———. 1987. 'History, Culture and the Comparative Method: A West African Puzzle', in L. Holy (ed.), *Comparative Anthropology*. Oxford: Basil Blackwell.

———. 1989. 'The Cultural Work of Yoruba Ethnogenesis', in E. Tonkin, M. MacDonald, and M. Chapman (eds), *History and Ethnicity*. London: Routledge.

———. 1995. 'For Who Hath Despised the Day of Small Things? Missionary Narratives and Historical Anthropology', *Comparative Studies in Society and History* 37 (3): 581–607.

———. 2000. *Religious Encounter and the Making of the Yoruba*. Bloomington IN: Indiana University Press.

Piot, C. 1996. 'Of Slaves and the Gift: Kabre Sale of Kin during the Era of the Slave Trade', *Journal of African History* 37 (1): 31–49.

———. 1999. *Remotely Global: Village Modernity in West Africa*. Chicago IL: University of Chicago Press.

———. 2010. *Nostalgia for the Future: West Africa after the Cold War*. Chicago IL: Chicago University Press.

Poku, K. 1969. 'People of Slave Origin in Ashanti', *Ghana Journal of Sociology* 5 (1): 33–7.

Ranger, T. 1989. 'Missionaries, Migrants, and the Mayinka: The Invention of Ethnicity in Zimbabwe', in L. Vail (ed.), *The Creation of Tribalism in Southern Africa*. Berkeley CA: University of California Press.

Rasmussen, S. J. 1999. 'The Slave Narrative in Life History and Myth, and the Problems of the Tuareg Cultural Predicament', *Ethnohistory* 46 (1): 67–108.

Rattray, R. S. 1959. *Art and Religion in Ashanti*. London: Oxford University Press.

Ray, B. C. 1993. 'Aladura Christianity: A Yoruba Religion', *Journal of Religion in Africa* 23 (3): 266–91.

Rivière, C. 1981. *Anthropologie réligieuse des Eve du Togo*. Lome: Les Nouvelles Editions Africaines.

Rosenthal, J. 1998. *Possession, Ecstasy, Law in Ewe Voodoo*. Charlottesville VA: University of Virginia Press.

———. 2002. 'Trance against the State' in C. Greenhouse, E. Mertz, and K. Warren (eds), *Ethnography in Unstable Places: Everyday Lives in Contexts of Dramatic Political Change*. Durham NC: Duke University Press.

———. 2005. 'Religious Traditions of Togo and Benin Ewe', in B. N. Lawrance (ed.), *A Handbook of Eweland: The Ewes of Togo and Benin*. Accra: Woeli Publishing Services.

Rossi, B. 2009. 'Slavery and Migration: Social and Physical Mobility in Ader (Niger)', in B. Rossi (ed.), *Reconfiguring Slavery: West African Trajectories*. Liverpool: University of Liverpool Press.

Rush, D. 2008. 'Indian Imagery in West African Vodun Art and Thought', in J. C. Hawley (ed.), *India in Africa, Africa in India: Indian Ocean Cosmopolitanisms*. Bloomington IN: Indiana University Press.

———. 2011. 'In Remembrance of Slavery: Tchamba Vodun', *African Diaspora Archaeology Newsletter* 14 (2): Article 1. Available at: <http://scholarworks.umass.edu/adan/vol14/iss2/1>.

———. 2013. 'In Remembrance of Slavery: Tchamba Vodun', in M. Klein, S. Greene, A. Bellagamba, and C. Brown (eds), *Finding the African Voice: Narratives of Slavery and Enslavement*. Cambridge: Cambridge University Press.

Sanneh, L. 2001. *Abolitionists Abroad: American Blacks and the Making of Modern West Africa*. Cambridge MA: Harvard University Press.

Shaw, R. 2002. *Memories of the Slave trade: Ritual and Historical Imagination in Sierra Leone*. Chicago IL: University of Chicago Press.

Skinner, K. 2007. 'Reading, Writing, and Rallies: The Politics of "Freedom" in British Togoland, 1953–56', *Journal of African History* 48 (1): 123–47.

Soothill, J. 2007. *Gender, Social change and Spiritual Power: Charismatic Christianity in Ghana*. Leiden: E. J. Brill.

Spieth, J. 1911. *Die Religion der Eweer*. Göttingen: Vandenhoekand Ruprecht.

———. 2011 [1906]. *The Ewe People: A Study of the Ewe People in German Togo* (translated by E. Tsaku, M. Edorh, R. Avornyo, M. E. Kropp Dakubu, edited by K. Amoaku). Accra: Sub-Saharan Publishers.

Stoller, P. 1995. *Embodying Colonial Memories: Spirit Possession, Power and the Hauka in West Africa*. London: Routledge.

Strickrodt, S. 2008. 'The Brazilian Diaspora to West Africa in the Nineteenth Century', in I. Phaf-Rheinberger and T. de Oliveira Pinto (eds), *AfricAmericas: Itineraries, Dialogues, and Sounds*. Frankfurt am Main: Vervuert, Bibliotheca Ibero-Americana.

Sundkler, B. and C. Steed. 2000. *A History of the Church in Africa*. Cambridge: Cambridge University Press.

Taussig, M. 1993. *Mimesis and Alterity: A Particular History of the Senses*. New York NY: Routledge.

Tonkin, E. 1992. *Narrating Our Pasts: The Social Construction of Oral History*. Cambridge: Cambridge University Press.

Turner, H. W. 1978. 'Patterns of Ministry and Structure within Independent Churches', in E. Fashole-Luke, R. Gray, A. Hastings, and G. Tasie (eds), *Christianity in Independent Africa*. London: Rex Collings Ltd.

Ustorf, W. 2001. *Bremen Missionaries in Togo and Ghana: 1847–1900*. Accra: Legon Theological Studies Series.

van den Besselaar, D. 2000. 'The Language of Igbo Ethnic Nationalism', *Language Problems and Language Planning* 24 (2): 123–47.

Venkatachalam, M. 2007. 'Slavery in Memory: A Study of the Religious Cults of the Anlo-Ewe of South-Eastern Ghana, *c.* 1850–present'. PhD thesis, School of Oriental and African Studies, University of London.

———. 2011. 'Between the Umbrella and the Elephant: Elections, Ethnic Negotiations and the Politics of Spirit Possession in Teshi, Accra', *Africa* 81 (2): 248–68.

———. 2012. 'Between the Devil and the Cross: Religion, Slavery and the Making of the Anlo-Ewe', *Journal of African History* 53 (1): 45–64.

Verdon, M. 1983. *The Abutia Ewe: A Chiefdom That Never Was*. Berlin: Mouton.

vom Bruck, G. 2005. *Islam, Memory, and Morality in Yemen: Ruling Families in Transition*. New York NY: Palgrave Macmillan.

Ward, W. E. F. 1958. *A History of the Gold Coast*. London: Allen and Unwin.

Welch, C. E. 1966. *Dream of Unity: Pan-Africanism and Political Unity in West Africa*. Ithaca NY: Cornell University Press.

Wendl, T. 1999. 'Slavery, Spirit Possession and Ritual Consciousness: The Tchamba Cult among the Mina in Togo', in H. Behrend and U. Luig (eds), *Spirit Possession: Modernity and Power in Africa*. Madison WI: University of Wisconsin Press.

Werbner, R. 1998. 'Beyond Oblivion: Confronting Memory Crisis', in R. Werbner (ed.), *Memory and the Postcolony: African Anthropology and the Critique of Power*. London: Zed Books.

West, H. 2008. *Ethnographic Sorcery*. Chicago IL: University of Chicago Press.

Westermann, D. 1906. *Wörterbuch der Ewe Sprache*. Berlin: D. Reimer.

———. 1935. *Die Glidyi-Ewe in Togo: Züge aus Ihrem Gesellschaftsleben*. Berlin: Walter de Gruyter.

Wilks, I. G. 1975. *Asante in the Nineteenth Century: The Structure and Evolution of a Political Order*. Cambridge: Cambridge University Press.

Winsnes, S. A. (ed.) 1992. *Letters on West Africa and the Slave Trade: Paul Erdmann Isert's Journey to Guinea and the Caribbean Islands in Columbia (1788)*, London: British Academy.

Archival Sources

National Archives, Accra

PRAAD/A/ADM 11/1/228: Quittah Lagoon
PRAAD/A/ADM 11/1/272: Appointment of Dzodze chiefs (1910)
PRAAD/A/ADM 11/1/404: Awuna Native Affairs
PRAAD/A/ADM 11/1/430: Fetishes at Atiavo
PRAAD/A/ADM 11/1/637: Kune (Kunde) Fetish
PRAAD/A/ADM 11/1/680: Whuti Native Affairs
PRAAD/A/ADM 11/1/751: Dente Fetish
PRAAD/A/ADM 11/1/768: Fetish Atigo at Battor

PRAAD/A/ADM 11/1/886: Witchcraft
PRAAD/A/ADM 11/1/1091: Fia Adama of Agbosome vs Sri
PRAAD/A/ADM 11/1/1387: Suppression of Atti fetish (1908)
PRAAD/A/ADM 11/1/1679: Native Customs and Fetish
PRAAD/A/ADM 41/4/1: Quitta Criminal Case Files
PRAAD/A/ADM 41/4/2: Quitta Criminal Case Files
PRAAD/A/ADM 41/4/20: Quitta Criminal Case Files
PRAAD/A/ADM 41/4/22: Quitta Criminal Case Files

Websites

'The Afrikania Mission', Web Url: http://members.tripod.com/afrikania/ (accessed 6 January 2013).
'The Blakhud Centre', Web Url: http://www.hypertextile.net/BLAKHUD/ (accessed 6 January 2013).
'Gbe Languages', Web Url: http://en.wikipedia.org/wiki/Gbe_languages (accessed 26 June 2006).
'Ghana census, on 'Ghana Home Pages', http://www.ghanaweb.com/ GhanaHomePage/general/ (accessed 17 June 2006).
PANAFEST 2007, Web Url, http://www.africa-ata.org/gh_panafest.htm (accessed 1 March 2007).
'African Ancestry', Web Url: http://www.africanancestry.com/ (accessed 15 June 2012).

Principal Interviews and Informants

Name, Occupation, Place, Date(s) of Interview(s)

Ablavi Amegbor, Fofie devotee, Anlo-Afiadenyigba: 18 November 2010
Adokomesi, *Fofiesi*, Klikor-Agbozume: 12 August 2000
Adzo Amevedzi, Church-goer, Anlo-Afiadenyigba: 6 March 2004
Agbodzi, Adzevodu initiate, Anlo-Afiadenyigba: 7 June 2004
Ajakoku, Head of the Fofie cult, Anlo-Afiadenyigba: 13 September 2003, 8 March 2004, 15 April 2004, 29 August 2005
Babaa, Fofie worshipper, Anlo-Afiadenyigba: 11 April 2004, 1 May 2004
Ben Afikpo, Nyigbla devotee, Afife: 21 December 2003
Blumesi, Fofie intiate, Anlo-Afiadenyigba: 13 September 2005
Christian Seeku, Mamaa devotee, Anlo-Afiadenyigba: 6 March 2004, 23 August 2005, 14 September 2006
Dadziezor, Yewe *vodusi*, Anlo-Afiadenyigba: 19 February 2004
David Davor, EP Church committee, Anlo-Afiadenyigba: 8 April 2004
David Kwatsikor, Anlo-Afiadenyigba: 27 August 2006
David Nyamesi, Anlo-Afiadenyigba: 8 December 2010, 9 December 2010
Denis, Adzevodu devotee, Anlo-Afiadenyigba: 3 May 2004
Dzogbesi, later Dzakpasi Metumisi, Fofie initiate, Anlo-Afiadenyigba: 23 November 2003, 30 November 2003, 5 December 2010
Elias Agboado, Anlo-Afiadenyigba: 27 August 2005, 7 December 2010
Esi, Yewe devotee, Anlo-Afiadenyigba: 8 March 2004
Faith Nyameshi, Mamma devotee, Anlo-Afiadenyigba: 10 April 2004, 29 August 2005
Felix, Diviner, Anloga: 6 October 2003, 8 October 2003
Gabriel Yevuagdi, Anlo-Afiadenyigba: 10 September 2005

Gawu Mortu, Afa diviner, Dagbamete: 25 February 2004
Gbara, Fofie initiate, Anlo-Afiadenyigba: 12 September 2005
Gideon Nyamesi, Fofie worshipper, Keta: 9 December 2010
Goku, Yewe shrine owner, Anlo-Afiadenyigba: 31 October 2003, 4 November
   2003, 10 September 2005
Foli, Yewe priest, Anlo-Afiadenyigba: 10 May 2004
Hlomesi, Gorovodu priestess, Pahou, Rep. of Benin: 14 June 2004
Hope Agboado, EP Church member, Anlo-Afiadenyigba: 27 August 2005
Hope Amevedzi, RC church, Anloga: 24 April 2005, 25 August 2005, 11 Septem-
   ber 2006
John Kuatsikor, Yewe priest, Anlo-Afiadenyigba: 19 September 2006
Justice Agboado, member of Fofie lineage, Keta: 9 December 2010
Ketaboko, Yewe priest, Anlo-Afiadenyigba: 19 February 2004
Kofi Ameve, Former Afrikania Mission Head, Accra: 3 August 2000, 10 August
   2000
Komla Donkor, Anlo-Afiadenyigba: 15 September 2007
Kwaku Amevedzi, Fofie worshipper, Anlo-Afiadenyigba: 23 November 2003
Kwasi Aku, Gorovodu priest, Anlo-Afiadenyigba: 19 February 2004
Kwabla Agodzi, Nunge priest, Atorkor: 17 September 2003
Kwadwo Jyameshi, Blekete drummer, Anlo-Afiadenyigba: 14 April 2004, 25 June
   2004
Kwadwo Tamakloe, Fofie devotee, Anlo-Afiadenyigba: 11 April 2004, 1 May
   2004
Mama Abena, Anlo-Afiadenyigba: 24 November 2003
Mama Acose, Yewe priestess, Pahou, Benin: 16 June 2004
Mama Adzima, Fofie shrine keeper, Dzita: 8 October 2003
Mamedu Badesi, Fofie initiate, Anlo-Afiadenyigba: 28 February 2004
Mansa Aidam, Yewe initiate, Atorkor: 19 September 2004
Metumisi, *Fofiesi*, Havedji: 6 December 2010
Midao Kazahlo, Yewe priest, Anlo-Afiadenyigba: 8 April 2004
Minao Gbanyaga, Yewe priestess, Anlo-Afiadenyigba: 4 November 2003
Miano Yorxor, Yewe priestess, Anlo-Afiadenyigba: 26 August 2006
Nana Dente, Chief priest of Dente shrine, Kete Krachi: 9 May 2004
Nanunsi (in trance), Fofie initiate, Anlo-Afiadenyigba: 3 June 2004
Nyomesi, Fofie initiate, Anlo-Afiadenyigba: 13 September 2005
Paulina Seeku, Mamma devotee, Anlo-Afiadenyigba: 13 April 2004
Peter Azumah, Gorovodu worshipper, Anlo-Afiadenyigba: 12 May 2004
Quasi Nyamesi, Anlo-Afiadenyigba: 19 May 2013
Rexford Smith, African-American visitor, Keta: 7 December 2010
Rose Aidam, Fofie devotee, Whuti: 3 April 2004
Sacrebode, Gorovodu spirit, Anlo-Afiadenyigba: 18 September 2005
Senchisro, Gorovodu priestess, Anlo-Afiadenyigba: 13 September 2003, 30
   November 2003, 27 August 2005
Slender, Gorovodu priest, Anlo-Afiadenyigba: 19 September 2005
Sogolum Kwashiga, Adzevodu shrine owner, Anlo-Afiadenyigba: 8 June 2004
Solomon Ocloo, Gorovodu worshipper, Blekusu: 10 June 2004
Togbi Akpate Akrobotu, Divisional Chief, Whuti: 17 September 2003
Togbi Mamma, Mamma shrine, Anlo-Afiadenyigba: 7 June 2004
Tunde Jyameshi, Afrikania Mission, Anlo-Afiadenyigba: 11 May 2004
Wango Adzinu, Gorovodu priest, Blekusu: 15 June 2004
Winston Churchill Van Lare, Anlo local historian, Accra: 22 April 2014

Index

Notes

The annotation 'f' is used to designate a reference to a figure, and is preceded by the page number on which the figure is to be found. (Maps are represented as figures.)

The annotation 'ff' when preceded by page/s number/s refers to an entry where information is contained only in a footnote and not in the main body of the text.

The annotation 'n' is used to indicate a footnote; it is usually followed by the number of the footnote, and preceded by the page number/s on which it is to be found.

Where there is a solitary footnote on a page, the number of the footnote is dropped.

Single footnotes that spill over two pages are represented by both page numbers separated by a dash. The footnote takes the form of either an 'ff' or an 'n' type depending on whether the entry is represented in the main text. Examples: 118–19ff; 118–19n34.

Consecutive footnotes on same page, containing information about the same entry, are usually represented as a single entry, separated by a dash between the footnotes, and indexed against the page number in which they appear. Example: 33n11–12.

Titles in the Series

Lightning Source UK Ltd.
Milton Keynes UK
UKHW040807210223
417374UK00001B/59